A **FALCON** GUIDE®

P9-DIW-929

Hiking the Columbia River Gorge

Second Edition

Russ Schneider

FALCON GUIDES®

GUILFORD, CONNECTICUT
HELENA, MONTANA
AN IMPRINT OF THE GLOBE PEQUOT PRESS

AFALCONGUIDE®

Falcon and FalconGuides are registered trademarks of
Morris Book Publishing, LLC.

All photographs by Russ Schneider unless otherwise
noted.

Maps by XNR Productions, Inc. © Morris Book Publishing,
LLC
The author used MapTech software to produce source
maps.

ISBN 978-0-7627-2962-3
ISSN 1549-7763

Manufactured in the United States of America
Second Edition/Second Printing

To buy books in quantity for corporate use
or incentives, call **(800) 962–0973**
or e-mail **premiums@GlobePequot.com.**

The Columbia River Highway
has not only unlocked the way
to the very heart of the wonder region but it has thrown
wide the door, and all are bid-
den to enter and to enjoy the
thrill of intimate touch with
one of nature's most stupen-
dous bits of handiwork.

—Ira Williams, 1916

Contents

Columbia River Gorge

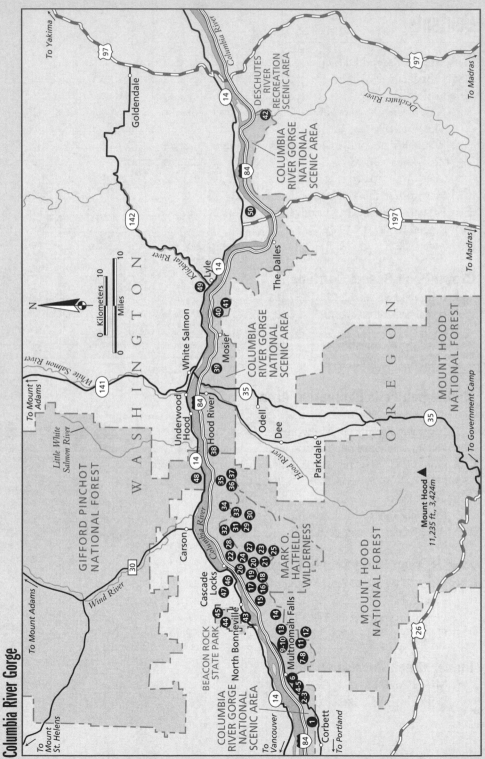

Pacific Crest Trail, Washington

Dog Mountain Trail System

The Dalles Area

Preface to the Second Edition

After spending many seasons revisiting the Columbia River Gorge, I still love it for what it is: a place for enjoying the healthy lifestyle of outdoor recreation and a place to bear witness to the resilience of nature amid overwhelming human enjoyment and use. Guidebook revisions are not as fun as hiking everything in the first place, but they are nostalgic and a case study in the permanence of a place over time.

I've also been struck by the general trend away from free outdoor recreation and toward heavily managed recreation areas partially supported by user fees. It's hard to just plop down by a lake, build a campfire, cook some fish, and go to bed without studying a book full of regulations and working hard not to violate any of them. This is true throughout the Northwest, and it often leaves me longing for simpler days—drive up, park, and throw on the knapsack for a walk in the woods. When I did the research for the first edition of this book, most of the trailheads were free, and the regulations were not complex.

It's a tough battle for public land managers to balance user freedom with preservation of the experience. Imagine unregulated camping on the lower reaches of Eagle Creek or on the shores of Wahtum Lake! Life means trade-offs, and after a trip up any of the cliffy trails in the gorge with a mounted safety cable, you might start thinking that the few bucks you pay at the trailhead are worth it—and still user fees pay only a small portion of the total cost of maintaining the recreation areas in the gorge. For example, Multnomah Falls Visitor Center is open 362 days a year, 7 days a week, quite an accomplishment in itself. Think of the new Highway State Trail and the preserved character of the historic highway, and you'll realize that any user fee is small in comparison to the total cost and effort being put forth on behalf of recreationists in the corridor.

The original edition of this book included an epilogue on Happy Hiking and Heavy Use—a theme that bears even more strongly on this edition: Masses of people can enjoy the gorge and still preserve it, at least to an extent, providing a broad exposure to the benefits of this place.

In compiling the second edition of this book, I enjoyed many wonderful excursions with my friends and family to continue my lifetime exploration of the gorge. I would like to thank my mother and family for driving and hiking (more on the driving side) the gorge looking for new trails, altered access, and opportunities for better pictures and perspectives. In addition, for the second edition of *Hiking the Columbia River Gorge,* I would like to thank the following organizations for their contribution either to this book or to the healthy management and preservation of the gorge: The Nature Conservancy, Columbia River Gorge National Scenic Area, Skamania Lodge Forest Service Visitor Center, Friends of Multnomah Falls, Washington State Parks, Mount Hood Ranger District, and FalconGuides editorial staff.

I enjoyed the process and I am proud of the results. Thank you.

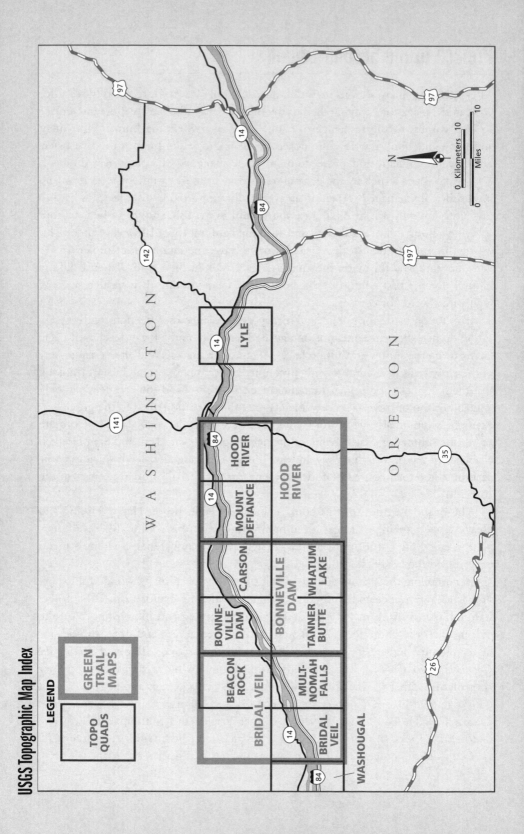

USGS Topographic Map Index

LEGEND

TOPO QUADS

GREEN TRAIL MAPS

Introduction

Driving through the Columbia River Gorge for the first time would fill anyone with wonder. Towering basalt cliffs and crashing waterfalls emphasize the steep walls of the gorge. The views of Mount Hood, Mount Adams, and Mount St. Helens are frequently stunning. The interstate is insignificant compared to the powerful forces that carved this river's passage. A massive flood caused by the overflowing of ancient Lake Missoula originally scored out this break in the mighty Cascade Mountains.

The Columbia River Gorge includes Mount Hood and Gifford Pinchot National Forests, the Mark O. Hatfield/Columbia Wilderness Area, the Historic Columbia River Highway, and twenty-two state parks. The area contains more than 300,000 acres of publicly accessible recreation land and over forty trails less than a two-hour drive from the city of Portland. Eighty percent of the Columbia River Gorge National Scenic Area is privately owned, but is managed cooperatively by the scenic area office, local citizens, private landowners, and municipalities. There are more than 200 miles of maintained trails and many unmaintained and primitive routes.

In putting the first edition of this guide together, I tried to include every hikeable trail between Portland/Vancouver and The Dalles area that featured public access, regardless how pretty it was, or how short or long—or whether it was really suited for hiking at all, rather than mountain biking or other modes of travel. In hindsight, however, some places just aren't worth visiting twice. I tried to leave some of these hikes out of this version, even at risk of losing comprehensiveness. This is a hiking guide, not a general tour guide, of which there are many on the gorge.

I also extended the range of the hiking area a little to include the Deschutes River Trail and the basalt cliffs of Horsethief Butte—hikes generally associated with the gorge at the eastern edge of the scenic area. These truly are places worth visiting more than twice. In addition, the core hikes of the gorge remain the prime reasons most of us travel here. Eagle Creek is still one of Oregon's wonders; Multnomah Falls is even more regular than Old Faithful. The flowers on Dog Mountain still bloom every spring, and we can still enjoy them.

The hikes in this guidebook range from fifteen-minute walks to 20-mile days and extended overnight backpacking vacations. There are hikes for all ages and abilities; hikes for waterfall lovers and mountain climbers. Check out the Vacation Planner for hike suggestions. And although it has been said many times in many guidebooks, it's always worth saying again—Happy Hiking!

A Geologic Overview of the Columbia River Gorge

You can spend a lifetime studying the geology of the Columbia River Gorge; the following is necessarily the short version!

The geologic history of the Columbia River Gorge includes three major events. First, a series of volcanic eruptions laid down the basalt rock and soil. Second, the flood of ancient Lake Missoula carved out the U-shaped valley. Third, landslides blocked the river channel, diverting the river and forming the great cascades.

Volcanoes erupted in the western Cascades eighteen to thirty million years ago, creating a layer of volcanic ash, lava, and mudflows several miles thick. The cliffs of the gorge expose about 1,000 feet of these mudflows. Probably the most visible rock formation in the Pacific Northwest, Columbia River basalt provides the cliff base for most of the gorge's current waterfalls. Between twelve and seventeen million years ago, eruptions began from dozens of mile-long fissures in eastern Washington and Oregon. The flows of hot and fluid basaltic lava spread over 60,000 square miles in both states. Only 16 of the more than 200 known basalt flows occurred in gorge cliffs. When a former valley of the Columbia filled with basaltic lava, the river was rerouted north and cut a new valley. Gray andesitic lava from the volcanoes built up the surface of the Cascade plateau. The lava flows caused a final diversion of the Columbia between two and three million years ago, by filling a deep canyon that the river had run through. This channel is now known as the Sandy River drainage. Now in its present track, the Columbia River cut itself a deep, V-shaped canyon. The erection of the fourteen major high Cascade volcanoes and more than 1,000 smaller peaks and cinder cones followed only in the last 700,000 years.

The second series of catastrophes began 15,000 years ago, near the end of the Ice Age. A glacial lobe from Canada formed an ice dam 2,500 feet high at Lake Pend Oreille. The dam backed water up the Clark Fork Valley of Idaho and impounded Lake Missoula, an ancient lake in Montana containing one-fifth of the amount of water in Lake Michigan. When the lake rose high enough to wash away the dam, 500 cubic miles of water poured across eastern Washington, scouring out Grand Coulee and hundreds of miles of other coulee valleys (now high and dry). This process was repeated anywhere from forty to more than a hundred times over a 3,000-year period: the ice dams re-formed, the lake refilled, and catastrophic floods reoccurred. In the Columbia River Gorge, these floods scoured away the valley walls, changed the V shape to its present U shape, and formed the cliffs and water-falls along the south side of the valley. Floodwaters were 1,000 feet deep at the Dalles, topped Crown Point at 700 feet, and covered the Portland area at 400 feet.

The final geologic catastrophe was the cascade landslide upon which Bonneville now rests. It's likely that a great earthquake started the landslide 750 years ago. Then the flood-steeped faces of Table Mountain displaced the river more than a mile to the south, building a debris dam 270 feet high across the river. By comparison, the modern-day Bonneville Dam is only 80 feet high. Forests along the river as far east as the Dalles were drowned as the lake filled behind the landslide debris dam. For as long as the dam existed, local Indians were able to cross the river dry shod. Eventually the dam washed away, leaving the series of Columbia River cascades that we know today. Native memories of the dam survive in the form of the legendary "Bridge of the Gods." This was adapted from a pamphlet published by the U.S. Army Corps of Engineers.

The Waterfalls

Because of its 600-foot-thick layer of Columbia River basalt, the gorge has more than thirty waterfalls easily accessible by maintained trails, most within an hour's drive of Portland.

The most common thing for a tourist to do when visiting the gorge is drive to Multnomah Falls, hike to the top, and then maybe stop at a couple of nearby trailheads for a brief look at Wahkeena or Horsetail Falls. Even this simple approach can make for a pleasant day, but if you really want to see all the waterfalls you can in a day, I suggest the following approach. Get up early and drive to the Bridal Veil exit off Interstate 84, take a right onto the Historic Columbia River Highway, and drive west to Latourell Falls.

Start your day with arguably the second most spectacular waterfall in the gorge, Latourell Falls, and a good early-morning stretch of the legs on a relatively gentle uphill loop. Next, while driving back east toward the Angels Rest Trailhead, stop at the bridge over Youngs Creek and walk down for a few pictures of Shepperds Dell Falls, hopping back in the car toward Angels Rest Trailhead shortly after. Next you might consider Coopey Falls; it's less than a mile in, and another easy falls to visit. After Coopey Falls, your next option is the famous Bridal Veil Falls. Take some time to enjoy this waterfall, another short and even flatter walk. It should be late morning when you get back to your car at the Bridal Veil Trailhead. Continue east on the Historic Columbia River Highway for the Wahkeena Trailhead. Do take the short walk up to Wahkeena Falls, though you may not want to hike all the way to Fairy Falls, which would definitely wind you. After Wahkeena, you really should brave the crowds for a jaunt up the somewhat steep paved trail to the top of Multnomah Falls. In addition, a trip farther up the Larch Mountain Trail will allow you to snag both Twanlaskie and Ecola Falls on the day's checklist, and they provide you with more waterfall per effort than Fairy Falls would have.

Depending on how fast you hiked or how far up each route you made it, you may still have time for more. The easiest cascade to the east is Horsetail Falls, right by the road, but if you have time, you can take the shorter loop to Ponytail Falls or the longer hike to Triple Falls. At this point, most people will be running out of waterfall hiking time; Triple Falls may have to wait for another trip. Still, snagging Triple Falls really makes for a complete tour along this famous section of the Historic Columbia River Highway.

If all these aren't enough waterfalls for you, plan on a Waterfall Day Two to include Elowah, Wahclella, and Tunnel Falls on the Eagle Creek Trail. Other options include Lancaster, Dry Creek Falls, Rodney Falls, and Hardy Falls. You should be able to get your fill.

Plunge

Horsetail

Block

Tier

Fan

Segmented

Punchbowl

Cascade

Waterfall Types of the Columbia River Gorge

Most people visit the gorge to see waterfalls. The erosion-resistant layers of basalt create ideal habitat for lots of waterfalls, with Multnomah Falls being the most spectacular. Unbelievably, there are even specific types of waterfalls. This is probably old hat for you veteran waterfall watchers, but there are eight forms of falls—plunge, horsetail, fan, cascade, punchbowl, block, tier, and segmented. Some of this nomenclature even originated from visitors trying to describe the look of different waterfalls throughout the Columbia River Gorge, where you can hike to Horsetail Falls and Punch Bowl Falls. Waterfall types vary, even on the same stretch of creek. For example, Punch Bowl Falls is a classic punchbowl, but Lower Punch Bowl Falls is actually a calm block-style waterfall.

The following definitions were adapted from a pamphlet published by the USDA Forest Service.

Block. A block pours over a wide section of a stream, short and fat. Examples include Twanlaskie Falls above Multnomah Falls, and Lower Punch Bowl Falls.

Cascade. A cascade borders on being simply a rustling stream, but is still spectacular enough to warrant waterfall consideration—usually a series of rocky slopes or narrows over which water rushes. Cascades are common throughout the steeper creeks of the gorge, but an easy-to-reach example is Ecola Falls above Multnomah Falls.

Fan. A fan starts similarly to a horsetail-type fall, but spreads or fans out toward the bottom. Fairy Falls on the Wahkeena Trail is a good example.

Horsetail. Horsetail-type falls (the name derives from the classic Horsetail Falls in the gorge) have a tendency to roughly maintain curved contact with rock along the descent, but also narrow to a solid tail between two large cheeks of rock on either side.

Plunge. A plunge drops vertically and away from the cliffside, losing contact with the bedrock. Examples include Multnomah, Elowah, Tunnel, and Latourell Falls.

Punchbowl. Just like pouring lemonade into bowl. The key to identifying a particular fall as a punchbowl is both a deep-pool bowl and a narrow spout falling into it. The classic Punch Bowl Falls is a must-see for any gorge traveler.

Segmented. Segmented falls separate into several vertical divisions as the falls progress; classic examples include Triple Falls and Upper McCord Creek Falls.

Tier. A tier falls, then falls, then falls again, in noticeable steps or tiers. One example is Wahkeena Falls.

Scenic Area Regulations

- Dogs are permitted on a 6-foot leash.
- Mountain bikes are not permitted on any gorge trails except for Larch Mountain Loop and sections of Gorge Trail 400.

- Horses are permitted on the Herman Creek Trail and the Pacific Crest Trail, but prohibited on all other trails.
- Some areas, such as Multnomah Falls, have trail-specific regulations, which are listed at the beginning of each section.
- Motor vehicles are prohibited on all trails in the gorge.
- Respect private property—not all open or forested lands are publicly owned.

Mark O. Hatfield/Columbia Wilderness Regulations

- A free permit is legally required and can be obtained at the entrance points to the Mark O. Hatfield/Columbia Wilderness Area.
- No campfires in the Eagle Creek Corridor, within 0.5 mile of Eagle Creek Trail 440 to the junction with Eagle–Tanner Trail 433.
- No campfires outside designated sites or within 200 feet of Wahtum Lake.
- No camping outside designated sites or within 200 feet of Wahtum Lake.
- A $5.00-per-day or $30.00-per-season permit is required for parking at certain trailheads in the Columbia River Gorge National Scenic Area and Mount Hood National Forest. In Oregon, these are Bridge of the Gods, Eagle Creek, Herman Creek, Larch Mountain, Wahclella, Wyeth, Rainy Lake, Wahtum Lake, and Warren Lake. In Washington, you'll need a permit at Bonneville, Beacon Rock, and Dog Mountain. For more information on the Northwest Forest Pass, call (800) 270–7504 or visit www.naturenw.org.
- A new $85 Washington and Oregon Recreation Pass will be honored throughout the Gorge. The pass is available online at www.naturenw.org or by calling (800) 270–7504.

Zero-Impact Travel

Nowadays most wilderness users want to walk softly, but some aren't aware that they have poor manners. Often their actions come from the outdated understanding of a past generation of campers who cut green boughs for evening shelters and beds, built fire rings, and dug trenches around tents. Today such behavior is unacceptable. The wilderness is shrinking, while the number of users keeps growing. More and more camping areas show unsightly signs of this trend.

Thus a new code of ethics is growing out of the need to cope with the unending waves of people wanting a perfect wilderness experience. Today we all must leave no clues that we have gone before. Canoeists can look behind them and see no trace of their passing. The same should be true of wild country recreation. Enjoy the wilderness, but leave only memories behind.

- Most of us know better than to litter—in or out of the wilderness. Be sure you leave nothing, regardless of how small it is, along the trail or at the campsite. This means you should pack out everything, including orange peels, flip tops, cigarette butts, and gum wrappers. Also, pick up any trash that others have left behind.

- Follow the main trail. Avoid cutting switchbacks and walking on vegetation beside the trail. Some of the terrain in the gorge is very fragile, so when going off-trail to get to a favorite lake or mountaintop, do your part not to create a new trail. Also, safety is a concern on many of the steep off-trail slopes and cliffs. If people continue to cut switchbacks, the trail crew will have to build unsightly fences along biologically sensitive areas, much like the lower part of the Multnomah Falls Trail. Please leave all rocks, antlers, and wildflowers. The next person wants to see them, too.

▶ **Marking your route is generally not a good idea from a zero-impact standpoint, but local volunteer trail organizations recommend carrying a pair of pruners to clear brush, Himalayan blackberry, and Scotch broom along maintained trails.**

- Avoid marking your route. Traditionally backcountry trails are marked by cairns or blazes. Cairns (small stacks of rocks) commonly mark confusing places on maintained trails, but avoid building cairns when traveling cross-country. They detract from the wilderness experience and can promote the repeated use of a specific route, eventually creating a new trail. Blazes, usually an upside-down exclamation point carved into the bark of trees, also mark many maintained trails, but individuals should never blaze trees in the backcountry.

- Try to camp below timberline. Alpine areas are delicate and require special care. Often it's only a short hike to a good campsite below timberline. When reasonable, keep your camp away from a shoreline or streambank, setting up the tent at least 100 feet from a lake or stream. If there is already an established campsite, use it, rather than creating additional damage by establishing a new one. When fetching water, use established paths or vary your route if there are none.

- Campfires probably cause more damage to the backcountry than any other aspect of camping. It's always better to use a lightweight camp stove instead. Although campfires are legal in most parts of the gorge, avoid building fires in alpine areas where the surface is fragile and wood is scarce. If a campfire is appropriate for the campsite, use the existing fire ring. If the area doesn't have a fire ring, don't build one. Dig out the native vegetation and topsoil and set it aside. When breaking camp, douse the fire thoroughly. After it's completely out, scatter the ashes and replace the native soil and vegetation. Build fires away from trees to prevent damage to root systems. Keep fires small and widely disperse any partially burned wood. Gather dead and down branches to burn, and avoid using a saw or ax.

Note that no campfires are permitted in the Eagle Creek Corridor.

- Avoid making loud noises that may disturb others. Remember, sound travels easily to the other side of the gorge.

- Be careful with food wastes to prevent unsightly messes and bad odors. Burn all flammable food packaging if you have a fire, and clean the remains out of the ashes. Always pack out garbage. Likewise, completely burn fish viscera. If fires are not allowed, place fish viscera and leftover food in plastic bags and carry them out. Never throw fish viscera into mountain streams and lakes. Broadcast wastewater at least 100 feet from open water and trails, after sifting out chunks with a wire screen. Never wash dishes in a mountain stream or lake. If you use soap, make sure it's biodegradable.

- Be careful with human wastes. Use white, unscented paper and bury it 6 to 8 inches deep along with human waste. Thoroughly bury human wastes to avoid any chance of bad odor or water pollution. This is a good reason to carry a light-weight trowel. Keep wastes at least 200 feet away from lakes and streams.

- Pack it in, pack it out. If you carry something into the backcountry, consume it, burn it, or carry it out.

For more information on zero-impact camping techniques, read *Leave No Trace* (Falcon 1997).

Safety: Be Prepared

The Boy Scouts of America have for decades adhered to what is perhaps the best single piece of safety advice—be prepared! For starters, carry survival and first-aid materials, proper clothing, a compass, and topographic maps—and know how to use them.

▶ Cell phone coverage is spotty at best in many areas of the Gorge, especially in the narrow valleys. Be prepared to go without one.

Perhaps the second best advice is to tell somebody where you're going and when you plan to return. Pilots must file flight plans before every trip, and anybody venturing into a blank spot on the map should do the same. File your "flight plan" with a friend or relative before taking off.

Next to preparedness and proper equipment is physical conditioning. Being fit not only makes wilderness travel more fun, it makes it safer.

To whet your appetite for more knowledge of wilderness safety and preparedness, here are a few basic tips:

- Check the weather forecast. Be careful not to get caught at high altitude by a snowstorm, and watch cloud formations closely so you don't get stranded on a ridge line during a lightning storm. Avoid traveling during prolonged periods of cold weather.

- If you start a fire, you are responsible for keeping it under control at all times and are accountable for the huge expense of fighting the fire and for any damage resulting from carelessness. Be extra careful if the fire danger is high. Check with the nearest Forest Service office for more information on fire danger and restrictions. If there is a fire in an area, consider that area off-limits to outdoor recreation.

- Avoid traveling alone in the wilderness.
- Never split up in the backcountry.
- Withstand the temptation to swim across a high mountain lake or large stream.
- Be wary of steep snowbanks with rocks or cliffs at the bottom.
- Know the preventive measures, symptoms, and treatment of hypothermia, the silent killer.
- Study basic survival and first aid before leaving home.
- Don't eat wild mushrooms or other plants unless you are positive of their identification.
- Before you leave, find out as much as you can about the route, especially its potential hazards.
- Don't exhaust yourself or weaker members of your party by traveling too far or too fast. Let the slowest person set the pace.
- Don't wait until you're confused to look at your maps. Follow them as you go along, from the moment you start moving up the trail, so you have a continual fix on your location.
- If you get lost, don't panic. Sit down and relax for a few minutes while you carefully check out your topo map and take a reading with your compass. Confidently plan your next move. It's often smart to retrace your steps until you find familiar ground, even if you think it might make the trip longer. Lots of people get temporarily lost in the wilderness and survive—usually by calmly and rationally dealing with the situation.
- Be extra cautious when fording a large stream. Use sandals or remove your socks and put your boots back on. This makes for more secure footing on the slippery stream bottom. Avoid the current's full force by keeping sideways to the flow. Slide—don't lift—your feet one at a time, making sure that one foot is securely anchored before seeking a new hold with the other one. Most often small rocks provide more stable footing than large, potentially slick rocks. Go slowly and deliberately. If you use a walking stick, keep it on the upstream side for additional support.
- Stay clear of all wild animals.
- Last but not least, don't forget that the best defense against unexpected hazards is knowledge. Read up on the latest in wilderness safety information before you go.

Survival Kit

A survival kit should include: compass, whistle, matches in a waterproof container, cigarette lighter, candle, emergency fishing gear (60 feet of six-pound line, six hooks, six lead shot, and six trout flies), signal mirror, fire starter, aluminum foil, water purification tablets, space blanket, and flare.

First-Aid Kit

Your first-aid kit should include: sewing needle, snakebite kit, aspirin, antibacterial ointment, two antiseptic swabs, two butterfly bandages, adhesive tape, four adhesive strips, four gauze pads, two triangular bandages, codeine tablets, two inflatable splints, moleskin, one roll of 3-inch gauze, CPR shield, rubber gloves, and lightweight first-aid instructions.

Hypothermia

Be aware of the danger of hypothermia—a condition in which the body's internal temperature drops below normal. It can lead to mental and physical collapse and death.

Hypothermia results from exposure to cold and is aggravated by wetness, wind, and exhaustion. The moment you begin to lose heat faster than your body produces it, you're suffering from exposure. Your body starts involuntary exercise such as shivering to stay warm, and it makes involuntary adjustments to preserve normal temperature in vital organs, restricting blood flow in the extremities. Both responses drain your energy reserves. The only way to stop the drain is to reduce the degree of exposure.

In full-blown hypothermia your energy reserves are empty and cold reaches the brain, depriving you of good judgment and reasoning power. You won't be aware that this is happening. You lose control of your hands. Your internal temperature slides downward. Without treatment, this slide leads to stupor, collapse, and death.

To defend against hypothermia, stay dry. When clothes get wet, they lose about 90 percent of their insulating value. Wool loses relatively less heat; cotton, down, and some synthetics lose more. Choose rain clothes that cover the head, neck, body, and legs, and provide good protection against wind-driven rain. Most hypothermia cases develop in air temperatures between thirty and fifty degrees Fahrenheit, but hypothermia can develop in warmer temperatures.

If your party travels in wind, cold, and wet, think hypothermia. Watch yourself and others for these symptoms: uncontrollable fits of shivering; vague, slow, slurred speech; memory lapses; incoherence; immobile, fumbling hands; frequent stumbling or a lurching gait; drowsiness (to sleep is to die); apparent exhaustion; and inability to get up after a rest.

When a member of your party has hypothermia, he or she may deny any problem. Believe the symptoms, not the victim. Even mild symptoms demand treatment, as follows: Get the victim out of the wind and rain. Strip off all wet clothes. If the victim has mild symptoms, give warm drinks, then get him or her into warm clothes and a warm sleeping bag. Place well-wrapped water bottles filled with heated water close to the victim. If the victim has serious symptoms, attempt to keep him or her awake. Put the victim in a sleeping bag with another person, skin to skin. If you have a double bag, put two warm people in with the victim.

Wood Ticks

Ticks are common throughout wooded, brushy, and grassy areas of the gorge. They are most active from March through early summer. All ticks are potential carriers of Rocky Mountain spotted fever. The western black-legged tick is responsible for transmitting Lyme disease, a bacterial infection named for the Connecticut town where it was first recognized.

Your best defense against ticks is to avoid areas infested with them and to wear clothing with a snug fit around the waist, wrists, and ankles. Wearing several layers of clothing is most effective in keeping ticks from reaching the body. Since ticks do not always bite right away (they often crawl around on a potential host for several hours before deciding where to feed on a victim's blood), a strong insect repellent can also be an effective deterrent against tick bites.

Poison Oak

In addition to Oregon oak, the gorge (especially the eastern part) is home to poison oak. In contact with skin, poison oak can cause an irritating rash that, although not life threatening, can ruin your outing. Resin produced by the plant causes redness, itching, and pain. The severity of the reaction varies, but the onset usually occurs within twelve hours of contact and can last for up to ten days.

Avoid contact with poison oak by learning to identify it. Remember: "Leaves of three, let it be." Poison oak often sprouts leaflets in groups of three on woody, rust-colored stems. Leaves are shiny or dull green, turning red, orange, or brown in fall. The leaves of poison oak are often heavily lobed around the edges.

To avoid contact, wear long pants and use care when choosing a cat hole. If you come into contact with poison oak, rinse the area immediately with lots of water, and if a rash develops apply calamine lotion to reduce itching.

Poison oak tends to be more prolific as you move toward the eastern side of the gorge and drier climates. Trails, such as McCall Point, Catherine Creek, and Wygant Point, deserve a little extra caution.

Lightning

Do not be caught on a ridge- or mountaintop, under large or solitary trees, in the open, or near open water during a lightning storm. Try to seek shelter in a low-lying area—a dense stand of small, uniformly sized trees is ideal. Stay away from anything that might attract lightning, such as metal tent poles, graphite fishing rods, or pack frames.

Water

Few backcountry pleasures can top a cool drink from a high-country lake or stream. That refreshing drink of water along the trail is almost a tradition, but now, like other grand traditions, this one is fading away.

A protozoan called *Giardia lamblia* has made this change permanent. This single-celled parasite, now found throughout the Columbia River Gorge and most other wild areas, causes severe intestinal disease. All wilderness users must now take appropriate measures to ensure that water is pure by taking one of the following steps:

- Pack water from the faucet. (This can be difficult on long trips.)
- Rapidly boil water for at least ten minutes before drinking.
- Purify water with a filter. Ceramic or carbon-based filtration systems are commonly sold in sporting goods stores.
- Add iodine tablets, drops, or other water purification tablets, available at sporting goods stores.
- Add two healthy bleach drops per quart and let set for twenty minutes before drinking.

Also, be aware of the source of your water. Snowmelt, springs, and small intermittent streams are safer than large streams or lakes. Take all water upstream from the trail.

One final note: If you become ill about two to four weeks after your backcountry visit, see a physician immediately.

Car Theft

Theft of property from unattended motor vehicles is becoming a significant problem in many areas—including the gorge. My strategy for avoiding vehicle theft has always been to not drive a car worth breaking into or leave anything worth stealing in sight. The latter is probably useful advice, since most people prefer to drive nice cars. It didn't used to be so, but now I do suggest taking your wallet and money with you securely fastened within a coat or knapsack. It is better, however, to go light on valuables; have a little money and some ID on you at all times, and don't leave anything in the car. If you do use a hide-a-key, make sure it's well hidden and that only people you trust know its location.

How to Use this Guidebook

This guidebook won't answer every question you have as you plan your excursions into the Columbia River Gorge. Then again, you probably don't want to know everything before you go—that would remove the thrill of making your own discoveries while exploring this magnificent landscape. Still, this book should provide you with all the basic information you need to plan a safe and exciting trip.

All Trails Start in the Gorge

This guide is limited to hikes that begin in the Columbia River Gorge, most of which are quite near the shore. Rather than cover a large area superficially, I've tried to cover the trails between Portland and the Dalles thoroughly. This sometimes makes for more climbing than might otherwise be necessary. Don't feel that you have to limit yourself to following the exact routes described—feel free to hike downhill all day if you like. My knees just happen to prefer going uphill, and you do get a better workout climbing. These hikes are equally memorable, however, whether you go uphill or down.

Distances

It's almost impossible to figure completely accurate lengths for hiking trails. The distances used in this guidebook are derived from a combination of actual experience hiking the trails, distances stated on Forest Service signs, and estimates made from looking at topo maps. In some cases the calculated distances here may be slightly off, so consider this in your planning. Keep in mind, too, that distance is often less important than difficulty—a rough and rocky cross-country trek of only 2 miles can take longer than 5 or 6 miles on a good trail.

Approximate Hiking Time

It's almost impossible to give an exact amount of time a hike will take, so I have provided a range for most of the hikes. Enthusiastic hikers may be able to complete most hikes faster than the low end of the range, and the contemplative may take more time. Either way the times I've given are intended to provide a general idea of the duration of the hikes.

Trail Difficulty Ratings

While I've estimated the difficulty of each trail as carefully as possible, keep in mind that rating is subjective; my estimates should serve as a general guide only, not the final word. What is difficult to one person may seem easy to the next. In this guidebook, difficulty ratings consider both how long and how strenuous the route is. Here are some general definitions of the ratings:

Easy. Suitable for any hiker, including small children or the elderly, without serious elevation gain, off-trail or hazardous sections, or places where the trail is faint and hard to follow.

Moderate. Suitable for hikers who have some experience and at least an average fitness level; probably not suitable for small children or the elderly unless they have an above-average level of fitness. These trails may include short sections where route finding is difficult, and often have some big hills to climb.

Difficult. Suitable for experienced hikers at an above-average fitness level. Often some sections of these trails are difficult to follow, or there are off-trail sections that could require knowledge of route finding with a topo map and compass. In addition, these trails often involve serious elevation gain, as well as the possibility of hazardous conditions and obstacles such as difficult stream crossings, snowfields, or cliffs.

Note: When the difficulty of a trail deserves special attention, this will be mentioned within the hike description. Some trails, like the Mount Defiance Trail, are considered extreme climbs suitable only for the experienced and very fit. Please consider your fitness level before attempting any of the trails listed as Strenuous Hikes in the Vacation Planner.

Traffic

Each hike description lists the volume of traffic as light, moderate, or heavy. Heavy use indicates that you will likely see many other hikers on a sunny day. Moderate use means you'll probably see other hikers, but not that many. Light use is a rating I reserve for little-used or hard-to-reach places in the gorge.

Following Faint Trails

If a trail is described as an unmaintained route, orienteering skills are necessary, but most of these trails were at least maintained in the past and are still followable. The few Columbia Gorge trails that receive infrequent use tend to fade away in overgrown vine maple and deadfall, on ridges, or through rocky sections. Don't panic. Usually such sections are short, and you can look ahead to see where the trail goes. Often you can see the trail going up a hill or through a corridor of trees ahead. If so, focus on that landmark and don't worry about being off the trail for a short distance.

Watch for other indicators that you are indeed on the right route, especially when the trail isn't clearly visible. These include cairns, blazes, downfall cut with saws, and trees with the branches whacked off one side. Only follow official Forest Service blazes that are shaped like the letter *i* (or an upside-down exclamation point); don't follow blazes made by hunters, outfitters, or other hikers marking the way to some special spot. Don't count on blazes. Not all trails are presently blazed.

Best Season

While it's possible to hike in the Columbia Gorge year-round, rain and snow can cause the trail conditions to vary widely on some trails, so the hiking season is usually best in the spring, summer, and fall.

Total Climbing

To give an idea of how much climbing there is on each hike, I have provided information on the sum of all the hills on each hike. This is in addition to the elevation profiles, which provide information on the duration of the hills and where they are located on each hike.

Canine Compatibility

Dogs like to go hiking, too. It is one of the great joys of life to have a dog along on a long hike, but there are hikes where they are not allowed or where it's better to leave them at home for environmental and safety reasons. For most of the hikes where dogs are allowed, they need to be on a leash.

Fees and Permits

With the heavy recreational use in the Columbia Gorge, permits and trail-use fees are a common fact of life. There are still a few hikes that are free, others are private and a donation is requested, still others require a Northwest Forest Pass for parking. To obtain a pass contact Nature of the Northwest at (800) 270-7504 or on the Web at www.naturenw.org. You can also buy passes at a number of shops, chambers of commerce, and other businesses. A yearly pass costs $30.00 and a day pass costs $5.00. A new $85 Washington and Oregon Recreation Pass will be honored throughout the Gorge. The pass is available online at www.naturew.org. or by calling (800) 270–7504.

Finding Maps

Good maps are easy to find, and they are essential to any wilderness trip. For safety reasons, you need maps for route finding and for "staying found." For nonsafety reasons, don't miss out on the joy of mindlessly whittling away untold hours staring at a topo map, and wondering what it's like here and there.

For trips into the Columbia River Gorge, you have several good choices for maps:

U.S. Geological Survey (USGS) topographic maps. Check sporting goods stores in the area or write directly to the USGS at the following address:

Map Distribution
U.S. Geological Survey
Box 25286, Federal Center
Denver, CO 80225
mapping.usgs.gov

To make sure you order the correct USGS map, refer to the grid on the USGS Topographic Map Index.

Maptech CD-ROM topographic maps. A nice way to store and manage all your USGS quads on a set of CD-ROMs and print only the areas you need.

Maptech
10 Industrial Way
Amesbury, MA 01913
(888) 839–5551
www.maptech.com

Trails of the Columbia Gorge. An excellent Columbia Gorge recreation map originally published by the Forest Service is called Trails of the Columbia Gorge. It does not, however, include most of the trips on the Washington side. It's available through most local Forest Service offices and Northwest Interpretive Association outlets, as well as from:

Nature of the Northwest
800 NE Oregon Street, Suite 177
Portland, OR 97232
(800) 270–7504
www.naturenw.org

Green Trails. A series of three hiking maps is published by Green Trails. You can find Green Trails maps at sporting goods stores in the area, or you can write to:

Green Trails
P.O. Box 77734
Seattle, WA 98177
(206) 546–6277
www.greentrails.com

In addition, there are several other maps of the Columbia River Gorge that are good for a bigger picture of the entire area, and Forest Service maps of the Gifford Pinchot and Mount Hood National Forests have the latest road information. A national scenic area map is now available from the Forest Service's scenic area office in Hood River. The Delorme Atlases for Oregon and Washington are good sources of map information for the Northwest. All of these maps are nice to have, but not necessary. All you really need is one of the four types of maps listed above describing the area you plan to visit.

Trail Contacts

Trail information sources are provided below and in an appendix at the back of the book. We have also provided the contact information for the primary land management organization or organizations in the Trail contacts section of each hike.

For Forest Service information, you can call, visit, or write to the Columbia River Gorge National Scenic Area office. Alternatively, stop by the visitor center at Multnomah Falls, Skamania Lodge, or the Gorge Discovery Center:

USDA Forest Service
Columbia River Gorge National Scenic Area
902 Wasco Street, Suite 200
Hood River, OR 97031
(541) 308–1700
www.fs.fed.us/r6/columbia/forest

Multnomah Falls Forest Service Interpretive Center
Multnomah Falls Lodge
Historic Columbia River Highway
(503) 695–2372

Skamania Lodge Forest Service Information Center
1131 Skamania Lodge Way
Stevenson, WA 98648
(509) 427–2528

Columbia Gorge Discovery Center
5000 Discovery Drive
The Dalles, OR 97058
(541) 296–8600
www.gorgediscovery.org

The best way to get up-to-date information on the gorge is to call (541) 386–2333 before you go. If you call the USDA Forest Service office, this is the number they will most likely refer you to. Information is updated weekly.

For wilderness-specific questions regarding the newly renamed Mark O. Hatfield/Columbia Wilderness Area, contact:

Mount Hood National Forest
16400 Champion Way
Sandy, OR 97055
(503) 668–1700
www.fs.fed.use/r6/mthood

How to Use the Maps in this Book

Elevation Profile: This helpful profile gives you a look at the cross-section of the hike's ups and downs. Elevation is labeled on the left, mileage is indicated on the top. Road and trail names are shown along the route, with towns and points of interest labeled in bold. Elevation profiles are not provided for hikes with less than 250 feet of elevation gain.

Route Map: This is your primary guide to each hike. It shows the accessible roads and trails, points of interest, water, towns, landmarks, and geographical features. It also distinguishes trails from roads, and paved roads from unpaved roads. The selected route is highlighted, and directional arrows point the way.

Map Legend

=(84)=	Interstate
=(26)=	U.S. highway
—(14)—	State highway
———	Paved road
═══	Gravel road
▬▬▬	Featured unimproved road
=====	Unimproved road
▬▬▬	Featured trail
---------	Optional trail
---------	Other trail
··········	Primitive route
++++++	Railroad
⊢——⊣	Tunnel
≍	Bridge
▲	Campground
∘	City
▬	Dam
•—•	Gate
🚶	Other trailhead
◼	Overlook/viewpoint
🅿	Parking
▲	Peak/elevation
⊞	Picnic area
▪	Point of interest
—•—	Power line
⌕	Spring
START 🚶	Trailhead
∥	Waterfall

Hike Index

34. Wyeth Trail to North Lake (can be combined with trip to Warren Lake and Bear Lake)

Hikes for Those Not Scared of Heights (trips with steep drop-offs near the trail)
13. Rock of Ages Ridge Trail
16. Upper McCord Creek Falls
18. Munra Point
23. Eagle Creek Trail to Wahtum Lake
25. Eagle Creek–Tanner Butte Loop
24. Metlako Falls
27. Ruckel Ridge Loop
32. Indian Point Loop (just the lookout)
43. Beacon Rock
45. Hamilton Mountain (southern face route)

Waterfall Lovers' Hikes
1. Latourell Falls
2. Bridal Veil Falls
3. Coopey Falls
5. Wahkeena Falls to Devils Rest
6. Multnomah Falls
10. Horsetail and Ponytail Falls
12. Oneonta Trail to Larch Mountain
15. Elowah Falls
16. Upper McCord Creek Falls
19. Wahclella Falls
23. Eagle Creek Trail to Wahtum Lake
24. Metlako Falls
28. Pacific Crest Trail to Dry Creek Falls
35. Lancaster Falls
44. Rodney and Hardy Falls

Author's Choice
4. Angels Rest–Devils Rest
6. Multnomah Falls
14. Nesmith Point and Yeon Mountain
25. Eagle Creek–Tanner Butte Loop
47. Table Mountain

Crown Point Scenic Corridor

As you drive east from Portland to begin your journey into the Columbia River Gorge, or as you drive west exiting the Gorge, your last vista is the cliff-top dome on Crown Point. Most often photographed from Portland Women's Forum Park, the Vista House provides the perfect foreground for the walls the mighty river cut through solid basalt.

The Vista House was built in 1916 and it makes a pleasant stop with a gift shop and interpretive displays. It is also the mid-point of the most traveled section of the Historic Columbia River Highway from Troutdale to Bridal Veil, Multnomah Falls, and Cascade Locks. You can start a trip to the Gorge by following the Historic Columbia River Highway from Troutdale through Corbett, stopping at the Vista House for a postcard and a picture, and continuing east to the waterfalls of the Bridal Veil Area. After that, Multnomah Falls is just a few miles down the road for a great introduction to the beauty of the Gorge. For more information or to contribute to the restoration of the Vista House contact: Friends of the Vista House, P.O. Box 204, Corbett, OR 97019; www.vistahouse.com.

1 Latourell Falls

A short, gentle hike up above 249-foot Latourell Falls to the calm roar of the upper falls.

Start: Latourell Falls Trailhead on the Historic Columbia River Highway.
Distance: 2.3-mile loop.
Approximate hiking time: 1 to 2 hours.
Difficulty: Easy.
Traffic: Heavy.
Trail type: Well maintained.
Best season: Year-round.
Total climbing: 800 feet.
Other trail users: None.
Canine compatibility: Dogs are allowed on leashes only.

Nearest town: The village of Latourell is just a few nice homes; for services, Troutdale is your best bet.
Fees and permits: None.
Maps: Bridal Veil Green Trails, Bridal Veil USGS, Geo-Graphics Trails of the Columbia River Gorge, and Maptech Oregon.
Trail contacts: Oregon State Parks, 725 Summer Street NE, Suite C, Salem, OR 97301; (503) 986-0707; www.prd.state.or.us.

Finding the trailhead: From Portland, take Interstate 84 east to exit 28, Bridal Veil. Follow the off-ramp to the intersection with the Historic Columbia River Highway. Turn right and head west for 2.8 miles to the Latourell Falls Trailhead. Park on the left. A paved trail starts on the south side of the parking lot. Bathrooms are available on the north side of the road by the bridge. An alternate and probably more scenic route is to take exit 17 or 18 in Troutdale and follow the Historic Columbia River Highway along the Sandy River, up and over Crown Point, and down to the Latourell Trailhead, the first developed waterfall trailhead on the way to Multnomah Falls.

Special considerations: This is the first well-known waterfall along the Historic Columbia River Highway driving from Portland and a popular place during peak visitation on weekends and sunny days.

The Hike

Latourell Falls is 249 feet tall, and even without too many cubic feet per second coming over the cliff, the height alone makes it spectacular. The trip to both the upper and main Latourell Falls is an easy hike and a good introduction to the waterfalls of the gorge. Overlooks provide several excellent views of both cascades, with the exception of the ill-placed tree branch or two that prevent a clean photo.

From the trailhead on the southeast side of the parking area, follow a paved path up to a lookout below Latourell Falls. The pavement ends shortly after the lookout, and a well-used dirt path begins. The trail climbs steeply up above the falls, with devil's-club and lady ferns along the way. After climbing about 300 feet in elevation, the trail flattens out.

Latourell Falls ▶

Latourell Falls

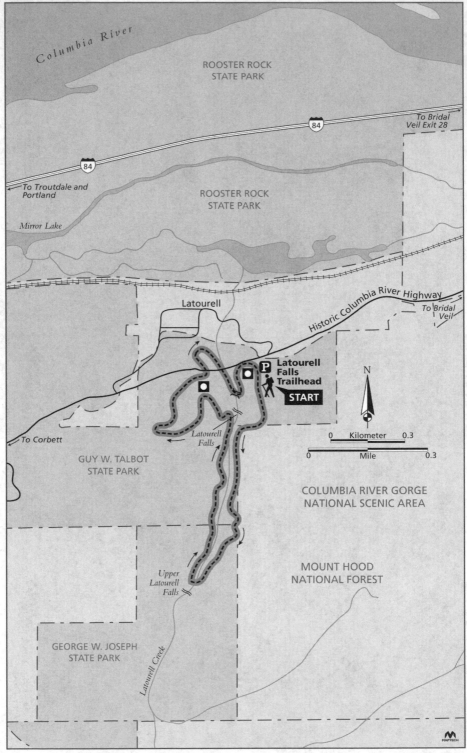

At 0.5 mile, you reach the junction with the cutoff trail to the return loop on the other side of Latourell Creek. Stay left, heading south, to see the upper falls. The trail continues at a gentle grade through cedar forest. Western red cedar trees are very shade tolerant and do not require a lot of sunlight, but they do need a lot of water. You cross several footbridges before reaching the upper falls.

At Upper Latourell Falls, the bridge crosses the stream just below the falls. You can take a short path on the opposite side of the creek, underneath the falls, but the rock is slippery and wet.

Most of the public land traversed by the Latourell Falls Trail was donated by Guy Webster Talbot and his family. It was once a private summer estate, but with good heart on the part of the Talbot estate it is forever accessible to future generations.

Past Upper Latourell Falls, the trail continues to level, then turns downhill to the north. On the other side, to reach the cutoff trail, stay left for the scenic highway and several lookout spots with benches for a moment of silence. There is a slight climb to the lookouts; then the trail drops on switchbacks past one of my favorite bigleaf maple trees. Bent into a U shape over the trail, it's easy to walk under. This is one way for a tree to capitalize on the sunlight left by the cleared trail, without getting in the way of the trail crew.

▶ This is one of the closest trailheads to the big city of Portland, and it's a good idea to get in the habit of not leaving valuables easily visible in your vehicle. Gorge trailheads receive a high volume of visitors, not all of whom are honest.

After 2.1 miles, the trail returns to the highway on the west side of the bridge over Latourell Creek. It's a 0.2-mile walk back to the trailhead. If you're not too tired and are anxious to see more waterfalls, drive east on the highway to Shepperds Dell, Bridal Veil, and beyond.

Lower Falls Trail Option

There is also a paved nature path leading below the lower falls. It leaves the parking lot on the south side of the highway, just before the bridge over Latourell Creek. It enables you to look up at the misty crash of water and get some good pictures. If you follow the lower trail from the parking lot, it will take you along Latourell Creek to Guy W. Talbot State Park, but because the trail doesn't loop back to the parking lot at Latourell Falls, I suggest returning to the trailhead via the same route.

The Falls at Shepperds Dell Option

Just a mile east of Latourell Falls on your way to or from hiking Bridal Veil Falls, be sure to stop at the Shepperds Dell—not really a hike, but a nice cascade right underneath the historic highway. A visit will take you only about five minutes, leaving you with plenty of time to gaze in wonder at the series of cascades inside a rock-sheltered cove. A paved path winds around the sheer basalt rock face of the dell to a guardrailed

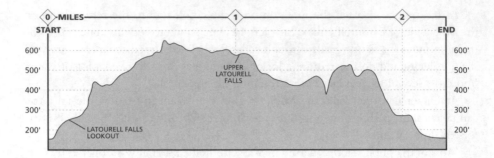

lookout above the falls. Shepperds Dell Falls is actually a combination of an upper 35- to 40-foot plunge and a lower 40- to 60-foot horsetail-type drop. Looking underneath the bridge gives you a feel for the height and erosive power of the rushing water that carved this dell.

Miles and Directions

0.0 **START** from Latourell Falls Trailhead on Historic Columbia River Highway.

0.2 Latourell Falls Lookout (end of pavement).

0.5 Junction with cutoff trail, where you can shorten loop, stay left (south).

1.0 Upper Latourell Falls.

1.5 Junction with the other side of the cutoff trail, stay left.

2.1 Return to highway west of the trailhead.

2.3 Return to Latourell Falls Trailhead.

2 Bridal Veil Falls

A short walk to an overlook above Bridal Veil Falls with a nature trail option afterward.

Start: Bridal Veil State Park Trailhead on the Historic Columbia River Highway.
Distance: 0.6 mile out and back to Bridal Veil Falls; 1.1 miles if you take the Overlook Loop option.
Approximate hiking time: 1 hour.
Difficulty: Easy.
Traffic: Heavy.
Trail type: Well maintained.
Best season: Year-round.
Total climbing: 150 feet.

Other trail users: None.
Canine compatibility: Dogs are allowed on leashes only.
Nearest town: Corbett.
Fees and permits: None.
Maps: Bridal Veil Green Trails, Bridal Veil USGS, Geo-Graphics Trails of the Columbia River Gorge, and Maptech Oregon.
Trail contacts: Oregon State Parks, 725 Summer Street NE, Suite C, Salem, OR 97301; (503) 986-0707; www.prd.state.or.us.

Finding the trailhead: From Portland, take Interstate 84 east to exit 28, Bridal Veil. Follow the off-ramp to the intersection with the Historic Columbia River Highway. Turn right and travel 0.8 mile; the trailhead will be on the right, just after crossing Bridal Veil Creek. Turn into the parking lot, and the trailhead is on the east end, near the bathrooms.

Special considerations: Watch for some poison ivy in the area. Staying on the trail and using the restroom at the trailhead should keep away the itchies.

The Hike

The hike to Bridal Veil Falls is an easy hike above one of the more nameworthy falls in the area.

At the trailhead, the path splits in two. Stay right, heading east, for the falls. The left fork becomes a nature trail that makes a nice walk after returning from the falls (see the Overlook Loop Option at the end of this hike). Soon the pavement ends and the often muddy trail leads into the deciduous forest down toward the falls.

At 0.1 mile, the trail comes to an unmarked intersection that often confuses hikers. Do not take the right trail to the south—it was a bushwhacker's attempt to reach the top of the falls. Stay left, heading east, and descend on a switchback to the bridge across the creek.

▶ In the little town of Bridal Veil, the post office is a popular place for local brides-to-be to postmark their wedding invitations. The post office is open Saturday for primarily this purpose; local mail volume is pretty low otherwise.

Bridal Veil Falls

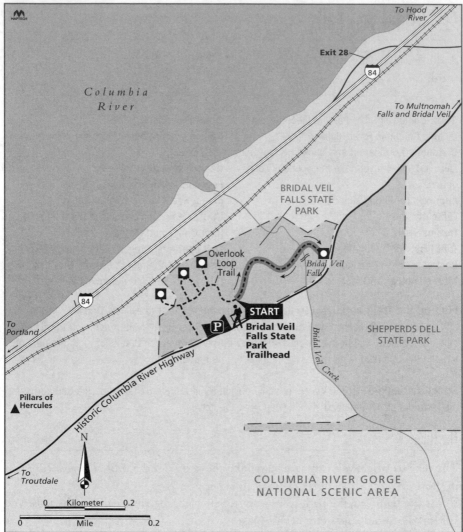

Once across the creek, the trail leads to a wooden staircase and lookout below Bridal Veil Falls. The large basalt rocks on which the platform is built offer a good foreground object for photographing the falls. The water demands of the logging industry and the reservoir above the falls used to reduce the falls to a trickle in late season, but the mill is no longer here and only its remnants are visible.

Bridal Veil Falls is a sharp double drop, with an upper drop of 60 to 100 feet and a lower drop of 40 to 60 feet forming a two-stage tier-type waterfall. The scene is spectacular, and once you gaze upon the falls, the source of the name *veil* is immediately apparent.

The platform is the end of this brief hike, but you can spend plenty of time with your flower book. Return via the same trail to the trailhead, and consider exploring the basalt plateau near the picnic area on the Overlook Loop Trail.

Overlook Loop Option

At the trailhead junction, take the left trail and head north. A paved path leads out onto the small plateau. A large interpretive sign announces the existence of camas lilies on this nature preserve. The Overlook Loop Trail offers several good lookouts for views of the Columbia and the Pillars of Hercules to the west. These eroded pinnacles of basalt are also visible from the interstate.

The Overlook Loop Trail does indeed have some camas lilies, as promised, but many invasive species like Scotch broom and Himalayan blackberry are threatening this preserve. Be careful to stay on the trail.

Miles and Directions

0.0 **START** from Bridal Veil Falls State Park Trailhead on Historic Columbia River Highway.

0.1 Junction with unmarked trail that dead-ends, stay left.

0.3 Bridal Veil Lookout.

0.6 Return to trailhead. Turn ringht to follow Overlook Loop Trail. **Option:** This will add another 0.5 mile to your hike.

3 Coopey Falls

A short, gentle hike to Coopey Falls.

Start: Angels Rest Trailhead.
Distance: 1.6 miles out and back.
Approximate hiking time: 1 hour.
Difficulty: Easy.
Traffic: Heavy.
Trail type: Well maintained.
Best season: Year-round.
Total climbing: 350 feet.
Other trail users: None.

Canine compatibility: Dogs are allowed on leashes only.
Nearest town: Corbett.
Fees and permits: None.
Maps: Bridal Veil Green Trails, Bridal Veil USGS, Geo-Graphics Trails of the Columbia River Gorge, and Maptech Oregon.
Trail contacts: Oregon State Parks, 725 Summer Street NE, Suite C, Salem, OR 97301; (503) 986-0707; www.prd.state.or.us.

Finding the trailhead: From Portland, take Interstate 84 east to exit 28, Bridal Veil. Follow the off-ramp to the intersection with the Historic Columbia River Highway and park to the right in a dirt lot. Angels Rest Trail 415 starts across the highway to the south.

The Hike

From the trailhead, Trail 415 climbs gradually, winding through forest into open slide areas. Burn marks are evident on many of the older trees that survived a 1991 fire. A more recent burn has allowed sunlight to reach the forest floor, fostering the growth of lots of bushy plants such as ocean-spray, thimbleberry, and wildflowers.

► Waterfalls in the gorge receive many visitors, and staying on the trail helps keep each waterfall just as it was the last time someone visited it.

At 0.8 mile, you reach Coopey Falls, a 150- to 175-foot horsetail-type waterfall. There are several spur lookout trails to the left for views down onto the crashing waters of the falls. Although not one of the most well-known

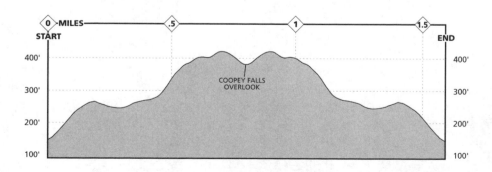

Coopey Falls

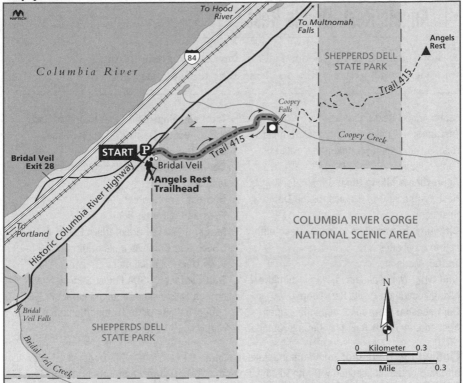

waterfalls in the gorge, Coopey does receive heavy traffic by those folks on the way to Angels Rest. If you're one of them, see the next hike description. Otherwise, follow the main trail back to the Angels Rest Trailhead.

Miles and Directions

0.0 **START** from Angels Rest Trailhead on Historic Columbia River Highway.

0.8 Reach Coopey Falls lookouts.

1.6 Return to Angels Rest Trailhead.

4 Angels Rest–Devils Rest

A short, gentle hike to Coopey Falls, an intermediate hike to Angels Rest Lookout for a view, and a long day hike to Devils Rest for more views.

Start: Angels Rest Trailhead.
Distance: 4.4 miles out and back to Angels Rest; 11.9 miles if you take the Devils Rest Loop option.
Approximate hiking time: 3 hours for Angels Rest and back; 6 to 8 hours for the Devils Rest Loop.
Difficulty: Intermediate to Angels Rest; difficult to Devils Rest.
Traffic: Moderate.
Trail type: Well maintained, with a primitive hiking section on Devils Rest Loop.
Best season: Year-round, depending upon frost line. Try Devils Rest May through October.

Total climbing: 1,540 feet to Angels Rest; 3,810 feet for Devils Rest Loop option.
Other trail users: None.
Canine compatibility: Dogs are allowed on leashes only.
Nearest town: Corbett.
Fees and permits: None.
Maps: Bridal Veil Green Trails, Bridal Veil USGS, Geo-Graphics Trails of the Columbia River Gorge, and Maptech Oregon.
Trail contacts: USDA Forest Service Multnomah Falls Visitor Center, Multnomah Falls Lodge, off I-84 or on Historic Columbia River Highway; (503) 695-2372.

Finding the trailhead: From Portland, take Interstate 84 east to exit 28, Bridal Veil. Follow the off-ramp to the intersection with the Historic Columbia River Highway and park to the right in a dirt lot. Angels Rest Trail 415 starts across the highway to the south.

The Hike

This trail is a good hike for people who don't want a really steep climb, but don't mind getting a little exercise. The views from Angels Rest are superb, and the trail up is gradual. This trail also offers a chance to see the forest recovering from a 1991 fire that burned these hills; many salmonberry and thimbleberry plants thrive in the open space left by the fire. Several loop options are available from this trailhead. They require a shuttle to Wahkeena or a longer trip back from Devils Rest.

From the trailhead, Trail 415 climbs gradually, winding through forest into open slide areas. Burn marks are evident on many of the older trees that survived the fire. A more recent burn has allowed sunlight to reach the forest floor, fostering the growth of lots of bushy plants such as ocean-spray, thimbleberry, and wildflowers.

At 0.8 mile, you reach Coopey Falls; there are several spur lookout trails to the left for views down onto the crashing waters. After the falls, bear right. The trail crosses the creek on a footbridge and climbs more steadily into the shade, then takes long switchbacks up another burn area with thick underbrush. The trail climbs right to the base of Angels Rest before veering south on one last long, gentle switchback

The Columbia River Gorge, from Angels Rest, with Hamilton and Table Mountains in the distance.

up to the top. On the last stretch the trail crosses a rocky section and seems to disappear. Look straight ahead for the trail, not uphill. It continues across flat rocks.

At 2.2 miles, you reach a junction before going out onto Angels Rest. To the right, heading east, is the continuation of Trail 415 to the Wahkeena area and Devils Rest. The left trail, heading north, is a lookout spur that extends all the way out to the end of Angels Rest, a prominent, flat, cliff-sided point. From the interstate, it looks like it would make a perfect helicopter landing pad. It's covered partially by bushes and large rocks, but offers excellent views and some good lunch-spot rocks. You can return to your car via the same trail or hike to Devils Rest or Wahkeena Trail. A trip to Wahkeena requires a shuttle car at the Multnomah Falls or Wahkeena Trailhead.

Continuing on for Devils Rest, return to the junction with the spur trail and turn left, heading east; the trail climbs gently up one switchback. Next, watch for a trail forking to the left at 2.3 miles—this is the main trail. Straight ahead is the Foxglove Trail area. Stay left, continuing east on Trail 415 for Wahkeena and Devils Rest. (You can reach Devils Rest by going right, but the trail is harder to follow.)

Angels Rest-Devils Rest

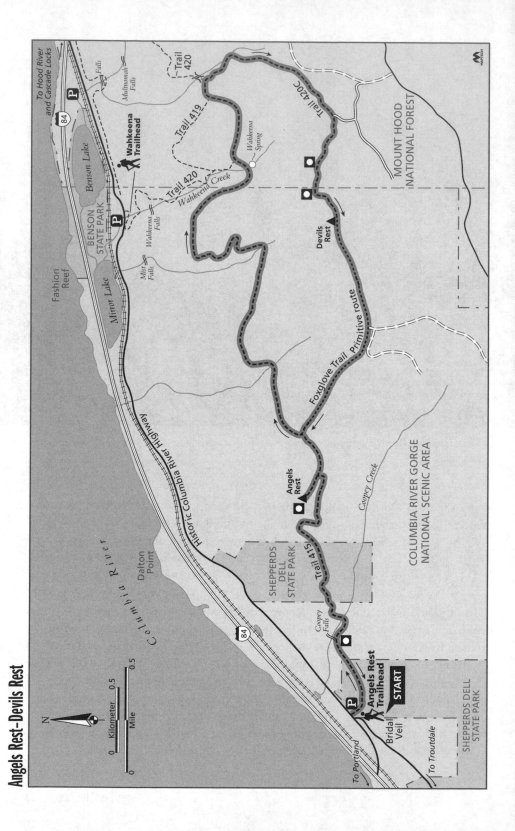

Trail 415 follows along the rim of the ridge. Through the trees you can get a view of Angels Rest, with the lower Columbia below. The trail crosses several small footbridges as it winds along through large Douglas firs and an understory less dense than in the burned area. After crossing a third creek on a foot-bridge, the trail begins to make gentle switchbacks down-ward. Some trees here survived the 1991 fire and have a competitive advantage over the bushy plants.

At 4.8 miles, the trail flattens out, climbing slightly. After crossing Wahkeena Spring on a footbridge, you will reach the junction with Wahkeena Trail 420. Turn left, heading north, for the Wahkeena Trailhead; stay right, continuing east for Devils Rest on what is now Trail 420 also. Taking the trail to Wahkeena is a good option for less experienced hikers. Trail 420 begins to climb steadily for 0.4 mile to the junction with Vista Point Trail 419. Several old stone trail markers lie around a pile of rocks that forms the junction. About 30 feet past this junction, to the east, Devils Rest Trail 420C veers right, turn-ing south.

▶ Volunteer habitat restoration opportunities are available. Inquire at the Multnomah Lodge Information Center at Multnomah Falls

After taking Devils Rest Trail 420C just past the junction, the trail climbs steep switchbacks for 0.5 mile before flattening out onto the narrow plateau toward Dev-ils Rest. One unmarked trail veers left, but stay right as the trail curves west. Then an old road intersects with the main trail—keep bearing right, to the west. There are two good viewpoints on the way to Devils Rest. The first, on a large rock, offers views of everything north of the river, including Table Mountain and Hamilton Mountain. The second lookout requires a short walk out to get a peek at the gorge. This cliffy but very scenic viewpoint is worth a stop. Continue past the lookout spur trails to Devils Rest.

Devils Rest is a good place for a rest, but it doesn't offer as good a view as the previous lookouts, because it's tree covered. Just before the top of Devils Rest, or the end of the maintained trail, is a marked junction with the Foxglove Trail. This route to the west is unofficial but straightforward and offers a shortcut back to Angels Rest Trail 415. The Foxglove Trail winds through shady forest before rejoining Trail 415 back to Angels Rest. Follow the main trail back to the Angels Rest Trailhead.

Miles and Directions

0.0 **START** from Angels Rest Trailhead on Historic Columbia River Highway.

0.8 Coopey Falls lookouts.

2.2 Angels Rest Lookout Trail, turn left (north) to reach Angels Rest. Return to Trail 415, turn left (east).

2.3 Junction with Foxglove Trail, stay left on Trail 415.

4.8 Wahkeena Spring.

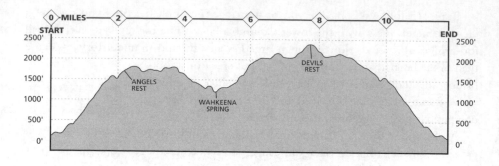

4.9 Junction with Wahkeena Trail 420, stay right on Trail 420.

5.2 Junction with Vista Point Trail 419, turn right. About 30 feet past this junction is the junction with Devils Rest Trail 420C, turn right (south).

5.7 Unmarked trail, stay right. Also stay right at the junction with an old road.

7.1 First lookout.

7.5 Second lookout.

8.6 Devils Rest and junction with Foxglove Trail, continue straight (west).

9.6 Junction with Trail 415, turn left (southwest).

11.9 Return to Angels Rest Trailhead.

5 Wahkeena Falls to Devils Rest

A popular day hike offering views of several famous Columbia Gorge waterfalls in the Multnomah Falls area.

Start: Wahkeena Trailhead.
Distance: 7.3 miles out and back.
Approximate hiking time: 4 to 6 hours.
Difficulty: Intermediate.
Traffic: Heavy.
Trail type: Well maintained.
Best season: Year-round.
Total climbing: 2,340 feet.
Other trail users: None.
Canine compatibility: Dogs are allowed on leashes only.

Nearest town: Corbett.
Fees and permits: None.
Maps: Bridal Veil Green Trails, Bridal Veil and Multnomah Falls USGS, Geo-Graphics Trails of the Columbia River Gorge, and Maptech Oregon.
Trail contacts: USDA Forest Service Multnomah Falls Visitor Center, Multnomah Falls Lodge, off I-84 or on Historic Columbia River Highway; (503) 695-2372.

Finding the trailhead: From Portland, take Interstate 84 east to exit 28, Bridal Veil. Follow the off-ramp and then turn left onto the Columbia River Highway; drive 2.5 miles to the Wahkeena Picnic Area and Trailhead. Parking is on the left (north) side of the road. The trail starts on the right. Bathrooms are available at the Multnomah Falls Lodge, 0.5 mile farther.

The Hike

Wahkeena Falls is a short walk up this trail, but the entire route is a pleasant alternative to often crowded Multnomah Falls Trail, featuring Fairy Falls, lush Wahkeena Spring, Lemmon and Vista Points, and a good healthy climb to Devils Rest.

Wahkeena Trail 420 climbs steadily from the start. The path is wide past several switchbacks and old slides. A stone bridge just below Wahkeena Falls makes for a misty rest spot. Wahkeena Falls has a height of 242 feet. *Wahkeena,* incidentally, means "most beautiful" in the Yakima language. In winter, if the temperature gets below freezing, the bridge becomes a sheet of ice and is practically impassable.

Just after the bridge is the junction with Old Perdition Trail 421, which was closed indefinitely after a 1991 fire and 1996 slides. Stay right, heading south, because entering a closed area is illegal and unsafe. The trail switchbacks steeply up the slope with nice masonry walls at crucial corners and benches.

▶ The gorge waterfalls are especially pretty when the spray is frozen and skirted by ice sculpture.

Next is the junction with two lookout trails. The more heavily used trail on the right leads out to Lemmon Viewpoint. It offers significant views across the mile-wide Columbia.

Hikers below Wahkeena Falls

Once you're back on the main trail, climb to Fairy Falls, a small cascade in a cool glen. Fairy Falls drops 20 to 30 feet and is a fan-type waterfall. A cedar log bench offers an opportunity for relaxation and contemplation.

At 1.2 miles up Wahkeena Trail 420 is the Vista Point junction with Trail 419. Stay right; you can return on the Vista Point route. Continuing south on Wahkeena Trail 420, the route is cool, and the rushing water drowns out highway sounds. At 1.6 miles is Angels Rest Trail 415; stay left, heading east. Trail 415 to the right takes you past Wahkeena Spring toward Angels Rest and longer hiking options. (See Hike 4, Angels Rest–Devils Rest.) The trail climbs gently before it is rejoined by Vista Point Trail 419.

At the well-marked Vista Point junction atop a small plateau in the trees, continue straight, heading east. Just 30 feet east of the junction with Trail 419 is another junction, with Trail 420C to Devils Rest. Turn right, heading south and up along Devils Rest Trail 420C. After the junction, the trail climbs steep switchbacks for 0.5 mile before flattening out onto the narrow plateau leading to Devils Rest. One

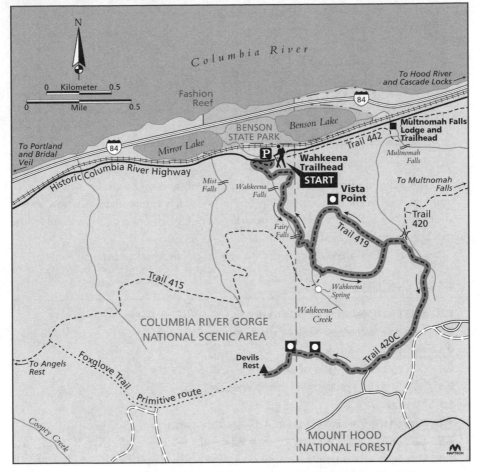

unmarked trail veers left; stay right. Then an old road intersects with the main trail—stay right again.

There are two viewpoints on the way to Devils Rest. The first, on a large rock, offers views of everything north of the gorge, including Table Mountain and Hamilton Mountain. The second lookout requires a short walk out to get a peek at the gorge. Don't miss these unmarked spur trails on your right as you climb toward Devils Rest. The top offers little in the way of views, but a lot in the way of satisfaction in completing the climb.

Return via Trail 420C to finish the Wahkeena Loop hike. Alternatively, follow the Foxglove Trail from the summit of Devils Rest down Angels Rest Trail 415, looping back around past Wahkeena Spring to rejoin the Wahkeena Loop.

After descending from Devils Rest back to the Vista Point junction, take the right or eastern descent back to the Wahkeena Trail. This route takes you past Vista

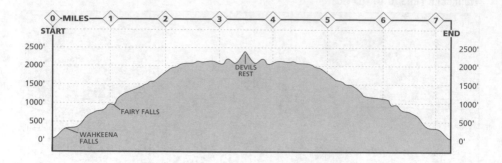

Point. You may end up wondering where Vista Point was. This point is in fact only a spur trail that veers off to the north of Trail 419 at an unmarked junction, at the end of a flat bend. Fire-scarred trees provide enough of an opening for a simple view across the gorge, even from the main trail.

Pass Fairy and Wahkeena Falls on the way back for another pleasant look.

Miles and Directions

0.0 **START** from Wahkeena Trailhead on Historic Columbia River Highway.

0.1 Junction with connecting Trail 442 to Multnomah Falls Lodge, turn right.

0.3 Wahkeena Falls Bridge.

0.4 Old Perdition Trail 421, closed indefinitely.

0.9 The trail on the right leads to Lemmon Viewpoint.

1.1 Fairy Falls.

1.2 Junction with Vista Point Loop Trail 419, stay right (south).

1.6 Junction with Angels Rest Trail 415, stay left (east).

1.9 Vista Point junction, continue straight (east). About 30 feet past this junction meet the junction with Trail 420C to Devils Rest, turn right (south).

2.4 Unmarked trail, stay right. Also stay right at the junction with an old road.

2.8 First lookout.

3.2 Second lookout.

3.5 Devils Rest, turn around.

5.1 Vista Point junction, turn right (east).

6.1 Rejoin Wahkeena Trail 420, turn right (north).

6.2 Fairy Falls.

7.3 Return to Wahkeena Trailhead.

Fairy Falls ▶

Multnomah Falls Recreation Area

I f you visit the gorge and only have time to do one thing, hiking to the top of Multnomah Falls definitely deserves consideration. At 620 feet, this is the second highest year-round waterfall in the United States. It is spectacular and spectacularly popular. The main 1.2-mile route at the falls is the shortest, fastest way to get to the top, look down, and come back, so if all you want to do is see this famous landmark from the best angle, choose Hike 6, Multnomah Falls.

Many things have been said about Multnomah Falls, but the one that really sticks out for me is that this waterfall has its own exit off Interstate 84. Not every waterfall can say that! In addition, Multnomah Falls boasts a full-service restaurant, ice cream stands, gift shop, and historic lodge. The lodge isn't really for overnight guests, but houses the restaurant and other visitor facilities.

Because Multnomah Falls receives such heavy use and is a national landmark besides, groups such as the Friends of Multnomah Falls were created to ensure its preservation. The interpretive center relies heavily on volunteers for its staff. If you would like more information on how you can help Multnomah Falls, and on attending events sponsored by the Friends of Multnomah Falls, please contact:

Friends of Multnomah Falls
P.O. Box 426
Troutdale, OR 97069
(503) 761–4751
www.multnomahfallsfriends.org

Multnomah Falls Interpretive Center
Multnomah Falls Lodge
Historic Columbia River Highway
(503) 695–2372

Besides this volunteer help, the scenic area staff has begun to manage the falls more like an urban park, with trail patrols to monitor switchback cutting and other problems. Off-trail activity is prohibited. You might ask how the wilderness experience is maintained. Well, it's not a wilderness experience to hike to Multnomah Falls, but it is a natural experience. No matter what conditions exist on the trail, in the parking lot, and at the top, Multnomah Falls keeps crashing down, and everyone gets to see, enjoy, and tell their friends about it.

Special Regulations for Multnomah Falls

- Off-trail travel is prohibited.
- Pets on a 6-foot leash only.
- The Upper Plunge Pool is closed.
- The trail closes from dusk until dawn.
- Camping is permitted 0.5 mile past the top of the falls.
- Climbing and other activities on the face of the falls are prohibited.

6 Multnomah Falls

The premier Columbia Gorge hike.

Start: Multnomah Falls Lodge and Trailhead.
Distance: 2.4 miles out and back.
Approximate hiking time: 1 to 2 hours depending on traffic and sight-seeing stops.
Difficulty: Moderate (short and easy to follow, but uphill all the way).
Traffic: Very heavy.
Trail type: Well maintained.
Best season: May through October.
Total climbing: 1,070 feet.
Other trail users: None.

Canine compatibility: Dogs are allowed on 6-foot leashes only.
Nearest town: Corbett.
Fees and permits: None.
Maps: Bridal Veil Green Trails, Multnomah Falls USGS, and Maptech Oregon; also, a handout on Multnomah Falls area trails at the visitor center.
Trail contacts: USDA Forest Service Multnomah Falls Visitor Center, Multnomah Falls Lodge, off I-84 or on Historic Columbia River Highway; (503) 695-2372.

Finding the trailhead: From Portland, drive east on Interstate 84 to exit 31, Multnomah Falls. Park and walk south, underneath the interstate and the train tracks, to the Multnomah Falls Lodge and Visitor Center. Trail 441 starts east of the lodge on a cement staircase. Multnomah Falls is visible from the highway and the parking area.

You can also reach the trailhead by taking exit 28, Bridal Veil, 3 miles before the Multnomah Falls exit. Alternatively, coming from the east, take exit 35, Ainsworth State Park, to access the Historic Columbia River Highway. Accessing the Historic Columbia River Highway from either the Bridal Veil or Ainsworth State Park exit allows you the flexibility to try other falls hikes in the area, such as Latourell Falls, Wahkeena Falls, and Horsetail Falls.

Special considerations: See the introduction to this section for special Multnomah Falls regulations.

The Hike

Multnomah Falls is the best-known and most visited spot in the Columbia River Gorge National Scenic Area. It receives more than two million visitors per year and has its own exit off Interstate 84. At the base of the falls, Multnomah Falls Lodge was constructed in 1925. It contains a restaurant, gift shop, Forest Service visitor center, and various concessions selling hot dogs, coffee, and ice cream.

If you don't like crowds, please avoid Multnomah Falls—but first consider that this waterfall is a national treasure. It's almost your duty as a visitor to the Columbia River Gorge to hike to the top at least once. At better than 620 feet, a classic plunge-type waterfall, Multnomah is the highest falls in the gorge and perhaps the most spectacular. In addition, after crashing from the top, the water flows under the famous Benson Bridge and drops again in a second-tier, wide block-type lower falls.

Multnomah Falls

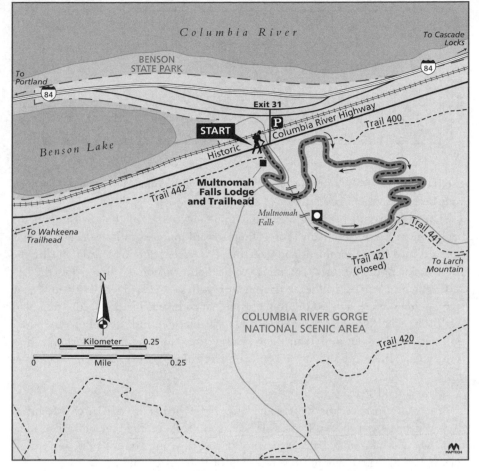

The combined picture of the two sections of the falls and the historic bridge seems to grace every piece of Oregon tourism promotional material.

Ira Williams put it best when describing Multnomah Falls: "Long have its praises been sung, and as our familiarity and knowledge of its idiosyncrasies grow, we come to realize that only the sweetest of strains can begin to express the love and reverence that this pygmy-giant but master stroke of Nature's busy hand must stir in every open heart. The rush of its waters is music that enthralls, and the picturesque surroundings are beyond the skill of the artist's brush to portray."

From this description, it's easy to understand why Multnomah Falls is the most popular hike in the gorge. All you need is patience, a friendly demeanor, and about an hour. The waterfall is easy to reach and clearly visible from the interstate. Where

◀ *Misty Multnomah Falls*

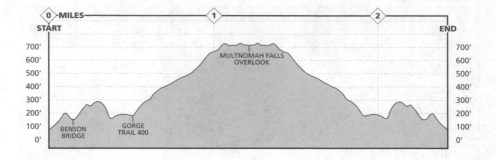

else is there a 1.2-mile-long paved trail for people with children in strollers? So open your heart and have a good hike.

The trail starts on a cement staircase within view of the falls. Follow this trail, the beginning of Larch Mountain Trail 441, up toward the famous Benson Footbridge. It was named for a prominent and generous Portlander, Simon Benson, during the construction of the Historic Columbia River Highway. After crossing below the falls and climbing a bit, you will reach the junction with Gorge Trail 400 at 0.5 mile. Stay right, heading south, toward the top. The asphalt path switchbacks up the slope just east of the falls. After cresting a slight ridge, the trail descends quickly to the junction with the lookout trail. Turn right, heading west, to view the falls. After a short walk, you reach a steel-and-wood platform. The railing is for resource protection as well as your safety.

Have a good stare.

You can return via the same route or explore farther up the Larch Mountain Trail. Wisendanger Falls and Ecola Falls are a short walk up the trail and a nice addition to your Multnomah Falls experience if you have an extra thirty or forty minutes and a little extra energy for some additional gradual climbing.

Miles and Directions

0.0 **START** from Multnomah Falls Lodge and Trailhead on Historic Columbia River Highway.

0.5 Junction with Gorge Trail 400, stay right (south).

1.0 Junction with lookout trail above falls, turn right (west).

1.2 Overlook, turn around.

2.4 Return to Multnomah Falls Lodge and Trailhead.

7 Larch Mountain from Multnomah Falls

A premier Columbia Gorge hike with spectacular waterfalls, old-growth forest, and clear, clean Multnomah Creek.

Start: Multnomah Falls Lodge and Trailhead.
Distance: 6.8 miles point to point.
Approximate hiking time: 4 to 6 hours.
Difficulty: Difficult.
Traffic: Heavy to moderate.
Trail type: Well maintained.
Best season: May through October.
Total climbing: 3,970 feet.
Other trail users: Mountain bikes are allowed on a short section of the trail near the summit.
Canine compatibility: Dogs are allowed on leashes only; they must be on 6-foot leashes on the Multnomah Falls paved path.

Nearest town: Corbett.
Fees and permits: A Northwest Forest Pass is required at the Larch Mountain Trailhead.
Maps: Bridal Veil USGS, Bridal Veil Green Trails, Geo-Graphics Trails of the Columbia River Gorge, and Maptech Oregon.
Trail contacts: USDA Forest Service Multnomah Falls Visitor Center, Multnomah Falls Lodge, off I-84 or on Historic Columbia River Highway; (503) 695-2372.

Finding the trailhead: From Portland, drive east on Interstate 84 to exit 31, Multnomah Falls. Park and walk south, underneath the interstate and the train tracks, to the Multnomah Falls Lodge and Visitor Center. The trail begins west of the lodge on a cement staircase. Multnomah Falls is visible from the highway and the parking area.

You can also reach the trailhead by taking exit 28, Bridal Veil, 3 miles before the Multnomah Falls exit. This allows you more freedom to take other falls hikes in the area, such as Latourell Falls and Wahkeena Falls.

To hike one-way to Larch Mountain, leave a car at the top. From Portland, take Interstate 84 east just past Troutdale and get off at exit 18, Lewis and Clark State Park. Follow the off-ramp until it ends at Historic Columbia River Highway, then turn left and follow the main road to Corbett. Two miles past Corbett, the road forks near Women's Forum Viewpoint, which offers a good view of the Vista House and Larch Mountain. Turn right at the fork, continuing east, onto Larch Mountain Road. Fourteen miles of pretty, paved, and winding road later is the Larch Mountain Trailhead.

The Hike

If you don't like crowds, please avoid Multnomah Falls. Past Multnomah Falls, however, the Larch Mountain Trail is less crowded, and the route follows cool, clear Multnomah Creek. The hike is easier going uphill because there are few flat spots to rest your downhill knees. Wisendanger Falls, a classic flat, block-type falls, and Ecola Falls, past Multnomah, provide additional scenery on the extended route. There isn't much of a view after the Multnomah Falls lookout, until the Sherrard Point option on the top of Larch Mountain.

The Benson Footbridge and Multnomah Falls

Larch Mountain Trail 441 starts on a cement staircase within view of the falls. Follow this up toward the famous Benson Footbridge, named for Simon Benson. It was built in 1915 and is one of the first continuously poured concrete structures in the United States. Benson was a prominent lumberman and generous Portlander during the construction of the Historic Columbia River Highway. He gave this land to the city of Portland as a park; it was later transferred to the USFS. After crossing below the falls and climbing a bit, at 0.5 mile you reach the junction with Gorge Trail 400. Stay right, heading south, toward the top.

The asphalt path switchbacks up the slope just east of the falls. After cresting a slight ridge, the trail descends quickly to the junction with the lookout trail. Hiking out and back to the lookout will add 0.4 mile to your hike.

Once you're back on the main trail, if you aren't too tired, cross the bridge over Multnomah Creek, heading south. Stay left, continuing south past Old Perdition Trail 421, which has been closed indefinitely thanks to a fire in 1991 and flooding in 1996.

The trail climbs steadily to Wisendanger Falls, which has a nice pool but a short drop. Beyond is Ecola Falls, which drops farther and makes a bigger splash. Neither of the upper falls is as spectacular as Multnomah, but each has its own beauty.

Larch Mountain from Multnomah Falls

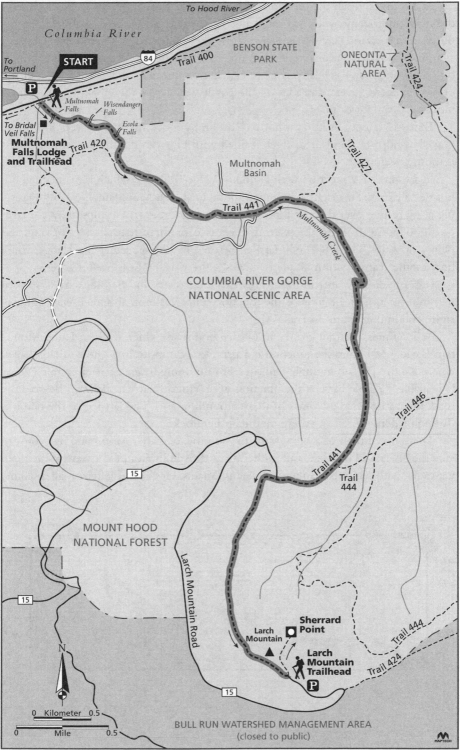

At 1.8 miles, reach the junction with Wahkeena Trail 420. This section is one of the most photogenic, with moving water, large rocks, and mosses. Stay left, continuing south, toward Larch Mountain. Cross the bridge over Multnomah Creek; a campsite is located up on the left 0.2 mile past the bridge. It has room for one or two tents, and water is relatively close by. There is another campsite with a tent site or two opposite several cascades on the basalt wall across the creek. It makes for a pleasant overnight or picnic spot.

Trail 441 is cool even on a hot day. It climbs above the basalt layers into more gravelly sandstone bands. The creek is filled with big, round boulders, and the forest is mostly deciduous.

At 3.0 miles is a junction with Franklin Ridge Trail 427, which is maintained but not heavily used. Stay right, continuing south, for Larch Mountain. Next, after crossing a log bridge over the east fork of Multnomah Creek, is a campsite by the river on the opposite bank to the west. It offers two or three tent sites, a fire ring, and plenty of water. Then, 0.1 mile farther, before crossing a second log bridge, you'll find another camp with multiple tent sites, a fire ring, and easy water access.

Pass a rock-slide area into old-growth Douglas firs and hemlock trees up to 6 feet in diameter. At 4.8 miles is the junction with Multnomah Creek Way 444; stay right, continuing south on Trail 441.

At 5.3 miles, the trail crosses an old logging road, which leads to Larch Mountain Road. Just before the junction is a primitive campsite in a grove of large trees. There is a fire pit and multiple tent sites, but no immediately available water. (Water is available 0.7 mile back, at the junction with Multnomah Creek Way.) Beyond the road, the trail offers few views of the surrounding area. The last leg of the climb is through a dense forest of young mountain hemlock.

There isn't much of a view from the summit of Larch Mountain, but you can take the Sherrard Point hike out to the site of the old lookout for a view of the main Cascades, with Mounts Rainier, St. Helens, Adams, Hood, and Jefferson all in a line.

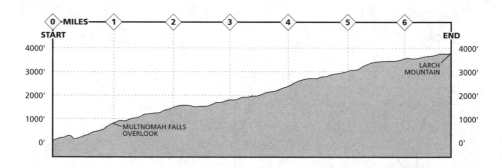

Miles and Directions

0.0 **START** from Multnomah Falls Lodge and Trailhead.

0.5 Junction with Gorge Trail 400, stay right (south).

1.0 Junction with lookout trail above Multnomah Falls. Continue south across bridge. **Option:** Turn right for a view of the falls. This spur trail will add 0.4 miles to the hike.

1.1 Junction with Old Perdition Trail 421. This trail is closed indefinitely.

1.8 Junction with Wahkeena Trail 420, stay left (south).

3.0 Junction with Franklin Ridge Trail 427, stay right (south).

4.8 Junction with Multnomah Creek Way 444, stay right (south).

5.3 Junction with jeep road, continue straight (west).

6.8 Larch Mountain Trailhead. **Option:** Hike out to Sherrard Point, north of the trailhead, for views north and south along the Cascades.

8 Larch Mountain Loop

A fairly easy loop walk in the heavily forested Larch Mountain area.

Start: Larch Mountain Picnic Area and Trailhead.
Distance: 6.1-mile loop.
Approximate hiking time: 3 to 4 hours.
Difficulty: Moderate.
Traffic: Moderate.
Trail type: Well maintained.
Best season: May through October.
Total climbing: 2,090 feet.
Other trail users: Mountain bikes are allowed on this loop section.

Canine compatibility: Dogs are allowed on leashes only.
Nearest town: Corbett.
Fees and permits: A Northwest Forest Pass is required.
Maps: Bridal Veil USGS, Bridal Veil Green Trails, Geo-Graphics Trails of the Columbia River Gorge, and Maptech Oregon.
Trail contacts: Mount Hood National Forest, 16400 Champion Way, Sandy, OR 97055; (503) 668-1700; www.fs.fed.us/r6/mthood.

Finding the trailhead: From Portland, take Interstate 84 east just past Troutdale and get off at exit 18, Lewis and Clark State Park. Follow the off-ramp until it ends at the Historic Columbia River Highway and turn left, heading south. Follow the scenic highway through Corbett. Two miles past Corbett, the road forks; make a right onto Larch Mountain Road. Fourteen miles of pretty, paved, and winding road later is the Larch Mountain Trailhead.

The Hike

Larch Mountain Trail is one of the few gorge trails open to mountain bikes. Stay alert for other users. While you're at the top, I suggest a quick walk out to Sherrard Point, which is 0.2 mile from the parking lot. It's just a short walk from the summit.

The Larch Mountain Trail starts just to the left of the bathrooms. It doesn't offer much in the way of views of the surrounding area, but it can be peaceful. From the top, the trail passes through the picnic area and past several cutoff trails joining the main trail. Keep going straight, heading north.

After 1.5 miles, the trail crosses an old logging road, which is now a popular shortcut to Larch Mountain Road. Just after the junction is a primitive campsite in a grove of large hemlocks and firs. There is no water, but you'll find a fire pit and multiple tent sites. Water is available 0.7 mile farther near the junction of Multnomah Creek Way with the main trail.

At 2.0 miles is the junction with Multnomah Creek Way 444, which gives you three loop options. The longest continues down the Larch Mountain Trail to Franklin Ridge Trail 427 and follows Multnomah Creek through some pretty cascades and rock gardens. It's 4.3 miles longer, and Franklin Ridge Trail 427 back isn't very scenic.

Larch Mountain Loop

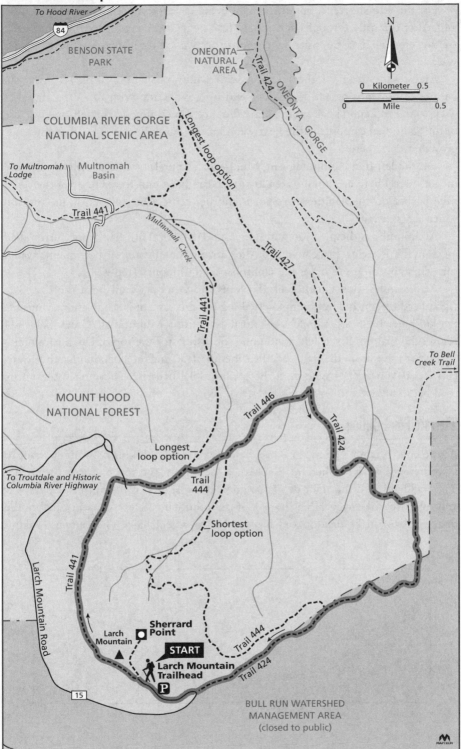

For the two shorter loops, turn right, heading east, on Multnomah Creek Way 444. After 0.2 mile through increasingly lush vegetation, cross Multnomah Creek. At the crossing is a campsite with room for two or three tents, a fire ring, and water access.

Across the stream, at the junction with Multnomah Spur Trail 446, you can choose to go right or left. Both trails end up connecting with Oneonta Trail 424 back to the top and are about the same distance. I recommend the left one because of the additional campsite at the next water crossing and the presence of serious old-growth cedars there.

On the left trail continuing east, Multnomah Spur Trail 446 is relatively flat and in the trees. There are more water-loving cedars here, and fewer firs. Another 0.25 mile farther on the Multnomah Spur is another camp. One tent site, a fire pit, and water access await.

At 3.0 miles is the junction with Oneonta Trail 424. This shady spot, surrounded by giant firs, is a great place for a nap. After dozing for a bit and drinking some water, turn right, heading south, for the climb back up Oneonta Trail 424.

At 3.8 miles, Bell Creek Trail 459 joins the Oneonta Trail from the east. Stay right, heading south. The young forest along the final ascent is dense and permits little sunshine. In another mile the return trail from Multnomah Creek Way 444 rejoins the main trail; stay left, continuing southwest, for the top of Larch Mountain.

At 5.7 miles from the trailhead, the Oneonta Trail ends at a bend in Larch Mountain Road. You are 0.4 mile from the parking lot. Turn right, heading west, on the road back to your car.

Sherrard Point Option

At the end of Larch Mountain Road, before you do any hiking, you might want to take the easy walk to Sherrard Point for a view from the top of Larch Mountain. The trail begins to the right of a large interpretive sign. It is paved most of the way and offers the best view from the top of the mountain. A few stairs just before the final platform make this lookout inaccessible to wheelchairs. The cement lookout

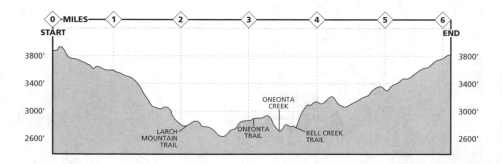

offers interpretive plaques in the direction of each dormant volcano on the horizon. On a clear day it's a special experience to pick out Mounts Jefferson, Hood, St. Helens, Adams, and Rainier. It gives you a big picture of the gorge area. Sometimes the best views are the easiest to reach.

Miles and Directions

0.0   **START** from Larch Mountain Picnic Area.

1.5   Junction with jeep trail to Larch Mountain Road, continue straight (east).

2.0   Junction Multnomah Creek Way Trail 444, turn right (east). **Option:** Continue on Larch Mountain Trail to Franklin Ridge Trail 427. Follow this trail to the junction of Multnomah Spur Trail 446 and Oneonta Trail 424, where it will rejoin the featured loop. This will add 4.3 miles.

2.2   Junction Multnomah Spur Trail 446, turn left. **Option:** Turn right for a different loop that is about the same length and joins Oneonta Trail 424 at mile 4.8 of the featured hike.

3.0   Oneonta Trail 424, turn right (southwest). This is where the longest loop rejoins the featured hike.

3.8   Bell Creek Trail 459, stay right (south).

4.8   Multnomah Creek Way Trail 444, stay left (southwest). This is where the shorter loop option joins the featured hike.

5.7   Larch Mountain Road, turn right (west).

6.1   Return to Larch Mountain Trailhead.

9 Gorge Trail 400—Multnomah Falls to Ainsworth State Park

A flat to rolling walk from Multnomah Falls through the trees paralleling the Historic Columbia River Highway to Ainsworth Campground.

Start: Multnomah Falls Lodge and Trailhead.
Distance: 6.2 miles point to point.
Approximate hiking time: 3 hours.
Difficulty: Easy to moderate.
Traffic: Heavy at the start, light at the finish.
Trail type: Well maintained.
Best season: Year-round.
Total climbing: 1,660 feet.
Other trail users: Mountain bikes on sections east of Multnomah Falls.
Canine compatibility: Dogs are allowed on leashes only.

Nearest town: Cascade Locks.
Fees and permits: None.
Maps: Bridal Veil Green Trails, Bridal Veil USGS, Geo-Graphics Trails of the Columbia River Gorge, and Maptech Oregon.
Trail contacts: Oregon State Parks, 725 Summer Street NE, Suite C, Salem, OR 97301; (503) 986-0707; www.prd.state.or.us. USDA Forest Service Multnomah Falls Visitor Center, Multnomah Falls Lodge, off I-84 or on Historic Columbia River Highway; (503) 695-2372.

Finding the trailhead: From either direction on Interstate 84, take exit 35, Ainsworth State Park, to access the Historic Columbia River Highway. Follow the historic highway west for about 0.5 mile. Ainsworth State Park and Campground is on the left, or south side. Leave a car at the day-use parking and continue west on the historic highway to drive your other car to Multnomah Falls Lodge and Trailhead.

The Hike

Like everyone else who frequents Multnomah Falls, you must first climb the cement staircase within view of the falls. Follow this trail, the beginning of Larch Mountain Trail 441 and the main route to the Multnomah Falls overlook, toward the famous Benson Footbridge.

The Benson Bridge, a part of every postcard depicting Multnomah Falls, was built in 1914 and named after a prominent and generous Portlander, Simon Benson, during the construction of the Historic Columbia River Highway.

After crossing the Benson Bridge below the falls and climbing a bit, you will reach the junction with Gorge Trail 400 at 0.5 mile. Hang a left, heading east on Gorge Trail 400 as the cliffside trail hovers above the historic highway.

The Historic Columbia River Highway is famous for its panoramic views up the mighty Columbia Gorge and its signature whitewashed guardrail, cement arching, and buttresses. Gorge Trail 400 maintains a relatively flat grade and stays close enough

Gorge Trail 400—Multnomah Falls to Ainsworth State Park

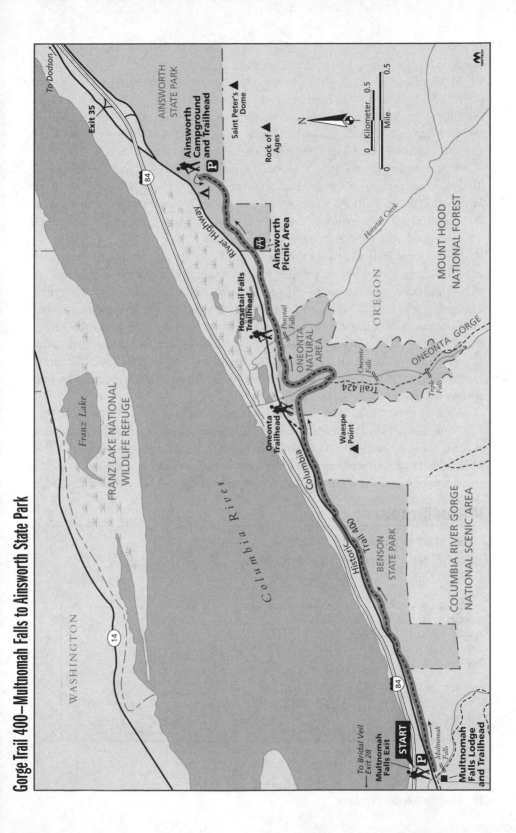

to Interstate 84 and the historic highway so there is still a high level of traffic noise, but it does offer a unique perspective on this corridor.

At 1.4 miles from Multnomah Falls Lodge, Gorge Trail 400 bumps into the historic highway. After a short bounce on the road, Gorge Trail 400 lingers just above the highway until the intersection with Oneonta Trail 424, where the combined trail picks up heavier traffic bound for Triple Falls. At the next junction, head down and east over Oneonta Creek. Ponytail Falls is just a bit farther east.

After visiting Ponytail Falls, the combined Gorge Trail 400 and Horsetail Falls Trail descends over several switchbacks. Gorge Trail 400 heads east just before the Horsetail Falls Trailhead. As soon as you take the right continuing on Gorge Trail 400, the crowds of waterfall watchers fall away and the quiet forest walk continues. This is a good time for conversation and reflection.

Next, Gorge Trail 400 passes the Ainsworth Loop Trail, an alternate entry point at a picnic area. I recommend bringing a plant, wildflower, or tree field guide as this section of trail is a great place to get a feel for the common plants of the Columbia Gorge. Douglas fir is the most common evergreen. Bigleaf maple is the most common deciduous tree. Bushy vine maple is also common. The most noticeable fern is the sword fern, which has a little hitch where the leaves connect to the stem. Oregon grape is also common. It has holly-like leaves and yellow bunches of flowers.

From Ainsworth Picnic Area, it is a mile to the Ainsworth Campground where you parked your vehicle.

Although many folks hike the short section of Trail 442 between the Wahkeena and Multnomah Falls Trailheads as if it was a connecting piece of Trail 400, it is not and neither is the section of Trail 415 on the Angels Rest route. Nevertheless, if you want to make an east-west trek along the historic highway through the falls area, you could start at Angels Rest and work your way to Trail 400 at Multnomah Falls Lodge.

Miles and Directions

0.0 **START** from Multnomah Falls Lodge.

0.5 Junction with Gorge Trail 400, turn left (east).

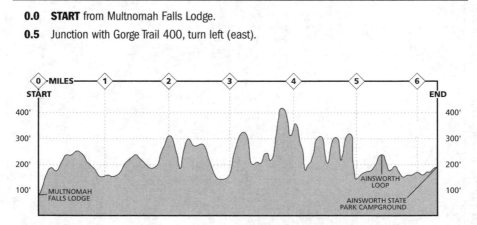

1.4 Historic Columbia River Highway.

2.3 Junction with Oneonta Trail 424, turn left (east).

3.0 Junction with Horsetail Falls Trail 438, turn right (east). Trails 438 and 400 merge here.

4.1 Leave Horsetail Falls Trail 438, turn right to continue on Gorge Trail 400.

5.2 Junction with Ainsworth Loop Trail.

6.2 Ainsworth Campground and Trailhead.

10 Horsetail and Ponytail Falls

A short day hike underneath Ponytail Falls that can easily be extended to Triple Falls.

Start: Horsetail Falls Trailhead on the Historic Columbia River Highway.
Distance: 2.7-mile loop.
Approximate hiking time: 1 to 2 hours.
Difficulty: Easy.
Traffic: Heavy.
Trail type: Well maintained.
Best season: Year-round, depending upon frost line.
Total climbing: 1,200 feet.
Other trail users: None.

Canine compatibility: Dogs are allowed on leashes only.
Nearest town: Cascade Locks.
Fees and permits: None.
Maps: Bridal Veil Green Trails, Multnomah Falls USGS, Geo-Graphics Trails of the Columbia River Gorge, and Maptech Oregon.
Trail contacts: USDA Forest Service Multnomah Falls Visitor Center, Multnomah Falls Lodge, off I-84 or on Historic Columbia River Highway; (503) 695-2372.

Finding the trailhead: From Portland, take Interstate 84 east to exit 28, Bridal Veil. Follow the off-ramp to the intersection with the Historic Columbia River Highway. Turn left, heading east on the historic highway for 5.5 miles to the Horsetail Falls Trailhead. Park in the lot on the north side of the road. Trail 438 is just across the highway, to the left of the Horsetail Falls Picnic Area. There is ample parking, but no public restrooms.

The Hike

Horsetail Falls and Ponytail Falls are part of an easy hike that includes spectacular views, waterfalls, and Oneonta Gorge. You can also extend your trip to take in Triple Falls. These features, along with easy accessibility, make for heavy use on weekends. Still, this route is good for hikers of most ages and abilities.

From the trailhead, gentle switchbacks climb around Horsetail Falls. Horsetail Falls, at 176 feet high, is the textbook example of the "horsetail" formation or category of waterfalls. At 0.2 mile is the intersection with Gorge Trail 400. Stay right, heading south, for Ponytail Falls. Trail 438 continues to climb until it turns west,

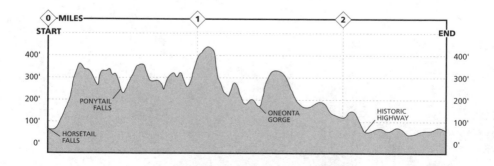

Oneonta Gorge

where cliffs block further climbing. It levels out as the trail rounds the bend. At 0.4 mile, Ponytail Falls is on the left. The trail goes directly underneath Ponytail Falls, another obviously horsetail-type fall, with sheer rock above and the falls crashing down in front of you.

The trail is flat and runs parallel to the highway. Then, at 0.8 mile, turn right, to the north, for a lookout above cliffs several hundred feet high. A marker warns of the dangerous nature of these cliffs; a thirteen-year-old boy fell and died near this lookout in 1988. If you don't like heights, stay to the left and skip this lookout.

The main trail turns south and descends into the Oneonta Gorge. Follow a few steep switchbacks down, cross a footbridge, and then climb a few more short switchbacks up the other side of Oneonta Gorge. At 1.3 miles is the intersection with Oneonta Trail 424. Turn right, heading north, to finish this loop; a left would take you south to Triple Falls.

If you're skipping Triple Falls, after turning right, head north for 0.7 mile until you reach the intersection with Gorge Trail 400. Then turn right and head northeast for the last 0.2 mile until you reach the Historic Columbia River Highway.

It's 0.5 mile back along the road to Horsetail Falls. As you follow the road back, be sure to look up the narrow section of Oneonta Gorge. This natural gorge offers

Horsetail and Ponytail Falls

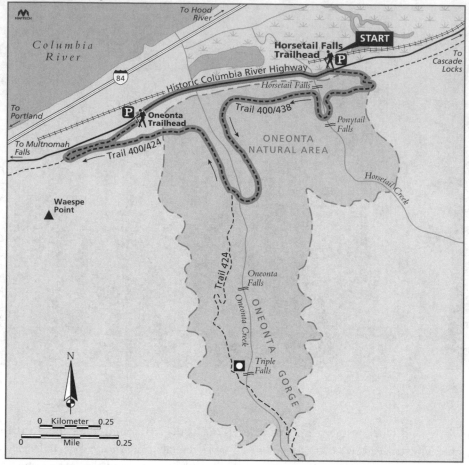

wading opportunities. About 1,000 feet up the gorge is 100-foot-high Oneonta Falls. The falls used to be closer to the highway, but as they cut a slit in the basalt, they worked their way upstream, forming a box canyon.

Miles and Directions

0.0 **START** from Horsetail Falls Trailhead.

0.2 Junction with Gorge Trail 400, stay right (south).

0.4 Ponytail Falls.

0.8 Junction with lookout spur, turn right (north).

1.3 Junction with Oneonta Trail 424, turn right (north).

2.0 Junction with Gorge Trail 400, turn right (northeast).

2.2 Return to Historic Columbia River Highway, turn right (east).

2.7 Return to Horsetail Falls Trailhead.

11 Triple Falls

A pleasant day hike up Oneonta Creek to a great example of a segmented-type waterfall, Triple Falls, with excellent old-growth forest along the way.

Start: Oneonta Trailhead.
Distance: 4.2 miles out and back.
Approximate hiking time: 3 to 4 hours.
Difficulty: Moderate.
Traffic: Moderate to heavy.
Trail type: Well maintained.
Best season: Year-round, depending upon frost line.
Total climbing: 1,200 feet.
Other trail users: None.

Canine compatibility: Dogs are allowed on leashes only.
Nearest town: Cascade Locks.
Fees and permits: None.
Maps: Bridal Veil Green Trails, and Multnomah Falls USGS, Geo-Graphics Trails of the Columbia River Gorge, and Maptech Oregon.
Trail contacts: USDA Forest Service Multnomah Falls Visitor Center, Multnomah Falls Lodge, off I-84 or on Historic Columbia River Highway; (503) 695-2372.

Finding the trailhead: From Portland, take Interstate 84 east to exit 28, Bridal Veil. Follow the off-ramp to the intersection with the Historic Columbia River Highway. Turn left, heading east on the historic highway for 5 miles to a turnoff to the Oneonta Trailhead. The dirt parking area is on the north side of the road; Oneonta Trail 424 starts across the highway to the south.

The Hike

From the trailhead, the trail climbs 0.2 mile to the junction with Gorge Trail 400. Stay left, continuing south and up. The trail leads through older fir trees with little sunlight. It rounds a bend into the Oneonta Valley and flattens out until 0.9 mile, the junction with Trail 438 from Horsetail Falls. Stay right, continuing south. The Oneonta Trail to Triple Falls is mostly level, with one or two steep sections. The trail climbs two long switchbacks and then runs level again until Triple Falls. Along the way, you can see down into the steep sides of Oneonta Gorge.

At 2.1 miles is Triple Falls, which features several good lunch spots with views. These falls are a classic example of a segmented-type waterfall. From the crest, Oneonta Creek splits into three separate falls; the drop to the canyon floor is almost 135 feet. The bridge just past the falls marks the start of a less drastic valley. Oneonta Creek, above the basalt layer, is just a lush Oregon stream.

Miles and Directions

0.0 **START** from Oneonta Trailhead on Historic Columbia River Highway.
0.2 Junction with Gorge Trail 400, stay left (south).

Triple Falls

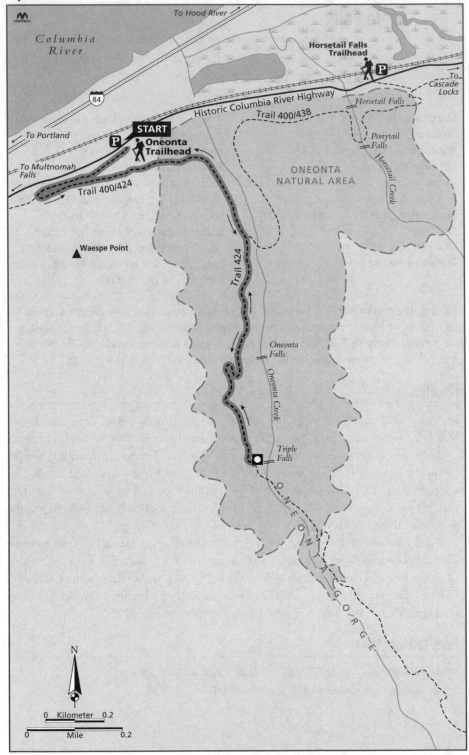

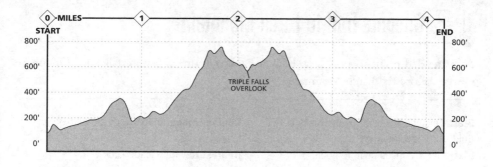

0.9 Junction with Horsetail Falls Trail to Ponytail Falls, stay right (south).

2.1 Triple Falls Overlook, turn around.

4.2 Return to Oneonta Trailhead.

12 Oneonta Trail to Larch Mountain

An extended point-to-point day hike or backpack through waterfall-filled Oneonta Gorge to forested Larch Mountain.

Start: Oneonta Trailhead on the Historic Columbia River Highway.
Distance: 8.7 miles point to point.
Approximate hiking time: 4 to 6 hours.
Difficulty: Difficult.
Traffic: Heavy to moderate.
Trail type: Well maintained.
Best season: May through October.
Total climbing: 5,570 feet.
Other trail users: None except mountain bikes near Larch Mountain.

Canine compatibility: Dogs are allowed on leashes only.
Nearest town: Cascade Locks.
Fees and permits: A Northwest Forest Pass is required to park at Larch Mountain.
Maps: Bridal Veil Green Trails, Multnomah Falls USGS, Geo-Graphics Trails of the Columbia River Gorge, and Maptech Oregon.
Trail contacts: USDA Forest Service Multnomah Falls Visitor Center, Multnomah Falls Lodge, off I–84 or on Historic Columbia River Highway; (503) 695-2372.

Finding the trailhead: From Portland, take Interstate 84 east to exit 28, Bridal Veil. Follow the off-ramp to the intersection with the Historic Columbia River Highway. Turn left, heading east on the historic highway for 5 miles to a turnoff to the Oneonta Trailhead. The dirt parking area is on the north side of the road; Oneonta Trail 424 starts across the highway to the south.

This trip requires a shuttle vehicle left at Larch Mountain. From Portland, take Interstate 84 east just past Troutdale, getting off at exit 18 for Lewis and Clark State Park. Follow the off-ramp until it ends at the Historic Columbia River Highway and turn left. Follow the main road to Corbett. Two miles past Corbett, the road forks; turn right onto Larch Mountain Road. Fourteen miles of pretty, paved, and winding road later is the Larch Mountain Trailhead.

The Hike

Oneonta Gorge Trail has all the elements that make for a good overnight trip in the Columbia River Gorge: waterfalls, steep creek-weathered basalt cliffs, and good campsites.

From the trailhead, the trail climbs 0.2 mile to the junction with Gorge Trail 400. Stay left, continuing south and up. The trail leads through older fir trees with little sunlight. It rounds a bend into the Oneonta Valley and flattens out until 0.9 mile, the junction with Trail 438 from Horsetail Falls. Stay right, continuing south. The trail climbs two long switchbacks and then runs level again until Triple Falls. Along the way, you can see down into the steep sides of Oneonta Gorge.

Cascade along Oneonta Creek ▶

Oneonta Trail to Larch Mountain

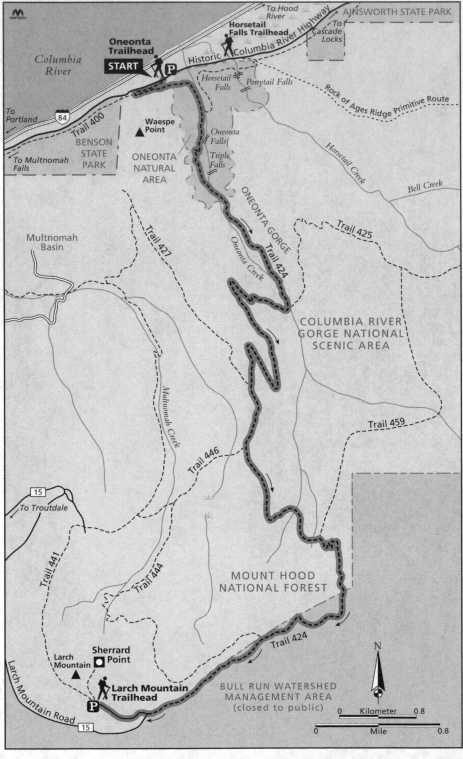

At 2.1 miles is Triple Falls, which is composed of three spouting 100-foot seg-mented drops, which fall a total of 135 feet. This makes an excellent place for lunch. The bridge just past the falls marks the start of a less drastic valley. Oneonta Creek, above the basalt layer, is just a lush Oregon stream. After crossing the bridge, there is a possible tent site, but I don't recommend camping here because of the heavy day use.

Past the falls, the trail climbs up the east side of the valley through moss-covered maples and deadfall. The sword ferns add a green touch, while licorice ferns grow out of the moss-covered trunks. The climb is gentle. The trail crosses Oneonta Creek on a bridge, then quickly reaches a heavily used campsite at the junction with Horsetail Creek Trail 425 from Nesmith Point. This camp has easy access to water and a good fire ring, but it isn't very far off the trail.

Turn right, continuing on Trail 424, for a climb up the west ridge. The elevation gain really picks up here; it's wise to tank up and rest up here at the creek before beginning the climb. You might even stay here a night.

At 5.2 miles, the trail intersects Franklin Ridge Trail 427. Only a little sunlight pokes through the dense forest. Stay left for Larch Mountain to the south.

At 5.7 miles is the junction with Multnomah Spur 446. This spot, surrounded by giant firs, is a great place for a nap. After dozing for a bit and drinking some water, turn right, heading southwest, for the climb up Oneonta Trail.

At 6.4 miles into the trip, Bell Creek Trail 459 joins Oneonta Trail 424 from the east. Stay right, heading south. The young forest along the final ascent is dense and allows little sunshine to break through. In another mile the return trail from Mult-nomah Creek Way 444 joins the main trail. Stay left, continuing southwest, for the top of Larch Mountain.

At 8.3 miles from the start, the Oneonta Trail ends at a bend in Larch Mountain Road. You are 0.4 mile from the parking lot. Turn right, heading west on the road to the Larch Mountain Trailhead.

Miles and Directions

0.0 **START** from Oneonta Trailhead on Historic Columbia River Highway.

0.2 Junction with Gorge Trail 400, stay left (south).

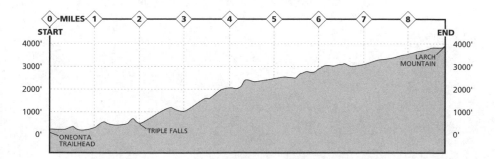

0.9 Junction with Trail 438 from Horsetail Falls, stay right (south).

2.1 Triple Falls.

3.5 Junction with Horsetail Creek Trail 425, turn right (south).

5.2 Junction with Franklin Ridge Trail 427, stay left (south).

5.7 Junction with Multnomah Spur 446, turn right (southwest).

6.4 Junction with Bell Creek Trail 459, stay right (south).

7.4 Junction with Multnomah Creek Way 444, stay left (southwest).

8.3 Oneonta Trail ends at bend in Larch Mountain Road.

8.7 Larch Mountain parking lot.

13 Rock of Ages Ridge Trail

A steep, primitive scramble up Rock of Ages Ridge, with abundant views of cliffs and basalt formations.

Start: Horsetail Falls Trailhead on the Historic Columbia River Highway.
Distance: 6.0 miles out and back to junction with Horsetail Creek Trail 425; 10.2 miles following the Oneonta Gorge option; 7.6 miles point to point on John B. Yeon State Scenic Corridor option.
Approximate hiking time: 3 to 6 hours.
Difficulty: Difficult.
Traffic: Light.
Trail type: Primitive.
Best season: May through October.
Total climbing: 2,940 feet to Trail 425.

Other trail users: None.
Canine compatibility: Dogs are allowed on leashes, but this isn't really a good hike for pets.
Nearest town: Cascade Locks.
Fees and permits: None.
Maps: Bridal Veil Green Trails, and Multnomah Falls USGS, Geo-Graphics Trails of the Columbia River Gorge, and Maptech Oregon.
Trail contacts: USDA Forest Service Multnomah Falls Visitor Center, Multnomah Falls Lodge, off I-84 or on Historic Columbia River Highway; (503) 695-2372.

Finding the trailhead: From Portland, take Interstate 84 east to exit 28, Bridal Veil. Follow the off-ramp to the intersection with the Historic Columbia River Highway. Turn left and head east on the historic highway for 5.5 miles to the Horsetail Falls Trailhead. Park in the lot on the north side of the road. (From Hood River, take exit 35, Warrendale/Dodson, and drive west on the historic highway for 1.5 miles to Horsetail Falls.) Trail 438 is just across the highway, to the left of the Horsetail Falls Picnic Area. There is ample parking, but no public restrooms.

Special considerations: This isn't really a maintained route. It's cliffy, requires good scrambling skills, and is definitely not a good trail for the young ones.

The Hike

The trail up Rock of Ages Ridge is unmaintained, little used, and very steep. But it offers breathtaking cliffside views, cool forests, and a good workout. The trail isn't as severe as Ruckel Ridge, but it does have a few adrenaline-rush spots. Rock of Ages Ridge is also a useful segue to loop options down Nesmith Point Trail or via Horsetail Creek and Oneonta Gorge.

From the trailhead, gentle switchbacks climb around Horsetail Falls. At 0.2 mile is the intersection with Gorge Trail 400. Stay right, heading south, for Ponytail Falls. The trail continues to climb, then turns west where cliffs block further climbing. As the now level trail rounds the bend, to the left at 0.4 mile is Ponytail Falls. Just as the trail rounds the corner to Ponytail Falls, look up and to the left for the fainter trail. A sign reading TRAIL NOT MAINTAINED is the only marker. Turn left, heading southeast, onto this primitive trail. It heads straight up the slope, splitting and rejoining in several places.

A hiker enjoys the view from Rock of Ages Ridge.

At 0.8 mile is a junction marked only by a cut branch on a fir tree. Straight east is a spur trail to a lookout. At the lookout, you need to climb over some rocks to see the sheer cliffs on the other side. This ascent is dangerous. If you want to take a look, be sure to crawl on all fours. On the basalt cliffs you can see an arch-protected cave. Up the ravine, look for a lonely tree in the crevice at the top.

Back down at the cut-branch junction, turn southeast and continue around and up this steep, primitive trail. The trail climbs for another 0.5 mile before reaching a large rock spine on a ridge covered in moss. Climb to the left around this outcropping to a viewpoint. To the east you can see Beacon Rock, Hamilton Mountain, and Mount St. Helens. Out on the rock spine, you can look farther east and get a glimpse of Rock of Ages next to Saint Peter's Dome, but it's not a very good angle. The trail continues through the trees up the ridge to the southeast.

After crossing the rock spine, the trail levels out; then climbs again through the trees; then, after about 2 miles, levels again. Along the way are cedars and ancient snags from a long-ago fire. Through the trees you'll catch a view of Yeon Mountain. The trail ends at Horsetail Creek Trail 425 on top of Nesmith/Yeon Plateau. Return

Rock of Ages Ridge Trail

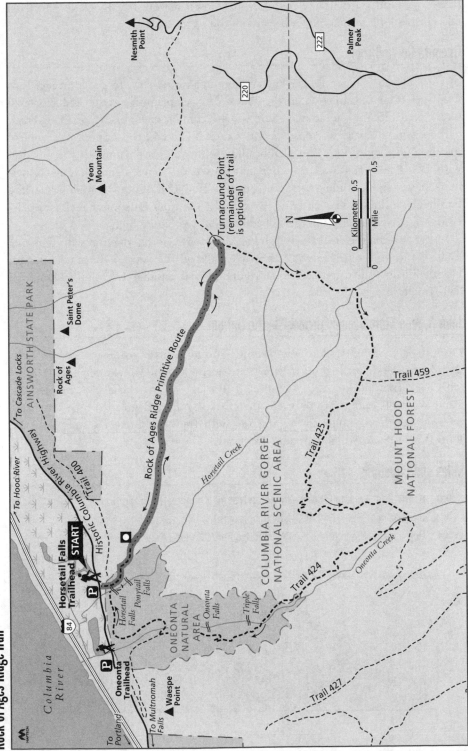

to the trailhead via the same trail or your chosen option. The Rock of Ages Trail takes just as long to hike down because of the steep grade.

Oneonta Gorge Option

It is possible to follow a longer but more gradual route back to the Horsetail Falls Trailhead from the junction of the Rock of Ages primitive route and Horsetail Creek Trail 425. You should make sure you are comfortable crossing a rushing creek because you will need to cross Oneonta Creek if you take this option. To complete the loop turn right onto Trail 425, heading southwest. At 4.3 miles is the junction with Bell Creek Trail 459, which is not shown on some maps. This junction is marked; stay right, heading west, for Oneonta Trail 424. About 0.5 mile farther the trail begins a drastic descent along switchbacks. Crossing Oneonta Creek is treacherous, especially in early summer when the water levels are high.

After crossing the creek, turn right, heading north, at the junction with Oneonta Trail 424 at mile 6.6. You will pass Triple Falls on the way to the junction with Horsetail Falls Trail at mile 8.6. Turn right and walk another 1.3 miles to Horsetail Falls Trailhead.

John B. Yeon State Scenic Corridor Shuttle Option

From the end of the Rock of Ages primitive route, it is also possible to make a shuttle hike that ends at the John B. Yeon State Scenic Corridor. Turn left onto Horsetail Creek Trail heading east. At mile 2.0 is a logging road that leads to Nesmith Point. You will continue south briefly then make a ninety-degree left turn. Continue on Trail 428 for 4.5 miles to the junction with Trail 400. Continue straight to the John B. Yeon State Scenic Corridor Trailhead.

Miles and Directions

- **0.0** **START** from Horsetail Falls Trailhead on Historic Columbia River Highway.
- **0.2** Junction with Gorge Trail 400, stay right (south).
- **0.4** Unmarked junction for Rock of Ages Ridge Trail, turn left (southeast).

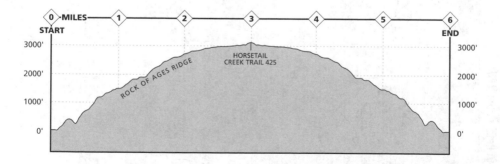

0.8 Junction with lookout spur on left (east).

3.0 Junction with Horsetail Creek Trail 425, turn around. **Option 1:** To complete a loop through Oneonta Gorge to Horsetail Falls Trailhead, turn right (southwest) onto Trail 425 and continue past the junction with Trail 459 to Oneonta Creek. After crossing the creek turn right (north) onto Trail 424 to the junction with Horsetail Falls Trail. Turn right (east) to reach Horsetail Falls Trailhead. **Option 2:** To complete a shuttle hike to the John B. Yeon State Scenic Corridor, turn left (east) onto Trail 425. Go 2.0 miles to an old logging road to Nesmith Point. Continue past this point on Trail 428 for 4.5 miles to the junction with Trail 400, then continue straight for 0.1 mile to the John B. Yeon State Scenic Corridor Trailhead.

6.0 Return to Horsetail Falls Trailhead.

John B. Yeon State Scenic Corridor

Along with Samuel Lancaster, John B. Yeon was one of the principal architects of the Historic Columbia River Highway and the reason this magnificent state scenic corridor bears his name. Few areas can boast as spectacular a waterfall as Elowah Falls, or crags as steep and rocky as the cliffs along Yeon Mountain. In addition, the bowl or basin pours frequent mudslides down the remnant villages of Warrendale and Dodson, periodically burying trails and private property. In fact, one slide closed what used to be a section of Gorge Trail 400 from Dodson to John B. Yeon State Scenic Corridor permanently, and slides periodically close the cliffy trails around McCord Creek.

The hike to Nesmith Point and around to Oneonta Creek is one of my favorites in the gorge: few fellow travelers, a good trail, steady climbing, and not nearly as punishing a trip as, say, Mount Defiance. Upper McCord Creek is also spectacular, but the cliff scares me a bit; I prefer more gradual hillsides or the view from below Elowah Falls.

Access to John B. Yeon from the west is at exit 35; continue on the frontage road to the trailhead. Access from the east is at exit 37—an on-ramp only, for eastbound traffic. If you're coming from Portland and miss exit 35, you won't be able to exit at exit 37 but will have to drive to exit 40, the Tanner Creek Trailhead Complex, and turning around.

14 Nesmith Point and Yeon Mountain

A long day hike through pristine forests, with incredible views of the Washington Cascades.

Start: John B. Yeon State Scenic Corridor Trailhead.

Distance: 13.1 miles point to point; 9.4 miles out and back from Nesmith Point.

Approximate hiking time: 6 to 8 hours.

Difficulty: Strenuous.

Traffic: Light.

Trail type: Maintained.

Best season: May through October.

Total climbing: 3,700 feet.

Other trail users: None.

Canine compatibility: Dogs are allowed on leashes only.

Nearest town: Cascade Locks.

Fees and permits: None.

Maps: Bridal Veil and Bonneville Dam Green Trails, Bonneville Dam and Multnomah Falls USGS, Geo-Graphics Trails of the Columbia River Gorge, and Maptech Oregon: Bonneville Dam.

Trail contacts: Oregon State Parks, 725 Summer Street NE, Suite C, Salem, OR 97301; (503) 986-0707; www.prd.state.or.us. Mount Hood National Forest, 16400 Champion Way, Sandy, OR 97055; (503) 668-1700; www.fs.fed.us/r6/mthood.

Finding the trailhead: From Portland, take Interstate 84 east to exit 35, Warrendale/Dodson. This loop requires you to leave a shuttle car at the Oneonta Trailhead. From exit 35, turn right and head west for 2 miles, past Horsetail Falls to the next marked trailhead on the left just past Oneonta Gorge. The Oneonta Trailhead is on the left, and a shaded dirt parking lot is across the road. Leave a car here and drive back on the Historic Columbia River Highway to exit 35. (Note that exit 37 past the John B. Yeon corridor is a westbound exit and eastbound on-ramp only.)

At exit 35, head east on the Historic Columbia River Highway for 2.5 miles to the John B. Yeon State Scenic Corridor Trailhead on the right. There is ample parking, but no public restrooms. Trail 428 to Nesmith Point begins on the west end of the parking lot.

Special considerations: Doing the loop does involve a tricky ford of Oneonta Creek—something to consider before choosing this hike, especially in the spring and early summer.

The Hike

The trail to Nesmith Point and farther to Yeon Mountain offers some intense hiking and some incredible views of Mount St. Helens, Mount Adams, and Mount Rainier. From a lookout near Yeon Mountain, you can see all three. Check the weather for a clear forecast. The trail to Nesmith Point can either be a up-and-back hike or a loop, depending upon whether you choose to leave a car at the Oneonta Trailhead. The loop option is longer and involves a ford across Oneonta Creek, but the extra view along the way and the more gradual descent are worth it. I highly recommend the loop option. Either way, however, this trail is a steep 3,700-foot climb—most of it in less than 3 miles.

Moss-covered slopes along the Nesmith Point Trail.

From the trailhead, after a sign at 0.1 mile, is Trail 428 to Nesmith Point. Take the right fork, heading west. The trail continues along a gentle grade for 0.6 mile, through the trees, until a huge landslide is visible on the right. This slide happened during the "Great Flood of '96," as the local media billed it. Huge boulders and mounds of dirt surround a few solitary trees that weathered the slide. Luckily the trail turns just before entering the slide. Trail 400, which would have continued west at this point, is no longer there; it may or may not be rebuilt in the future.

After a mile of long switchbacks is a spur trail, on your left, heading north, to a small lookout. From this lookout is the first of the good views to come. Table and Hamilton Mountains are visible across the gorge. After this short side trip, the trail flattens out for a few hundred yards before again climbing steeply on switchbacks.

There are several examples of old-growth fir and cedar as the trail climbs higher. Also watch out for devil's-club, which has huge leaves much like cow parsnip, but the stems have slivery spikes and emit a chemical that can cause uncomfortable itching and scratching, similar to that caused by nettles. Devil's-club does, however, bear a very pretty stack of bright red berries late in the season. Look, but don't touch, and definitely don't eat.

When you enter the most shaded and oldest grove of cedars, you are close to the end of the steepest climbing. Cresting the ravine makes you appreciate this legitimate power climb. From here it's still 1.5 miles to the top, but the climb is nowhere near as steep as what you've just completed. The trail continues to climb gradually, turning west through younger trees. You get a short glimpse of the McCord Creek Valley to the left.

Just before the junction with the old logging road to the top, the trail make a ninety-degree right turn to the north. At one point a straight trail connected this trail with Horsetail Creek Trail 425 to make a loop, but it no longer does. Stay right, heading north, at this unmarked junction. At 4.6 miles is a marked junction with an old logging road to the top of Nesmith Point. Turn right to Nesmith Point.

▶ Topographic maps are only a guide to what trails existed at one time in an area, but they do allow you to figure out the contour of the land and the probable course of a now unmaintained or overgrown trail.

Congratulations, you've reached the top of a 4.7-mile, 3,720-foot climb. That's an average of 790 feet per mile. The summit is forested, but one spot offers a cliffside view of the Columbia Gorge, Vancouver, and beyond. There is enough room at the top for several parties to find solitude. There is an old abandoned outhouse, not recommended for use, and an old benchmark. Most of the top is protected from the wind and far from the sounds of the interstate below.

If hiking in the trees makes you hungry for more overlooks, continue on the loop instead of returning via the same route. The Horsetail Creek Trail has several more of these lookouts, similar to the one on top of Nesmith Point.

If continuing on is not an option, the return trip down to the John B. Yeon State Scenic Corridor Trailhead is a steep one. You might want to tighten your laces.

To continue on from the summit, return via the old logging road to the marked junction with the Nesmith Point Trail and the old logging road. Turn right, heading west, on the logging road, and less than 0.1 mile farther take another right onto Horsetail Creek Trail 425. The grade descends gradually before leveling off. The surrounding forest is thick and has small-diameter trees. When a stand of trees is young, there tend to be more trees with smaller diameters. As the forest ages, the weak trees die off, leaving the healthier survivors with more sunlight and less competition. The older a tree gets, the thicker it gets.

At two points, the trail passes along the edge of Yeon Mountain, offering views of the steep Tumalt Creek Valley. The first point offers a unique view of the bowl-shaped topography of the valley below. This area is where a major landslide started in 1996 that blocked Interstate 84 completely for several days. You can also see Mount St. Helens, Mount Adams, and Mount Rainier. From the second lookout,

Nesmith Point and Yeon Mountain

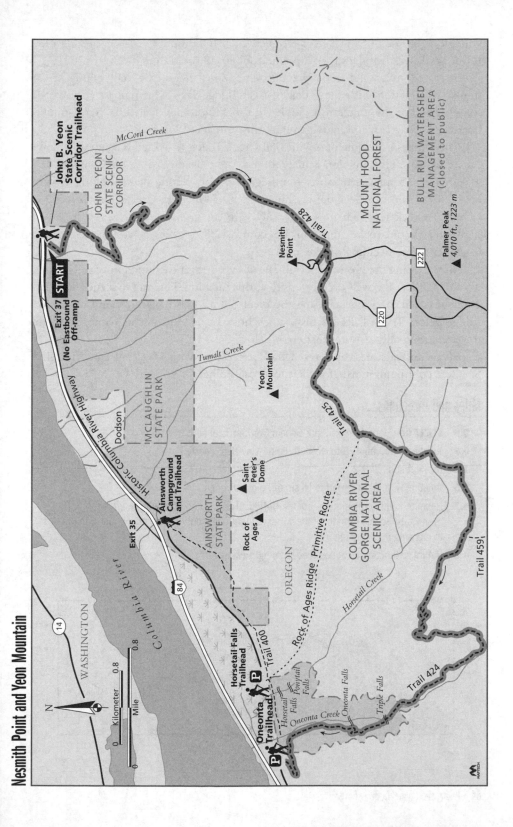

you get a glimpse of Saint Peter's Dome, which is a product of layers of Columbia River basalt weathered away to a pointed solitary formation.

After 6.8 miles and a couple of tremendous views, the trail comes to an unmarked junction with the Rock of Ages Ridge Trail. This trail isn't shown on some maps, but the junction is visible on the Multnomah Falls USGS 7.5-minute quadrangle. Stay left, continuing west, at this unmarked junction.

At 8.1 miles is the junction with Bell Creek Trail 459, which is again not shown on some maps. This junction is marked; stay right, heading west, for Oneonta Trail 424. About 0.5 mile farther, the trail begins a more drastic descent along switchbacks. Soon you can hear the crashing water of Oneonta Creek. The crossing of Oneonta Creek is treacherous, especially early in summer when water levels are high. You should make sure you are comfortable crossing a rushing creek like Oneonta before deciding on the loop.

After crossing the creek, turn right, heading north, at the junction with Oneonta Trail 424. There is a well-used campsite at this junction. The trail descends at stream gradient down the gorge, crossing the creek on a log bridge and again on a footbridge before Triple Falls. It's easy to see how Triple Falls got its name, given the three shooting tails of water that crash below.

After another mile, you'll reach the intersection with Horsetail Falls Trail 438. Stay left, continuing north, for the Oneonta Trailhead.

Miles and Directions

0.0 **START** from John B. Yeon State Scenic Corridor Trailhead.

0.1 Junction with Trail 428 to Nesmith Point, stay right (west).

1.2 Lookout spur.

4.6 Junction with logging road to Nesmith Point, turn right.

4.7 Nesmith Point Lookout, turn around. **Option:** This is a good place to return to John B. Yeon State Scenic Corridor, if the water is high in Oneonta Creek, or you just don't feel up to crossing a swift creek.

4.8 Return to junction with jeep road, turn right (west).

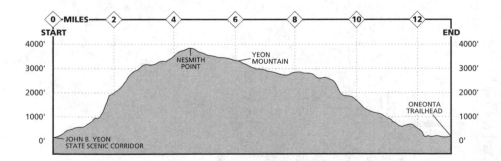

6.8 Unmarked junction with old Rock of Ages Ridge Trail, stay left (west).

8.1 Junction with Bell Creek Trail 459, stay right (west).

10.4 Junction with Oneonta Trail 424, turn right (north).

12.4 Junction with Horsetail Falls Trail, stay left (north).

13.1 Oneonta Trailhead.

15 Elowah Falls

A short day hike to 290-foot-high Elowah Falls.

Start: John B. Yeon State Scenic Corridor Trailhead.

Distance: 1.6 miles out and back.

Approximate hiking time: 1 hour.

Difficulty: Easy.

Traffic: Heavy.

Trail type: Well maintained.

Best season: Year-round, depending upon frost line.

Total climbing: 140 feet.

Other trail users: Trail 400 is open to mountain bikes heading to Tanner Creek and Eagle Creek.

Canine compatibility: Dogs are allowed on leashes only.

Nearest town: Cascade Locks.

Fees and permits: None.

Maps: Bridal Veil and Bonneville Dam Green Trails, Bonneville Dam and Multnomah Falls USGS, Geo-Graphics Trails of the Columbia River Gorge, and Maptech Oregon: Bonneville Dam.

Trail contacts: Oregon State Parks, 725 Summer Street NE, Suite C, Salem, OR 97301; (503) 986-0707; www.prd.state.or.us.

Finding the trailhead: From Portland, take Interstate 84 east to exit 35, Warrendale/Dodson. Turn left, heading east on the Historic Columbia River Highway for 2.5 miles, to the John B. Yeon State Scenic Corridor Trailhead on the right. There is ample parking, but no public restrooms. The trail to Elowah Falls begins on the west end of the parking lot. (Note that exit 37 past the John B. Yeon corridor is a westbound exit and eastbound on-ramp only.)

The Hike

At 290 feet, Elowah Falls is one of the tallest waterfalls in the gorge and produces an incredible amount of spray and mist that swirls around its base. The mist is cold and pure on the skin, especially on a hot day. The hike involves a gentle ascent and descent, is short, and does not climb on any ledges, unlike the trail to Upper McCord Creek Falls (Hike 16). It's a good hike for people of all ages.

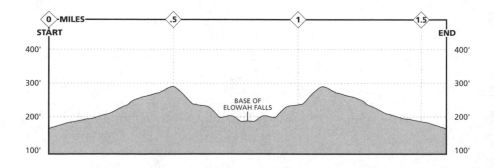

Elowah Falls

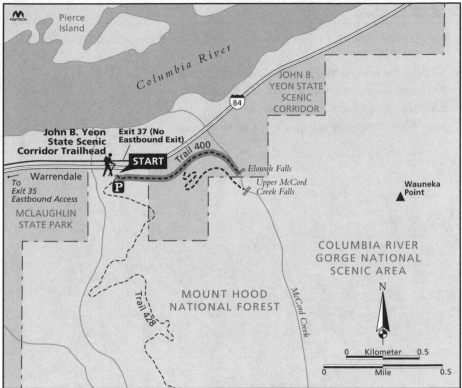

After leaving the trailhead, the trail forks. Take the left fork, heading east, for Elowah Falls. The trail climbs at a gentle grade through middle-age trees. In spring watch for trillium, a resident of moist forest floors. Trillium is a flower with three large white petals and three 2- to 6-inch-long, broadly ovate leaves.

At 0.4 mile is the second junction. The right trail climbs steeply up to Upper McCord Creek Falls. Take the left fork, Trail 400, continuing east for Elowah Falls. Trail 400 drops on switchbacks into the Elowah Glen below the falls. At 0.8 mile is Elowah Falls, crashing down from a height of 290 feet. This is a classic plunge-type waterfall, like Multnomah Falls. The spray from the falls blows across the bridge, especially in spring, making the wood planks slick—watch your footing.

After the bridge, Trail 400 continues, if 0.8 mile wasn't enough. The trail heads to the Wahclella Trailhead, passing Munra Point along the way.

From the other side of the bridge, you can look up to the cliffs above and see the Upper McCord Creek Trail cut into the face. If the sight of this excites you, try the Upper McCord Creek Trail on the way back. Return to the trailhead via the same route.

Miles and Directions

0.0 START from John B. Yeon State Scenic Corridor Trailhead (GPS waypoint: 10 05 77 738 E 50 51 254 N).

0.1 Junction with Nesmith Point Trail 428, stay left (east).

0.4 Junction with Upper McCord Creek Falls Trail, stay left (east).

0.8 Bridge below Elowah Falls, turn around.

1.6 Return to John B. Yeon State Scenic Corridor Trailhead.

16 Upper McCord Creek Falls

A short day hike above Elowah Falls to Upper McCord Creek Falls.

Start: John B. Yeon State Scenic Corridor Trailhead.
Distance: 2.2 miles out and back.
Approximate hiking time: 1 to 2 hours.
Difficulty: Moderate.
Traffic: Moderate.
Trail type: Maintained.
Best season: Year-round, depending upon frost line.
Total climbing: 540 feet.
Other trail users: None.
Canine compatibility: Dogs are allowed on leashes only.
Nearest town: Cascade Locks.
Fees and permits: None.
Maps: Bridal Veil and Bonneville Dam Green Trails, Bonneville Dam and Multnomah Falls USGS, Geo-Graphics Trails of the Columbia River Gorge, and Maptech Oregon: Bonneville Dam.
Trail contacts: Oregon State Parks, 725 Summer Street NE, Suite C, Salem, OR 97301; (503) 986–0707; www.prd.state.or.us.

Finding the trailhead: From Portland, take Interstate 84 east to exit 35, Warrendale/Dodson. Turn left and head east on the Historic Columbia River Highway for 2.5 miles to the John B. Yeon State Scenic Corridor. The trailhead is on the right. There is ample parking, but no public restrooms. The trail to Upper McCord Creek Falls begins on the west end of the parking lot. (Note that exit 37 past the John B. Yeon Corridor is a westbound exit and eastbound on-ramp only.)

Special considerations: Another really cliffy gorge hike—use caution.

The Hike

If you liked the view of Elowah Falls and want to see more of it, this is the trail for you. The path takes you along a sheer rock face to Upper McCord Creek Falls. The trail climbs almost 400 feet of switchbacks; the path along the cliff has a guardrail, but looking down can still give you the shivers.

After leaving the trailhead, the trail forks at 0.1 mile. Take the left fork, Trail 400, and head east for Upper McCord Creek Falls. The trail climbs at a gentle grade, with Douglas fir and Oregon grape below.

At 0.4 mile is the second junction. The left trail is to Elowah Falls. Take the right fork, heading south, and begin the climb to Upper McCord Creek Falls. The trail takes one very long switchback past several large, rusted water pipes. Plants and water are vigorously decaying these old pieces of metal, proving that even old metal pipes are biodegradable.

After the rusted water pipes, the trail traverses the ridge toward McCord Creek. The trail flattens out as you begin to walk on the face of a cliff. The steel railing on the left offers reassurance to the hiker, but in one spot the railing is missing. There

Upper McCord Creek Falls

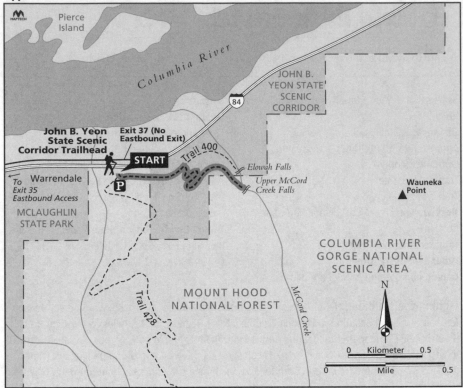

is plenty of room to safely hike this trail, but if you're prone to vertigo, I don't suggest it.

The view below is a new perspective on the 290 feet of Elowah Falls. The impact of the water on the rock cuts and shapes the landscape below. The steep basalt cliffs offer ideal habitat for the Columbia Gorge daisy.

After leaving the guardrail, the trail comes to the Upper McCord Creek Falls, which is less exhilarating than the hike to it. Upper McCord Creek Falls is a minor example of a segmented-type waterfall, splitting near the top. At less than 100 feet tall, it is hard to appreciate as much as the more spectacular Elowah Falls. If it were in an area without as many spectacular waterfalls as the gorge, Upper McCord Creek Falls might get more recognition.

Return to the trailhead via the same route.

Miles and Directions

0.0 **START** from John B. Yeon State Scenic Corridor Trailhead.

0.1 Junction with Nesmith Point Trail 428, stay left (east).

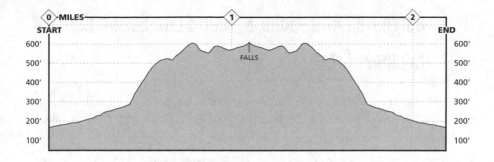

0.4 Junction with Gorge Trail 400 to Elowah Falls, turn right (south).

1.1 Upper McCord Creek Falls, turn around.

2.2 Return to John B. Yeon State Scenic Corridor Trailhead.

17 Gorge Trail 400–John B. Yeon State Scenic Corridor to Tanner Creek

A mix of singletrack trail and paved multiuse trail that connects the John B. Yeon State Scenic Corridor and Tanner Creek short day hike to 290-foot-high Elowah Falls.

Start: John B. Yeon State Scenic Corridor Trailhead.
Distance: 4.3 miles point to point.
Approximate hiking time: 2 hours one-way.
Difficulty: Easy.
Traffic: Moderate to light.
Trail type: Well maintained.
Best season: Year-round.
Total climbing: 760 feet.
Other trail users: Trail 400 is open to mountain bikes heading to Tanner Creek and Eagle Creek.

Canine compatibility: Dogs are allowed on leashes only.
Nearest town: Cascade Locks.
Fees and permits: None.
Maps: Bridal Veil and Bonneville Dam Green Trails, Bonneville Dam and Multnomah Falls USGS, Geo-Graphics Trails of the Columbia River Gorge, and Maptech Oregon: Bonneville Dam.
Trail contacts: Oregon State Parks, 725 Summer Street NE, Suite C, Salem, OR 97301; (503) 986-0707; www.prd.state.or.us.

Finding the trailhead: From Portland, take Interstate 84 east to exit 35, Warrendale/Dodson. Turn left and head east on the Historic Columbia River Highway for 2.5 miles to the John B. Yeon State Scenic Corridor. The trailhead is on the right. There is ample parking, but no public restrooms. The trail to Upper McCord Creek Falls begins on the west end of the parking lot. (Note that exit 37 past the John B. Yeon corridor is a westbound exit and eastbound on-ramp only.)

For a point-to-point hike ending at the Tanner Creek area, take Interstate 84 east from Portland to exit 40, Bonneville Fish Hatchery. Turn right and right again, heading south to the Wahclella Falls Trailhead. Follow the right loop around to find ample parking (but no public restrooms). Trail 436 to Wahclella Falls begins on the far end of the loop on an old road. You may want to park at the new Toothrock Trailhead just up the road toward the Tanner Butte Trail (Hike 21).

The Hike

If you're looking to really explore the gorge or an alternate access route to Munra Point with a little more scenery past Elowah Falls, this is a hike for you. The hike involves a gentle ascent and descent, is short, and does not climb on any ledges, unlike the trail to Upper McCord Creek Falls. This is a good hike for people of all ages.

After leaving the trailhead, the trail forks. Take the left fork, Trail 400, heading east, for Elowah Falls. The trail climbs at a gentle grade through middle-age trees. In spring watch for trillium, a resident of moist forest floors. Trillium is a flower with three large white petals and three 2- to 6-inch-long, broadly ovate leaves.

Gorge Trail 400–John B. Yeon State Scenic Corridor to Tanner Creek

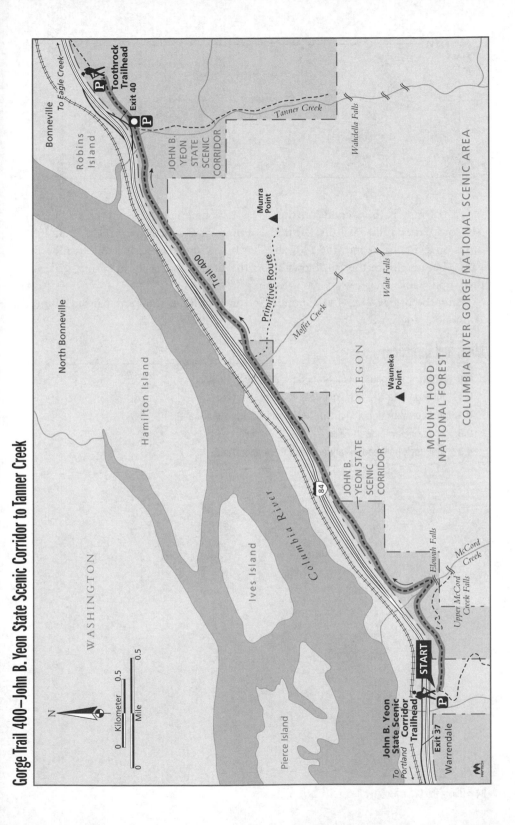

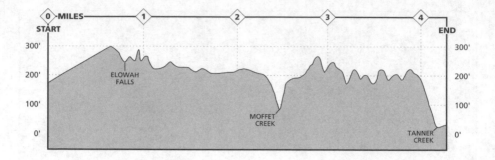

At 0.4 mile is the second junction. The right trail climbs steeply up to Upper McCord Creek Falls. Take the left trail, continuing east for Elowah Falls. Trail 400 drops on switchbacks into the Elowah Glen below the falls. At 0.8 mile is Elowah Falls. The spray from the falls blows across the bridge, especially in spring, making the wood planks slick—watch your footing.

After the bridge, Trail 400 continues to the Toothrock Trailhead, passing Munra Point along the way.

Miles and Directions

0.0 **START** from John B. Yeon State Scenic Corridor Trailhead.

0.1 Junction with Nesmith Point Trail 428, stay left (east).

0.4 Junction with Upper McCord Creek Falls Trail, stay left (east).

0.8 Bridge below Elowah Falls.

4.3 Toothrock Trailhead in Tanner Creek Recreation Area.

Tanner Creek Recreation Area

The nice thing about the Tanner Creek area is that exit 40 is just a plain old normal eastbound/westbound all-access exit. You don't have to remember which direction you're heading or to take another exit, as you do at the Eagle Creek and John B. Yeon exits. In addition, everything south of the interstate is totally developed for recreation.

Tanner Creek, like most streams in the gorge, is prone to occasional massive flushes and periodically washes out parts of nearby trails, but as of this printing things were in excellent shape. Upgrades to this recreation area include a nice new bridge on the way to Wahclella Falls, fancy new Toothrock Trailhead, and an extremely well-maintained, paved multiuse trail stretching from the other side of Interstate 84 from Moffet Creek all the way to the Bridge of the Gods.

There are many hiking options, but they don't all start in the same place. The Wahclella Falls Trailhead is straight south after leaving the off-ramp, while the route to Munra Point lies across the creek just before you head into the Wahclella Falls Trailhead area. The Toothrock Trailhead is a short drive to the east, after turning left before entering the Wahclella Falls Trailhead area. Forest Road 777 continues past the turnoff to the Toothrock Trailhead for 2.1 miles to the Tanner Butte Trailhead and is a nice road for both hiking and mountain biking. The multiuse paths along the Highway State Trail are better suited to mountain biking than hiking, but you may see all sorts of travelers along the way. In addition, the Toothrock Trailhead offers general parking and access to all the hikes or bikes in the area.

18 Munra Point

A steep scramble of a day hike up Munra Point on a primitive trail.

Start: Wahclella Falls Trailheads in Tanner Creek Recreation Area.
Distance: 5.2 miles out and back.
Approximate hiking time: 4 to 9 hours.
Difficulty: Difficult.
Traffic: Light.
Trail type: Unmaintained.
Best season: May through October.
Total climbing: 1,600 feet.
Other trail users: Mountain bikes.
Canine compatibility: Dogs are allowed on leashes only.
Nearest town: Cascade Locks.

Fees and permits: A Northwest Forest Pass is required for Tanner trailheads.
Maps: Bonneville Dam Green Trails, Maptech Oregon: Bonneville Dam. The route up Munra Point does not appear on USGS or Trails of the Columbia Gorge.
Trail contacts: Oregon State Parks, 725 Summer Street NE, Suite C, Salem, OR 97301; (503) 986-0707; www.prd.state.or.us. Mount Hood National Forest, 16400 Champion Way, Sandy, OR 97055; (503) 668-1700; www.fs.fed.us/r6/mthood.

Finding the trailhead: From Portland, take Interstate 84 east to exit 40, Bonneville Fish Hatchery. Turn right, then right again, heading south toward the Wahclella Falls Trailhead. Follow the right loop around to find ample parking (but no public restrooms). The trail to Munra Point begins on Gorge Trail 400 heading west. It starts on the old scenic highway on the west side of the road just as you enter the trailhead drive. You can also access this hike from the John B. Yeon State Scenic Corridor Trailhead; see previous hike descriptions.

Special considerations: Once you leave Trail 400 this is less a trail than a scramble climb.

The Hike

The Hike up Munra Point is short, steep, and often treacherous if you're not used to steep ascents without many switchbacks. The trail doesn't take you all the way up, but the views are nice and the trail is one of the least used in the area.

▶ When scrambling up a steep slope, use stable trees to pull yourself up as you'd use the railing on a staircase.

From the trailhead, Trail 400 crosses Tanner Creek immediately on a bridge of the Historic Columbia River Highway on the newly constructed Highway State Trail. The trail veers left and uphill at a marked junction toward John B. Yeon State Scenic Corridor.

At 1.4 miles, just before dropping into Moffet Creek, an unmarked trail forks to the left. Take it, and head south on the Munra Point Trail. This trail is not maintained and less used than most, but it's not hard to spot. If you cross Moffet Creek, you've gone too far.

Hamilton Mountain from Munra Point.

After the junction, the trail climbs through a mixed forest of fir and oak trees along switchbacks, then heads straight up. The path splits and veers around trees as you scramble up. When you have to choose between a left or right fork, go right for an easier path. This primitive trail is almost vertical and often requires going on all fours.

Just before the top, the trail forks; the right fork continues up the ridge over steep rock climbs. The left trail takes you out onto a lookout. This gives you a nice tunnel view down the gorge, with Table Mountain and Hamilton Mountain on the other side.

On the way back, to get away from the sounds of Interstate 84, turn left at the unmarked junction and drop down to a trail leading to a new bridge across Moffet Creek. The rushing water drowns out the sounds of the outside world and offers a soothing rest spot after your adventurous climb.

Return via Trail 400 to the Wahclella Falls Trailhead.

Munra Point

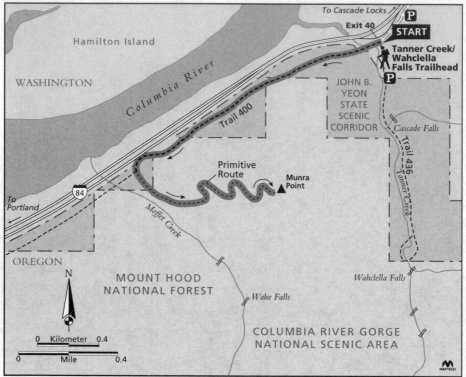

Miles and Directions

0.0 **START** from Wahclella Falls Trailhead.

0.2 Junction with jeep road, stay right.

1.4 Junction with Munra Point Trail, turn left.

2.6 Junction with lookout spur, turn left.

5.2 Return to Wahclella Falls Trailhead.

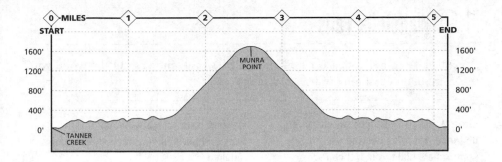

19 Wahclella Falls

A gentle hike to a spectacular falls. Wahclella Falls easily drowns out the world with the calm sound of rushing water.

Start: Wahclella Falls Trailhead off exit 40.
Distance: 1.8 miles out and back.
Approximate hiking time: 2 hours.
Difficulty: Easy.
Traffic: Heavy.
Trail type: Well maintained.
Best season: Year-round.
Total climbing: 240 feet.
Other trail users: None.
Canine compatibility: Dogs are allowed on leashes only.

Nearest town: Cascade Locks.
Fees and permits: A Northwest Forest Pass is required.
Maps: Geo-Graphic Trails of the Columbia Gorge, Bonneville Dam Green Trails, and Maptech Oregon: Bonneville Dam. The trail does not appear on USGS maps.
Trail contacts: Oregon State Parks, 725 Summer Street NE, Suite C, Salem, OR 97301; (503) 986-0707; www.prd.state.or.us.

Finding the trailhead: From Portland, take Interstate 84 east to exit 40, Bonneville Fish Hatchery. Turn right and right again, heading south to the Wahclella Falls Trailhead. Follow the right loop around to find ample parking (but no public restrooms). Trail 436 to Wahclella Falls begins on the far end of the loop on an old road. If the parking lot is full, you may want to park at the new Toothrock Trailhead, just up the road toward the Tanner Butte Trail.

The Hike

Wahclella Falls Trail 436 is very pretty and flat. It showcases one of the Columbia River Gorge's most memorable waterfalls. This hike doesn't have any scary ledges for those who don't like heights, and it's a good hike for children. Still, families may want to stay on the lower or western trail to the base of the falls.

From the trailhead, Wahclella Falls Trail 436 travels 0.3 mile on an old road next to Tanner Creek. It then crosses a short bridge. A cascade of water is on the left. The

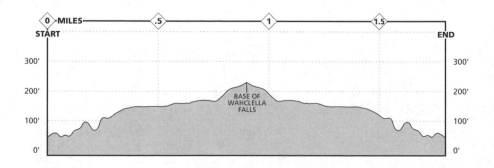

Cascade along the Wahclella Falls Trail.

trail continues along Tanner Creek until 0.7 mile, where the trail forks. Both forks lead to Wahclella Falls, but the right fork is slightly more gentle. This description follows the left fork, continuing south.

The left fork climbs up for a bit before dropping through a grove of cedars to Wahclella Falls. Here you'll get a good up-front view of the falls and the narrow shoot of water above it. Wahclella Falls has an upper tiered drop of 14 to 25 feet and a lower tiered drop of 50 to 70 feet, but the total cascade drops more than 350 feet. The large pool at its base forms a place for spawning salmon in fall.

▶ **On hot days, waterfalls are the coolest places to hike.**

After you stop to gaze in wonder, follow the trail across the creek next to shiny, water-beaten logs. Next, you pass a small cave underneath the perspiring rock. The loop follows the creek downstream before crossing another bridge to rejoin the main trail. Follow the main trail downstream to the trailhead.

Wahclella Falls

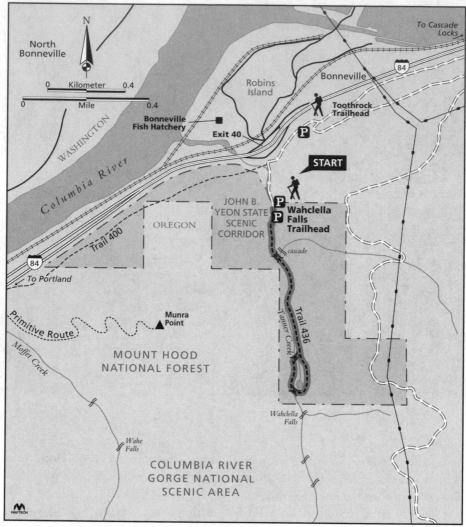

Miles and Directions

0.0 **START** from Wahclella Falls Trailhead.

0.7 Junction with top loop, stay left. **Option:** The right fork also leads to Wahclella Falls and is slightly more gentle.

0.9 Wahclella Falls, turn around.

1.8 Return to Wahclella Falls Trailhead.

20 Tanner Creek Trail

A short day hike in some less traveled temperate forest away from the crowds.

Start: Forest Road 777 gate, shortly after the Tanner Butte Trailhead.
Distance: 7.5 miles out and back.
Approximate hiking time: 3 to 5 hours.
Difficulty: Moderate.
Traffic: Light.
Trail type: Maintained.
Best season: Year-round, depending upon frost line.
Total climbing: 2,100 feet.
Other trail users: Mountain bikes are allowed on the gated portion of FR 777.

Canine compatibility: Dogs are allowed on leashes only.
Nearest town: Cascade Locks.
Fees and permits: A Northwest Forest Pass is required.
Maps: Bonneville Dam Green Trails, and Tanner Butte USGS, Geo-Graphics Trails of the Columbia River Gorge, and Maptech Oregon: Bonneville Dam.
Trail contacts: Mount Hood National Forest, 16400 Champion Way, Sandy, OR 97055; (503) 668-1700; www.fs.fed.us/r6/mthood.

Finding the trailhead: From Portland, take Interstate 84 east to exit 40, Bonneville Fish Hatchery. Turn right and then left, heading east, up Forest Road 777. This road is only open to the public for 2.1 miles, to a little way past the Tanner Butte Trailhead. Park at Tanner Butte Trailhead. The remaining portion of the road that leads to the Tanner Creek Trail is only used by and open to Bonneville Power Administration vehicles for the maintenance of its transmission towers up the drainage.

Special considerations: I found this trail best as a combo mountain bike and hike, biking up the road and hiking the singletrack.

The Hike

Tanner Creek Trail 431 isn't as scenic as the road to it, but it offers relatively secluded camping opportunities after just a short walk. Forest Road 777 is only open to the public for roughly 2.1 miles to the Tanner Butte Trailhead. The remaining portion of the road that leads to Tanner Creek Trail is only used and open to Bonneville Power Administration vehicles for the maintenance of its transmission towers in the drainage. With the closure to most vehicles, the walk along the road is very pleasant and gives a little distance to the end of the short Tanner Creek Trail 431. When I did this hike I found it was nice to mountain bike on the road section and then hike on the singletrack, but hiking on the doubletrack is just as pleasant.

Once you reach the start of Tanner Creek Trail 431, you will pass two trailhead signs. The trail goes through young, mostly deciduous forest with lush vegetation. It crosses several streams at a level grade.

Tanner Creek Trail

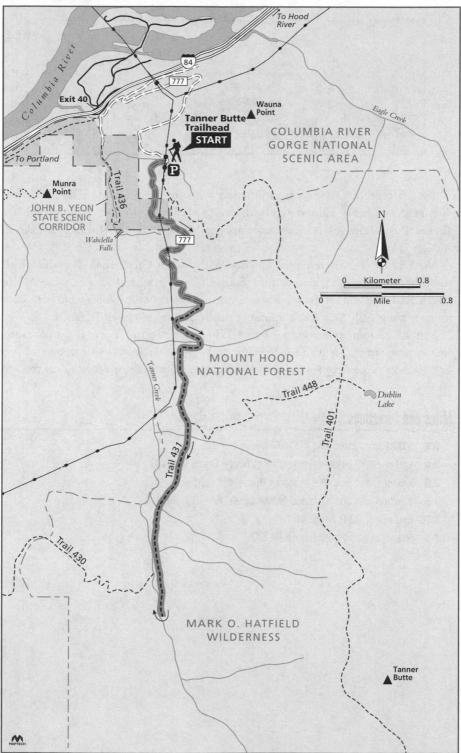

◀ *The ghost-like evidence of a past forest along the Tanner Creek Trail.*

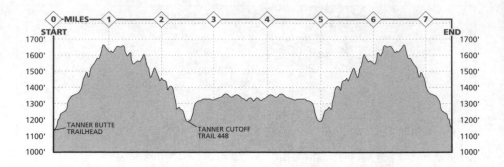

At 2.5 miles in is the marked junction with the Tanner Cutoff Trail. This trail doesn't receive heavy use and may be difficult to follow up to Tanner Butte Trail 401. Tanner Butte Trail 401 is more easily accessed back a couple of miles on FR 722 access road.

At 3.5 miles in, you reach the junction with Moffet Creek Trail 430, which forks right, heading west. It's hard to ford Tanner Creek in spring to access the Moffet Creek Trail. The trail on the other side is not well used, but it is followable with good route-finding skills. Stay left, continuing south on Tanner Creek Trail 431.

After 1.25 more miles, Tanner Creek Trail 431 peters out. There is a small campsite with one to two tent sites, a fire ring, and easy water access. A large, burned root nearby hints at the fiery past of this area. Stay the night or return to your car the way you came.

Miles and Directions

0.0   **START** from gated end of FR 777 from exit 40.

2.0   End of FR 777 doubletrack; start of Tanner Creek Trail 431.

2.5   Tanner Cutoff Trail 448 to Tanner Butte, stay right.

3.5   Junction with unmaintained Moffet Creek Trail 430, stay left.

3.75 End of Trail 431; campsite.

7.5   Return to gated trailhead on FR 777.

21 Tanner Butte

A strenuous, waterless climb to Tanner Butte and Dublin Lake.

Start: Tanner Butte Trailhead.
Distance: 18.3 mile loop.
Approximate hiking time: All day or overnight.
Difficulty: Difficult.
Traffic: Moderate to light.
Trail type: Maintained.
Best season: May through October.
Total climbing: 4,100 feet.
Other trail users: None.
Canine compatibility: Dogs are allowed on leashes only.

Nearest town: Cascade Locks.
Fees and permits: A Northwest Forest Pass required.
Maps: Bonneville Dam Green Trails and Tanner Butte USGS, Geo-Graphics Trails of the Columbia River Gorge, and Maptech Oregon: Bonneville Dam.
Trail contacts: Mount Hood National Forest, 16400 Champion Way, Sandy, OR 97055; (503) 668-1700; www.fs.fed.us/r6/mthood.

Finding the trailhead: From Portland, take Interstate 84 east to exit 40, Bonneville Fish Hatchery. Turn right and then left, up Forest Road 777. This road is only open to the public for 2.1 miles, to a little way past the Tanner Butte Trailhead. Park at the Tanner Butte Trailhead. The remaining portion of the road that leads to the Tanner Creek Trail is only used by and open to Bonneville Power Administration vehicles for the maintenance of its transmission towers up the drainage.

Special considerations: Carry plenty of water for the climb, until you can get to Dublin Lake.

The Hike

Tanner Butte isn't the easiest hike in the gorge, and there isn't much water along the trail. It does, however, go to one of the most prominent high points on the Oregon side, and offers some spectacular views. The best way to do this hike is to make a two-night stay at Dublin Lake with a day trip to the top of Tanner Butte. If you want to go farther, the next good camping spot is Big Cedar Springs on Eagle–Tanner Trail 433. I don't recommend staying at Tanner Springs, especially late in the season when there might not be any water there. Besides, it's one of the least pleasant camping spots I've come across in the gorge.

Begin at the Tanner Butte Trailhead or however far up Tanner Road you made it. The Tanner Butte Trailhead is well marked, and the trail leaves the road just before crossing a rushing creek; this is a good place to filter water if you didn't pack enough. The next water source is Dublin Lake. The trail climbs steeply on switchbacks, with virtually no views.

At 2.2 miles, you reach the junction with an old trail to Wauna Point (not to be confused with the Wauna Viewpoint Trail from Eagle Creek). This unmaintained trail receives quite a few curious hikers and is well worn. It dead-ends in the trees at a

Tanner Butte from Ruckel Creek Trail.

sign reading WAUNA POINT. The only view is of a tree-carved smiley face, because the joke is on you: This isn't actually Wauna Point. To reach the real Wauna Point, you would have to scramble down another 0.25 mile and out onto a treacherous ledge. I don't recommend this side trip—it could scare the daylights out of you. At the junction with the unmaintained trail to Wauna Point, there is a campsite. It has room for two or three tents and a nice fire ring, but there is no water.

To continue toward Tanner Butte, turn right and head south on Tanner Butte Trail 401. The trail is pretty much level up to the junction with Tanner Cutoff Trail 448, which receives light use and is hard to follow. Continue straight, heading south for another 0.1 mile to the junction with the Dublin Lake Trail.

At 4.4 miles, turn left, heading east for Dublin Lake. Even if you don't camp at Dublin Lake, you'll want to stop for water. Dublin Lake is a small pond that supports a healthy population of brook trout and salamanders, which, when swimming along the bottom of the sunlit lake, can look like brook trout. They aren't as tasty, though.

There isn't a lot of room for tents at Dublin Lake—but maybe you'll find a spot that works. If someone already has that spot, it could be hard to find a place to pitch

Tanner Butte

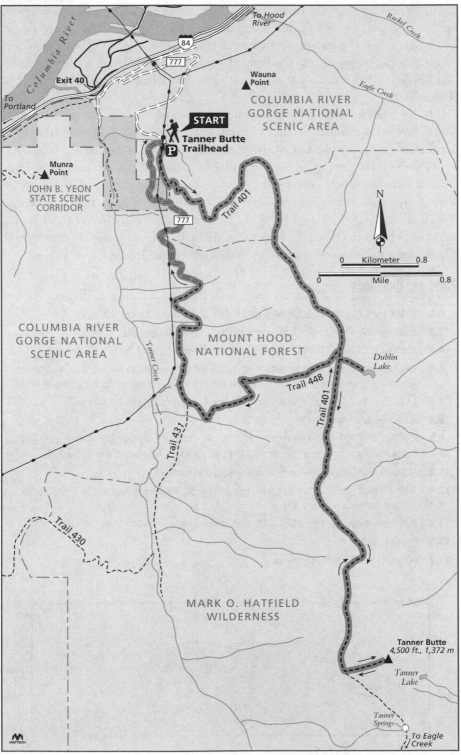

a tent. After setting up your base camp and relaxing for the night, return to the main trail. Take Tanner Butte Trail 401 south; the trail is flat and eventually becomes an old logging road. The canopy opens into meadows of bear grass and other subalpine plants. You can see down into the Tanner Creek Valley to the west, and toward Benson Plateau to the east. To the south you can see the half-tree-covered summit of Tanner Butte.

At 7.8 miles from the trailhead is a primitive cutoff route to the top of Tanner. Since there is no maintained trail to the summit, work your way through the dense spruce and fir forest to the top, where it opens up to views of the surrounding peaks.

Return via the same route to camp at Dublin Lake or all the way back to the trailhead. If you want a little variety, you have two options: You can continue toward the Eagle Creek Trail, or you can take the Tanner Cutoff Trail down to the Tanner Creek Trail and then walk back on FR 777 to the trailhead. This also offers an additional overnight option to extend this into a three-day trip. You can spend the first night at Dublin Lake and the second night near the south end of Tanner Creek Trail 431.

Miles and Directions

0.0 **START** from Tanner Butte Trailhead on FR 777, 2.1 miles from exit 40.

2.2 Junction with Wauna Point Trail (unmaintained), turn right (south).

4.3 Junction with Tanner Cutoff Trail 448, continue straight (south).

4.4 Junction with Dublin Lake spur, turn left (east) for the campsites at Dublin Lake. After visiting the lake, return to Trail 401, and turn left (south) to continue toward Tanner Butte.

7.8 Junction with scramble route up Tanner Butte, turn left (east).

8.3 Tanner Butte, turn around.

8.8 Junction with Trail 401, turn right to return to the trailhead. **Option:** Continue toward Eagle Creek Trail for a long loop hike ending at Eagle Creek Campground and Picnic Area.

12.2 Junction with Dublin Lake spur, continue straight (north).

12.4 Junction with Tanner Cutoff Trail 448, turn left (west). **Option:** Return to the trailhead the way you came, along Trail 401.

15.8 Junction with Tanner Creek Trail 431, turn right (north).

16.3 Forest Road 777.

18.3 Return to Tanner Butte Trailhead.

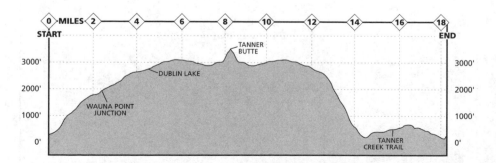

Eagle Creek Recreation Area

E agle Creek Recreation Area is second only to Multnomah Falls in popularity with gorge visitors. Eagle Creek is said to be the most popular hiking trail in Oregon, but I have a hard time believing it receives more visitors than Mult-nomah Falls—some folks must not consider Multnomah a "hike."

There's good reason for Eagle Creek's popularity. There are waterfalls around every bend, old-growth trees, and lush moss-covered cliffsides. It has long been an escape for Portlanders and westerners alike. In fact, Eagle Creek Campground is the oldest national forest campground in the United States and still serves visitors every summer. It dates back to 1916, when it was one of the first public recreation sites in Oregon. You can still visit the Civilian Conservation Corps–era log buildings at the picnic area.

The Eagle Creek Trail has more waterfalls than any other hike in the gorge and offers day, overnight, and extended trip options. You can see three major waterfalls in a day trip to Tunnel Falls. You can spend a night at Tenas Camp and hike out. You can shuttle a car to Wahtum Lake. Or you can do a two- to four-day loop via Tan-ner Butte—or cut your trip short at any time. My favorite spot, however, is the Big Cedar Camp. It's hard to reach, but the old-growth cedar is the best in the gorge.

Also, with the addition of the Highway State Trail connecting the Tanner Creek area and Cascade Locks, you can make Eagle Creek a great base for days of explo-ration—or even better, grab a nice hotel room in Cascade Locks and spend a week hiking all the trails you can, amen.

Eagle Creek Recreation Area Regulations

- No fires in the Eagle Creek Corridor.
- Camping is allowed only upstream of the High Bridge.
- No fires outside designated campsites or within 200 feet of Wahtum Lake.
- No camping outside designated sites or within 200 feet of Wahtum Lake.
- Dogs are allowed on leashes only.

- A free wilderness use permit is required May 15 through October 15, and can be obtained at the Mark O. Hatfield/Columbia Wilderness boundary before reaching Tunnel Falls. This is required for both overnight and day hikers.
- Group size is limited to twelve heartbeats (counting people and stock) in the Mark O. Hatfield/Columbia Wilderness.

Eagle Creek Campground

There are twenty sites at the campground, available on a first-come, first-served basis; reservations are not taken. The cost is $10 per night. The maximum RV length is 22 feet.

Eagle Creek Overlook Picnic Area

You can reserve the shelter and picnic area for group camping and picnicking by calling (541) 308–1712 or (541) 308–1713. The site holds up to ninety people and forty cars. Sunday through Thursday the cost is $40 per night; on Friday, Saturday, and holidays, it runs $80 per night.

22 Highway State Trail–Tanner Creek, Eagle Creek, and Bridge of the Gods

A wide, paved multiuse path connecting the Tanner Creek, Eagle Creek, and Cascade Locks areas for nonmotorized recreationists.

Start: The Toothrock Trailhead off exit 40 in the Tanner Creek Recreation Area.
Distance: 7.0 miles out and back.
Approximate hiking time: 1 to 2 hours, depending upon your mode of transport.
Difficulty: Easy.
Traffic: Moderate.
Trail type: Well maintained.
Best season: Year-round.
Total climbing: 1,640 feet.
Other trail users: Open to most nonmotorized, nonequestrian modes of transport.
Canine compatibility: Dogs are allowed on leashes only.

Nearest town: Cascade Locks.
Fees and permits: A Northwest Forest Pass is required.
Maps: Bridal Veil and Bonneville Dam Green Trails, Bonneville Dam and Multnomah Falls USGS, Geo-Graphics Trails of the Columbia River Gorge, and Maptech Oregon: Bonneville Dam.
Trail contacts: Oregon State Parks, 725 Summer Street NE, Suite C, Salem, OR 97301; (503) 986-0707; www.prd.state.or.us. Mount Hood National Forest, 16400 Champion Way, Sandy, OR 97055; (503) 668-1700; www.fs.fed.us/r6/mthood.

Finding the trailhead: From Portland, take Interstate 84 east to exit 40, Bonneville Fish Hatchery. Turn right and then left onto Forest Road 777, then left again into the Toothrock Trailhead for the Historic Columbia River Highway State Trailhead.

The Hike

This trail—and I use the word *trail* loosely—is part of a massive reconstruction effort to restore a bike-hike route east and west through the gorge without traveling on sections of the busy Interstate 84. If you have a mountain bike, you may want to take a side trip or two, either to Elowah Falls on Gorge Trail 400 or up FR 777 in the

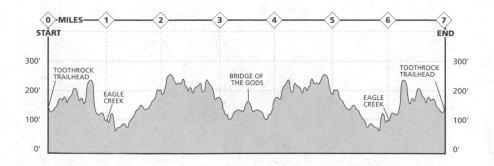

Highway State Trail—Tanner Creek, Eagle Creek, and Bridge of the Gods

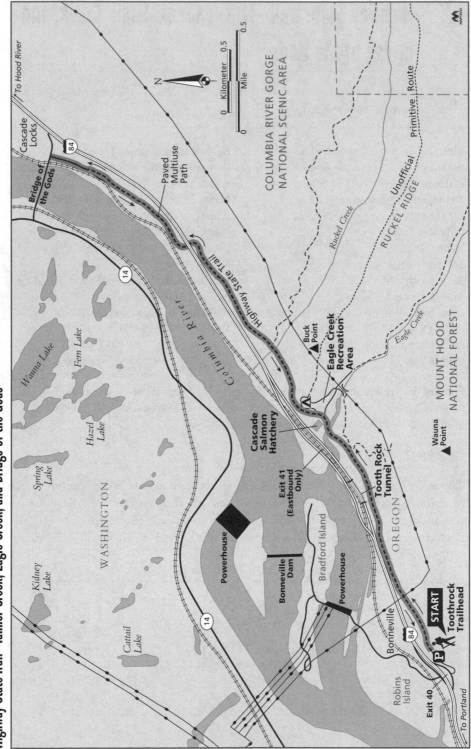

Toothrock Trailhead on the Highway State Trail

Tanner Creek area. For hikers, this is a nice stroll, and the staircase just west of Eagle Creek is your only advantage.

Miles and Directions

0.0 **START** from Toothrock Trailhead/Tanner Creek Recreation Area.
1.0 Eagle Creek Campground.
3.5 Cascade Locks, turn around.
7.0 Return to Toothrock Trailhead.

23 Eagle Creek Trail to Wahtum Lake

The second most famous and perhaps most enjoyable hike in the gorge, or even the entire state of Oregon.

Start: Eagle Creek Campground and Picnic Area.
Distance: 13.3 miles point to point to Wahtum Lake; 12.0 miles out and back to Tunnel Falls.
Approximate hiking time: 5 to 8 hours or overnight.
Difficulty: Difficult to Wahtum Lake.
Traffic: Heavy.
Trail type: Well maintained.
Best season: May through October.
Total climbing: 3,900 feet to Wahtum Lake; 1,200 feet to Tunnel Falls.
Other trail users: No mountain bikes or horses are allowed on the trail, and they'd be crazy to ride it anyway.

Canine compatibility: Dogs are allowed on leashes only (you will see a lot of dogs on this trail).
Nearest town: Cascade Locks.
Fees and permits: A Northwest Forest Pass is required.
Maps: Geo-Graphics Trails of the Columbia Gorge, Bonneville Dam, Tanner Butte and Wahtum Lake USGS, Bonneville Dam Green Trails, and Maptech Oregon: Bonneville Dam.
Trail contacts: Mount Hood National Forest, 16400 Champion Way, Sandy, OR 97055; (503) 668–1700; www.fs.fed.us/r6/mthood.

Finding the trailhead: From Portland, take Interstate 84 east to exit 41, which is accessible only from the eastbound side. Turn right, heading south past the fish hatchery, and stay along the creek for 0.3 mile to the Eagle Creek Trailhead. Heading in from Cascade Locks or points east, you will have to drive to exit 40 and turn around to access exit 41, Eagle Creek, from the west.

To make this trip one-way to Wahtum Lake, you must leave a vehicle at Wahtum Lake. To get there, drive east to exit 62, Hood River, turning right and following the signs toward the city center on Oak. Turn right at the 13th Street stoplight and head south. Follow the main route. Stay left on Tucker Road, following the signs to Dee after bending left and right. At Dee, turn right onto Lost Lake Road, cross the railroad tracks, and stay left at the fork. Follow the well-marked, paved Forest Road 1310 for 10 miles to the Wahtum Lake Trailhead, which is on the right.

Special considerations: The trail along Eagle Creek is often cut right into the bedrock and can be narrow, with steep drop-offs. Most of these sections have a solid handrail cable, but caution is warranted. The trail is easy to hike safely, but not easy to enjoy if you are scared of heights. As my mother put it, "There are lots of places along this trail where if you fell off, it is far enough down to kill you." Also see the introduction to this section for Eagle Creek Recreation Area regulations.

Tunnell Falls PHOTO MARNIE SCHNEIDER ▶

Eagle Creek Trail to Wahtum Lake

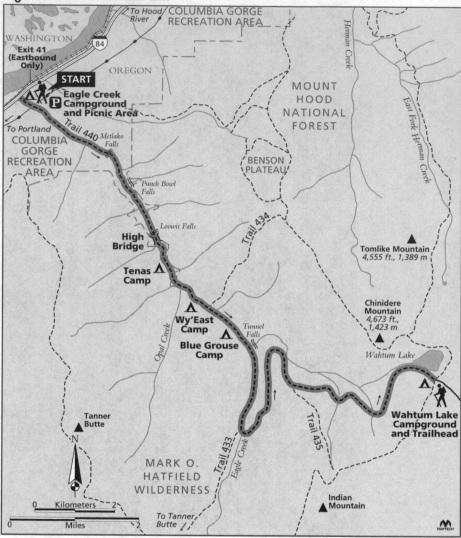

The Hike

Eagle Creek Trail 440 is second only to Multnomah Falls in popularity, being the hike with more waterfalls than any other in the Columbia Gorge. It's also one of the most flexible, offering day, overnight, and extended backpacking options.

The path is well beaten and wide as it follows rushing Eagle Creek. The first stretch is a little cliffy; one spot has a 20-foot drop. There is a cable handrail to steady your stride. The trail is flat and high above Eagle Creek. At 1.5 miles there are two spur trails, both of which grant excellent views of Metlako Falls, which drops 100 to 150 feet and is named for the goddess of the salmon. Unfortunately for many hikers tuckered out by the hike to Metlako Falls, the best is yet to come.

At 1.8 miles is the lower Punch Bowl Overlook Trail—this gives you a view of Punch Bowl from a distance. At 2.1 miles, you reach the Punch Bowl overlook. A guardrail prevents hikers from scrambling below, but you can still get a good picture from the lookout. The guardrail is here for good reason: It would be treacherous to venture past the fence. Safety is worth more than a good picture. The Punch Bowl Falls is definitely not a notable waterfall when it comes to the height of the drop, but the size of the deep pool or "bowl" makes it a spectacular scene—like a fountain in a lake. This is probably why the name emphasizes water punching into a bowl rather than the actual fall.

Along the trail, in between cliffs, the trail passes several talus slopes with nice oldgrowth Douglas fir along the edges. In this temperate rain forest climate, Douglas fir dominate the early stages of succession, but in the absence of a major fire, the more shade-tolerant hemlock and cedar make up the climax forest.

There are several high bridges across tributaries to Eagle Creek before you reach the official High Bridge. The section between Punch Bowl and High Bridge always seems a bit longer than indicated by the trail mileage.

The trail continues on a level grade. High Bridge, at 3.3 miles, crosses Eagle Creek on a steel span above a narrow gorge much like Oneonta Gorge. The trail is cliffy, but again there is protective cable along the way. The 6 miles above High Bridge burned in 1902 and features some smaller-diameter trees, but it's a nicely recovered and mature forest. Along the trail are mostly regrown Douglas fir and a covering of vine maple.

At 3.5 miles, shortly after High Bridge, is the first camp on the right. It has two or three tent sites, but no easy access to water. There is another camp at 3.6 miles with one or two tent sites, but again there is no water access.

At 3.7 miles is the Tenas Camp, with multiple tent sites and an outhouse, old fire rings, and water access. Tenas Camp receives heavy use and is probably not your best option for privacy. There isn't much of a view, either. About 0.3 mile after crossing the next bridge is another camp. It is near water and has room for three to four tents.

Before reaching Wy'East Camp, you'll pass another camp near water with two or three tent sites. Then cross Wy'East Creek, which dries up in late September. Wy'East Camp is equipped with multiple tent sites right next to Eagle Creek. Water is easy to get. Fires are not permitted, though camp stoves are. At 5.0 miles is the junction with Eagle Benson Trail 434. The trail receives moderate use, but the junction is marked. Next is the Blue Grouse Camp, which has several tent sites and easy water access. It's a slightly more private setting than Wy'East Camp. The farther you get from the trailhead, the fewer people.

At 6.0 miles is Tunnel Falls, a classic plunge-type waterfall. The tunnel underneath the falls makes the name obvious, but it isn't a dry tunnel. The sweating rock and spray will wet your forehead if you don't wear a hat. After Tunnel Falls, look for

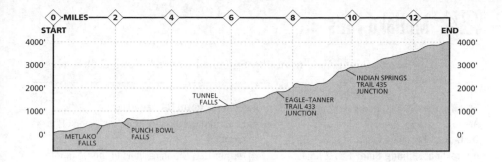

another falls on the main river and a camp just above it. There are several tent sites, and water is available if you go a second falls farther. It is remarkably scenic. After 7.0 miles is the "7.5 mile camp" by the stream. It has three or four tent sites, fire rings, and easy water access. You'll reach it just before crossing two streams. The trail here is in an old burn area with huge snags and dense foliage. At 7.6 miles is the junction with Eagle–Tanner Trail 433, which doesn't receive the heavy use that the path to Wahtum Lake does. Turn left, heading east, on the Eagle Creek Trail. There is one fantastic lookout along the way that gives you a view of the Eagle Creek Valley. At 9.8 miles is the junction with Trail 435 to Indian Springs. Stay left, heading east. There is one campsite on this last stretch, but you might want to wait for Wahtum Lake. You'll find several nice campsites on the south shore of the lake.

Miles and Directions

0.0 **START** from Eagle Creek Campground and Picnic Area.

1.5 Metlako Falls.

2.1 Punch Bowl Falls.

3.3 High Bridge.

3.7 Tenas Camp.

4.7 Wy'East Camp.

5.0 Junction with Eagle Benson Trail 434, continue straight (south).

5.3 Blue Grouse Camp.

6.0 Tunnel Falls.

7.6 Junction with Eagle-Tanner Trail 433, turn left (east).

9.8 Junction with Indian Springs Trail 435, stay left (east).

13.3 Wahtum Lake Campsite and Trailhead.

 Loowit Falls

24 Metlako Falls

A short, flat hike to the first and most photographed waterfall along Eagle Creek.

Start: Eagle Creek Campground and Picnic Area.
Distance: 3.0 miles round trip.
Approximate hiking time: 1 to 2 hours.
Difficulty: Easy.
Traffic: Heavy.
Trail type: Well maintained.
Best season: Year-round.
Total climbing: 200 feet.
Other trail users: None.
Canine compatibility: Dogs are allowed on leashes only (you will see a lot of dogs on this trail).

Nearest town: Cascade Locks.
Fees and permits: A Northwest Forest Pass is required.
Maps: Geo-Graphics Trails of the Columbia Gorge, Bonneville Dam, Tanner Butte and Wahtum Lake USGS, Bonneville Dam Green Trails, and Maptech Oregon: Bonneville Dam.
Trail contacts: Mount Hood National Forest, 16400 Champion Way, Sandy, OR 97055; (503) 668–1700; www.fs.fed.us/r6/mthood.

Finding the trailhead: From Portland, take Interstate 84 east to exit 41, which is accessible only from the eastbound side. Turn right, heading south past the fish hatchery, and stay along the creek for 0.3 mile to the Eagle Creek Trailhead. Heading in from Cascade Locks or points east, you will have to drive to exit 40 and turn around to access exit 41, Eagle Creek, from the west.

Special considerations: The trail along Eagle Creek is often cut right into the bedrock and can be narrow, with steep drop-offs. Most of these sections have a solid handrail cable, but caution is warranted. The trail is easy to hike safely, but not easy to enjoy if you're scared of heights. Also see the introduction to this section for Eagle Creek Recreation Area regulations.

The Hike

Eagle Creek Trail is a well beaten path on its lower reaches as it follows rushing Eagle Creek. The first stretch is a little cliffy; one spot has a 20-foot drop. There is a cable handrail to steady your stride. The trail is flat and high above Eagle Creek.

At 1.5 miles there are two spur trails, both of which offer excellent views of Metlako Falls, which is a plunge-type waterfall that drops 100 to 150 feet. It is named for the goddess of the salmon. Unfortunately for many hikers tuckered out by the hike to Metlako Falls, the best is yet to come. Consider extending your trip to Punch Bowl, Tunnel Falls, or beyond.

Metlako Falls ▶

Metlako Falls

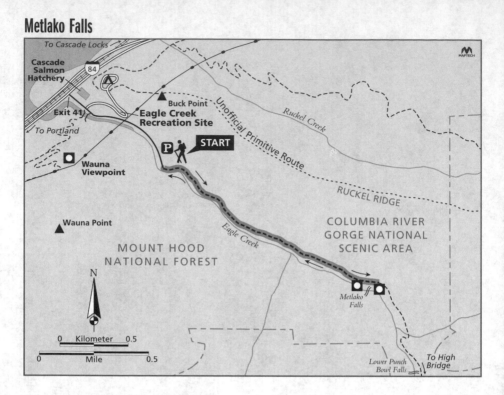

Miles and Directions

0.0 **START** from Eagle Creek Campground and Picnic Area.

1.5 Metlako Falls, turn around.

3.0 Return to Eagle Creek Trailhead.

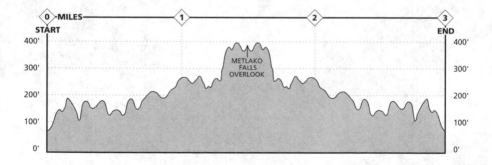

25 Eagle Creek-Tanner Butte Loop

The second most famous and perhaps most enjoyable hike in the gorge.

Start: Eagle Creek Campground and Picnic Area.
Distance: 21.8-mile loop to Tanner Butte Trailhead; 24.2-mile loop to Eagle Creek Campground.
Approximate hiking time: Overnight.
Difficulty: Difficult.
Traffic: Heavy to light.
Trail type: Well maintained.
Best season: May through October.
Total climbing: 5,570 feet.
Other trail users: No mountain bikes or horses are allowed on the trail, and they'd be crazy to ride it anyway.

Canine compatibility: Dogs are allowed on leashes only (you will see a lot of dogs on this trail).
Nearest town: Cascade Locks.
Fees and permits: A Northwest Forest Pass is required.
Maps: Geo-Graphics Trails of the Columbia Gorge, Bonneville Dam, Tanner Butte and Wahtum Lake USGS, Bonneville Dam Green Trails, and Maptech Oregon: Bonneville Dam.
Trail contacts: Mount Hood National Forest, 16400 Champion Way, Sandy, OR 97055; (503) 668-1700; www.fs.fed.us/r6/mthood.

Finding the trailhead: From Portland, take Interstate 84 east to exit 41, which is accessible only from the eastbound side. Turn right, heading south past the fish hatchery, and stay along the creek for 0.3 mile to the Eagle Creek Trailhead. To leave a shuttle vehicle at Tanner Butte Trailhead, turn right and then left off exit 40 onto Forest Road 777. Go 2.1 miles to the trailhead. The road is closed a little way past the trailhead.

Special considerations: The trail along Eagle Creek is often cut right into the bedrock and can be narrow, with steep drop-offs. Most of these sections have a solid handrail cable, but caution is warranted. The trail is easy to hike safely, but not easy to enjoy if you're scared of heights. Like my mother put it, "There are lots of places along this trail where if you fell off, it is far enough down to kill you." Also see the introduction to this section for Eagle Creek Recreation Area regulations.

The Hike

The Eagle Creek Campground dates back to 1916, when it was one of the first public recreation sites in Oregon. You can still visit the Civilian Conservation Corps–era log buildings at the picnic area. Eagle Creek, second only to Multnomah Falls in popularity, is the trail with more waterfalls than any other hike in the gorge and offers day, overnight, and extended trip options. You can see three waterfalls in a day trip to Tunnel Falls. You can spend a night at Tenas Camp and hike out, or you can do a two- to four-day loop via Tanner Butte. This description covers the entire route, but you can cut it short at any time. My favorite spot is the Big Cedar Camp—hard to reach, but its old-growth cedar is the best in the gorge.

The path is well beaten and wide as it follows rushing Eagle Creek. The first stretch is a little cliffy; one spot has a 20-foot drop. There is a cable handrail to steady your stride. The trail is flat and high above Eagle Creek.

At 1.5 miles there are two spur trails, both both of which feature grand views of Metlako Falls, which drops 100 to 150 feet and is named for the goddess of the salmon. And the best is yet to come: At 1.8 miles is the lower Punch Bowl Overlook Trail. This gives you a view of Punch Bowl from a distance. At 2.1 miles, you reach the Punch Bowl overlook. A guardrail prevents hikers from scrambling below, but you can still get a good picture from the lookout. The guardrail is here for good reason: It would be treacherous to venture past the fence. Safety is worth more than a good picture. The Punch Bowl Falls is definitely not a notable waterfall when it comes to the height of the drop, but the size of the deep pool or "bowl" makes it a spectacular scene—like a fountain in a lake. This is probably why the name emphasizes water punching into a bowl rather than the actual fall.

Along the trail, in between cliffs, the trail passes several talus slopes with nice old-growth Douglas fir along the edges. In this temperate rain forest climate, Douglas fir dominate the early stages of succession, but in the absence of a major fire, the more shade-tolerant hemlock and cedar make up the climax forest.

There are several high bridges across tributaries to Eagle Creek before you reach the official High Bridge. The section between Punch Bowl and High Bridge always seems a bit longer than indicated by the trail mileage.

The trail continues on a level grade. High Bridge, at 3.3 miles, crosses Eagle Creek on a steel span above a narrow gorge much like Oneonta Gorge. The trail is cliffy, but again there is protective cable along the way. The 6 miles above the High Bridge burned in 1902 and features some smaller-diameter trees, but it's a nicely recovered and mature forest. Along the trail are mostly regrown Douglas fir and a covering of vine maple.

At 3.5 miles, shortly after High Bridge, is the first camp on the right. It has two or three tent sites, but no easy access to water. There is another camp at 3.6 miles with one or two tent sites, but again there is no water access.

At 3.7 miles is the Tenas Camp, with multiple tent sites and an outhouse, old fire rings, and water access. Tenas Camp receives heavy use and is probably not your best option for privacy. There isn't much of a view, either. About 0.3 mile after crossing the next bridge is another camp. It is near water and has room for three or four tents.

Before reaching Wy'East Camp, you'll pass another camp near water with two or three tent sites. Then cross Wy'East Creek, which dries up in late September. Wy'East Camp is equipped with multiple tent sites right next to Eagle Creek. Water is easy to get. Fires are not permitted, though camp stoves are. At 5.0 miles is the junction with Eagle Benson Trail 434. The trail receives moderate use, but the junction is

◀ *Lower Punch Bowl Falls*

Eagle Creek-Tanner Butte Loop

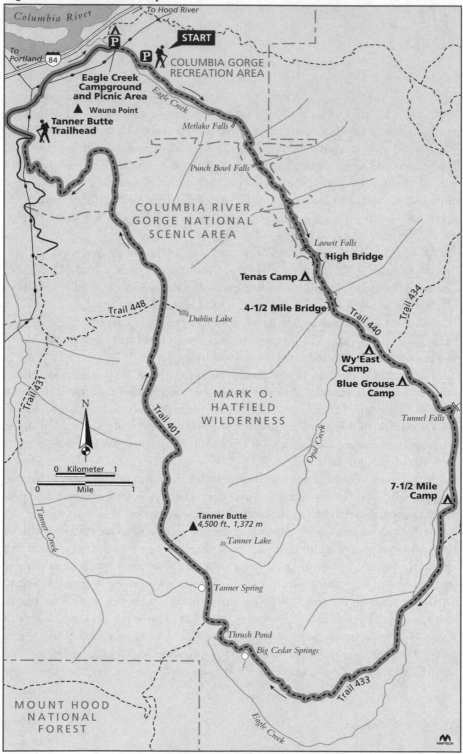

Columbia River

To Hood River

To Portland 84

START

COLUMBIA GORGE
RECREATION AREA

Eagle Creek
Campground
and Picnic Area

▲ Wauna Point

Tanner Butte
Trailhead

Eagle Creek

Metlako Falls

Punch Bowl Falls

COLUMBIA RIVER
GORGE NATIONAL
SCENIC AREA

Loowit Falls

High Bridge

Tenas Camp △

4-1/2 Mile Bridge

Trail 448

Dublin Lake

Trail 440

Trail 434

Wy'East
Camp △

Blue Grouse △
Camp

Trail 431

N

MARK O.
HATFIELD
WILDERNESS

Opal Creek

Tunnel Falls

Trail 401

0   Kilometer   1

0   Mile   1

7-1/2 Mile
Camp △

Tanner Butte
▲ 4,500 ft., 1,372 m

Tanner Lake

Tanner Creek

○ *Tanner Spring*

Thrush Pond

○ *Big Cedar Springs*

Trail 433

MOUNT HOOD
NATIONAL
FOREST

Eagle Creek

MAPTECH

marked. Next is the Blue Grouse Camp, which has several tent sites and easy water access. It's a slightly more private setting than Wy'East Camp. The farther you get from the trailhead, the fewer people.

At 6.0 miles is Tunnel Falls. The tunnel underneath the falls makes the name obvious, but it isn't a dry tunnel. The sweating rock and spray will wet your forehead if you don't wear a hat. After Tunnel Falls, look for another falls on the main river and a camp just above it. There are several tent sites, and water is available if you go a second falls farther. It is remarkably scenic. After 7.0 miles is the "7.5 mile camp" by the stream. It has three or four tent sites, fire rings, and easy water access. You'll reach it just before crossing two streams. The trail here is in an old burn area with huge snags and dense foliage. At 7.6 miles is the junction with Eagle–Tanner Trail 433, which doesn't receive the heavy use that the path to Wahtum Lake does.

Instead of turning left (east) at the 7.6-mile junction with Eagle–Tanner Trail 433, turn right (south). The path is less used because most travelers make the point-to-point hike to Wahtum Lake, but here is your chance to go deep in the heart of the Columbia Wilderness.

The trail is relatively flat, with some gradual climbing, until at 8.5 miles it crosses the West Fork of Eagle Creek. There is a camp just before the crossing in dense alder and maple forest. The ford is tough in spring. There is room for only a tent or two, and easy water access.

After the ford, the trail is overgrown with sword fern, vine maple, and devil's-club. There are many small-diameter fallen trees, which indicate light use. Don't plan on this section to be cleared: Because of its remoteness, it's not a top maintenance priority.

The trail climbs more steeply, passing through a very dense young forest. The canopy is so thick that in some places the forest floor cannot support shrubs. At 11.5 miles (3.9 miles after leaving the main Eagle Creek Trail) is Big Cedar Springs Camp. The camp rests among some excellent old-growth trees, the biggest I've seen in the gorge, as well as some 500-year-old cedar and fir. These are especially pretty after the dense forest on the trip in. The spring ensures water even in September, and there is room for only one tent.

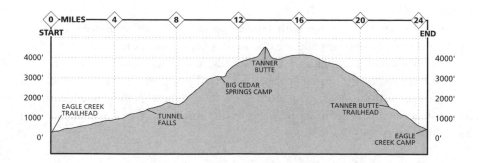

Punch Bowl Falls

The next bit of trail features large diameter logs requiring a little extra effort from the trail crew each pass. The trail has been cut out and is not too difficult to follow.

After the short climb, the trail goes past a pond. This muddy water is a better bet than counting on the supposed Tanner "Spring" camp appearing on some maps.

After 13.1 miles (5.0 miles after leaving the main Eagle Creek Trail), you'll reach the junction with Tanner Butte Trail 401, an old logging road. Turn right, heading north.

At 13.4 miles, the junction with Tanner "Spring" spur trail is marked. Turn left, heading west, to a campsite with one or two sites. Don't count on water here; if there is water early in the season, it's a 0.25-mile walk west. There's no view, either.

Past the spur to the "spring" camp is a marked junction with an unmaintained ascent of Tanner Butte. A scramble route works its way through the dense spruce and fir forest to the top. It opens up to views of the surrounding area, and you can cut back down (north) to the trail.

At 17.3 miles into the trip is the junction with a marked trail to Dublin Lake. It supports brook trout and has room for one to two tents, but the camp is right on the lake. About 0.2 mile farther is Tanner Cutoff Trail 448, which offers access to the lightly used Tanner Creek Trail 431.

At the border of the wilderness area, a trail to Wauna Point splits right. It's a scary thing to climb all the way down onto Wauna Point—I don't recommend it. It is no shortcut to Eagle Creek. At this junction, there is a campsite with room for two or three tents and no water. Stay left, heading west. The rest of the descent to Forest Road 777 is steep, with switchbacks and no water. Once you're on the road, turn right, heading east along the road and working your way back to Eagle Creek.

Miles and Directions

0.0 START from Eagle Creek Campground and Picnic Area.

1.5 Metlako Falls.

2.1 Punch Bowl Falls.

3.3 High Bridge.

3.7 Tenas Camp.

4.7 Wy'East Camp.

5.0 Junction with Eagle Benson Trail 434, continue straight (south).

5.3 Blue Grouse Camp.

6.0 Tunnel Falls.

7.0 7½ Mile Camp.

7.6 Junction with Eagle–Tanner Trail 433, turn right (south).

8.5 West Fork of Eagle Creek Camp.

11.5 Big Cedar Springs Camp.

13.1 Junction with Tanner Butte Trail 401, turn right (north).

13.4 Tanner Spring spur trail, turn left (west).

17.3 Dublin Lake spur trail, stay left (north).

17.5 Tanner Cutoff Trail 448, stay right (north).

19.6 Wauna Point Trail (unmaintained), stay left (west).

21.8 Tanner Butte Trailhead.

24.2 Return to Eagle Creek Campground.

26 Wauna Viewpoint

A short, but uphill, climb to a lookout beneath the power lines.

Start: Eagle Creek Trailhead bridge.
Distance: 3.6 miles out and back.
Approximate hiking time: 1 hour.
Difficulty: Moderate.
Traffic: Heavy.
Trail type: Well maintained.
Best season: Year-round.
Total climbing: 1,100 feet.
Other trail users: Mountain bikers.

Canine compatibility: Dogs are allowed on leashes only.
Nearest town: Cascade Locks.
Fees and permits: A Northwest Forest Pass is required.
Maps: Bonneville Dam Green Trails, and Bonneville Dam USGS.
Trail contacts: Mount Hood National Forest, 16400 Champion Way, Sandy, OR 97055; (503) 668-1700; www.fs.fed.us/r6/mthood.

Finding the trailhead: From Portland, take Interstate 84 east to exit 41, Eagle Creek Recreation Area, which is accessible only from the eastbound side. Turn right, heading south, and drive past the fish hatchery along the creek for 0.1 mile. Before reaching the visible suspension bridge over Eagle Creek, park on the left by the picnic area. Bathrooms are available back toward the hatchery or 0.2 mile farther, at the Eagle Creek Trailhead. The trail starts across the suspension bridge.

The Hike

Wauna Viewpoint is a commonsense alternative to actually ascending Wauna Point. It has one major drawback: the power lines. There's no getting around it, the view is just not as pretty with the power lines. This trail is similar to the one to Buck Point on the Ruckel Ridge Trail (Hike 27), but it offers a slightly better view of Bonneville Dam and Table Mountain.

Trail 402 starts across the bridge. After crossing, you reach a junction with the Shady Glen Interpretive Trail, one of the by-products of increased hiker participation in the outdoors. Stay right, heading west. The trail climbs along the side of the

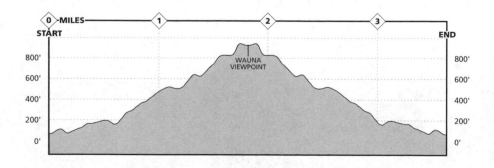

Wauna Viewpoint

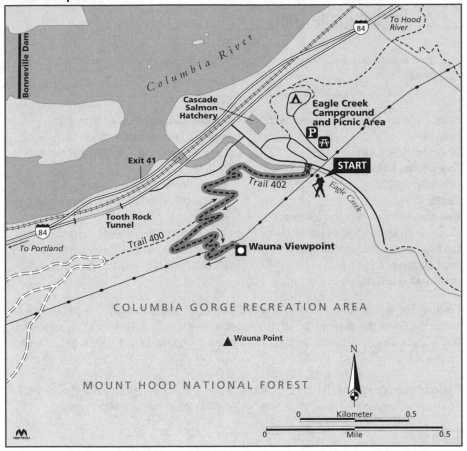

Eagle Creek Valley toward the Columbia. Large firs and plenty of sunlight add to the trail's atmosphere.

At 0.9 mile is a well-marked junction with Gorge Trail 400, which is straight ahead. Turn left, heading south up the hill. The trail climbs on switchbacks until the only cover is several large towers. BPA towers do mean that there are no trees—and no trees makes for a better view. You can see across to Table Mountain and the peaks of the Washington Cascades.

Return to the trailhead via the same route.

Miles and Directions

0.0 **START** from Eagle Creek Trailhead bridge.

0.1 Junction with Shady Glen Interpretive Trail, stay right (west).

0.9 Junction with Gorge Trail 400, turn left (south).

1.8 Wauna Viewpoint, turn around.

3.6 Return to Eagle Creek Trailhead.

27 Ruckel Ridge Loop

An adventurous day hike atop a rocky cliff–sided ridge into the Mark O. Hatfield Wilderness.

Start: Eagle Creek Campground on the Buck Point Trail.
Distance: 8.0-mile loop.
Approximate hiking time: 4 to 6 hours.
Difficulty: Difficult.
Traffic: Moderate.
Trail type: Primitive hiker trail up Ruckel Ridge; well-maintained down Ruckel Creek.
Best season: May through October.
Total climbing: 3,750 feet.
Other trail users: None.

Canine compatibility: Not compatible.
Nearest town: Cascade Locks.
Fees and permits: A Northwest Forest Pass is required.
Maps: Bonneville Dam Green Trails, Bonneville Dam and Carson USGS, and Maptech Oregon: Carson.
Trail contacts: Mount Hood National Forest, 16400 Champion Way, Sandy, OR 97055; (503) 668–1700; www.fs.fed.us/r6/mthood.

Finding the trailhead: From Portland, take Interstate 84 east to exit 41, Eagle Creek Recreation Area. Follow the off-ramp. Turn right, then left, and park at the lot in front of the restrooms. Do not try to drive up to the campground. The trailhead is 200 yards up the campground road on your left.

Special considerations: The climb up Ruckel Ridge is a very primitive route with some cliffy sections. It is an unofficial route and hikers should take care to minimize their impact.

The Hike

The Ruckel Ridge Trail is not for people who are scared of heights, out of shape, or without sturdy footwear. The primitive trail climbs up steep rock talus slopes and is on top of a narrow ridge; at one point it crosses a section of ridge only 4 feet wide. The experience is exhilarating, but also dangerous if taken lightly. If you want to avoid the ridge, a steep hike up the Ruckel Creek Trail is a good option, but not as scenic.

From the parking lot, walk up the campground road for about 200 yards to the trailhead marker on the left side of the road. Follow this trail around the campground to the intersection with Gorge Trail 400 at 0.1 mile and take the right fork. If you do the loop, you will return on this left trail. (If you are just hiking the Ruckel Creek Trail, keep left here to reverse the second half of the loop.) The trail goes around the campground, passing through an amphitheater for fireside chats. A large sign reads BUCK POINT 3/4 MILE.

▶ **Warning: This trail requires scrambling on all fours.**

Bridges of the Gods from Ruckel Creek Trail

From the Buck Point Trail 439 sign, a well-maintained trail switchbacks uphill. After about 0.5 mile, the trees are succeeded by power lines, and the trail crosses underneath them to reach Buck Point. The point isn't terribly scenic due to the power lines, but having an official destination enables the trail to remain maintained up to this point. This can be the end of the trip if all you want is a short walk with a view, but Wauna Viewpoint is a little better in the view department.

Head south, past Buck Point, and stay right. The trail drops slightly onto a rocky, mossy slope, then climbs through a slide area. Stay left, heading east, as you climb. Several cairns, or large piles of rocks, mark the faint trail. Climb back up to the crest of the ridge, then turn straight up the ridge before reaching the base of a cliff. Then skirt left around it. The trail is very steep, but there are roots and small trees to pull yourself up with.

You ought to get used to climbing up a steep trail on top of the ridge, because you'll continue to do this for the next 2.5 miles. In several spots you have to scramble up and down large rocks. There is one scary stretch that crosses a section of the rocky ridge just 4 feet wide.

Ruckel Ridge Loop

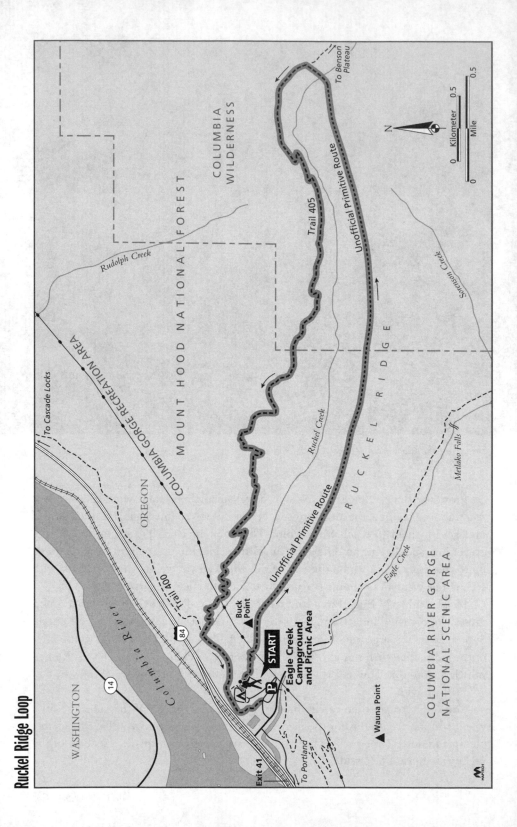

There are several good viewpoints along the way. From the ridge you can see Table Mountain, Hamilton Mountain, Tanner Butte, and Mount St. Helens if it's clear and the "mountains are out." The last stretch is also steep, and the trail is marked only by blazes.

As the grade flattens out, the trail crosses Ruckel Creek. There is no bridge. This is a good place to filter water because the trail down Ruckel Creek doesn't get very close to the creek. The forest is composed of mostly middle-age hemlock and fir trees and is well shaded.

Shortly after Ruckel Creek, climb up and to the left. A faint trail leads to the junction with Ruckel Creek Trail 405, where you have two choices. A right leads to the Benson Plateau and farther to Pacific Crest Trail 2000. Turn left to complete the loop. The Ruckel Creek Trail is well maintained and easy to follow.

Next is the steady descent into Ruckel Creek Valley. About 2 miles down are several hanging gardens of flowers. The open green slopes offer a pleasant break from hiking in the trees.

After 6.5 miles of hiking, the trail drops on steep, short switchbacks, passing an excellent view of the Bridge of the Gods. The trail is very steep on this last section. If you decide to reverse the route or just hike up Ruckel Creek, be ready for this section to get you winded. It might even slow you to less than a 1-mile-per-hour hiking speed.

After many more switchbacks, the trail levels off across an open rocky area. It then descends in forested slopes to Ruckel Creek. Just after you've seen Ruckel Creek for the first time since the top of the hike, the trail intersects Gorge Trail 400 on the old scenic highway. Turn left onto the stone bridge for the final 0.4 mile to the campground and back to the trailhead.

Miles and Directions

0.0 **START** from Eagle Creek Campground, Buck Point Trail 439.

0.1 Junction with Gorge Trail 400, stay right.

0.75 End Buck Point Trail 439, head south past Buck Point, then stay left after a short down-hill across a mossy slope following several cairns.

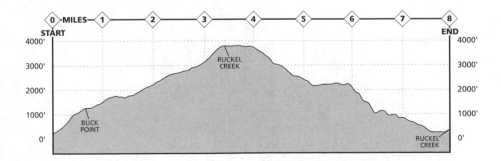

3.3 Junction with Ruckel Creek Trail 405, turn left (northwest). **Option:** Turning right on Ruckel Creek Trail leads to Benson Plateau and the Pacific Crest Trail.

3.7 Junction with Trail 405D, turn left (west).

7.6 Junction with Gorge Trail 400, turn left (southwest).

8.0 Return to Eagle Creek Campground; junction with Buck Point Trail 439.

Pacific Crest Trail, Oregon

Pacific Crest Trail National Scenic Trail 2000 extends from Mexico to Canada and encompasses miles of trail. The PCT was designated a national scenic trail by Congress in 1968. The section through the Columbia River Gorge offers at least four good hiking options—more if you like. On the Oregon side the best way to break the trail up is to make a short day hike from the Bridge of the Gods to Dry Creek Falls. For longer trips, try starting at Herman Creek for quicker access.

For volunteer opportunities and more information:

Pacific Crest Trail Association
5325 Elkhorn Boulevard, PMB 256
Sacramento, CA 95842-2526
(888) 728–7245
www.pcta.org

28 Pacific Crest Trail to Dry Creek Falls

An easy hike to a little-known waterfall.

Start: Bridge of the Gods Toll Booth Park.
Distance: 4.4 miles out and back.
Approximate hiking time: 2 to 3 hours.
Difficulty: Easy.
Traffic: Moderate.
Trail type: Well maintained.
Best season: May through October.
Total climbing: 580 feet.
Other trail users: Horses.
Canine compatibility: Dogs are allowed on leashes only.

Nearest town: Cascade Locks.
Fees and permits: A Northwest Forest Pass is required.
Maps: Carson USGS, USFS Pacific Crest Trail Oregon, Bonneville Dam Green Trails, and Maptech Oregon: Carson.
Trail contacts: Mount Hood National Forest, 16400 Champion Way, Sandy, OR 97055; (503) 668-1700; www.fs.fed.us/r6/mthood.

Finding the trailhead: To reach the Pacific Crest Trail's Bridge of the Gods Trailhead, drive east from Portland on Interstate 84 and take exit 44, Cascade Locks. Follow the off-ramp toward the town; just as you pass under the steel girders of the Bridge of the Gods, turn right and then right again into the parking lot before the tollbooth. The trail starts to the south, across the road.

The Hike

The Pacific Crest Trail 2000 (PCT 2000) is one of the best-known trails in the gorge. This particular section of the PCT is part of a longer route to the Benson Plateau; for extended trips, then, it's more efficient to start at the Herman Creek Work Center. This short section does, however, offer a hidden waterfall without the crowds of the other gorge cascades.

From the trailhead, cross the street and follow Trail 2000 under the interstate and up a road to the right, just under the overpass. One hundred yards up the road is the junction with Gorge Trail 400 and the PCT 2000. Turn left, heading east, on Trail 2000, leading into the trees. This area was the site of some interesting vandalism,

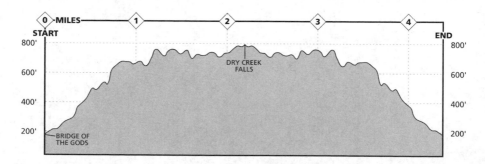

Pacific Crest Trail to Dry Creek Falls

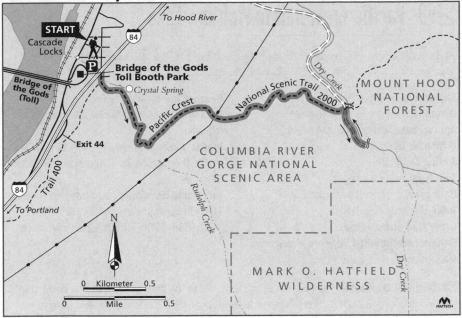

which involved decorating trail signs with underwear, the last time I passed through. It may not be as entertaining now.

The trail runs uphill slightly but is mostly level. The forest of young trees muffles the sounds of the interstate rather quickly. Familiar banana slugs dot the trail.

At 2.0 miles, the PCT 2000 reaches the junction with old Trail 405D to Ruckel Creek. You will not notice this junction without looking hard for it; it comes just before you reach a gravel road. I don't recommend trying this route to Ruckel Creek unless your route-finding skills are quite refined.

Instead, take a right, heading south, on the gravel road just before the bridge. A short distance later you'll find a little waterfall above the trail and an old water-regulating gate. Dry Creek Falls is a single spout of water less than 50 feet tall. It's not the most spectacular cascade in the area, but it isn't on the map and therefore not in most people's travel plans. Think of it as your own private waterfall.

Return to the trailhead via the same route or access areas farther along on the PCT 2000.

Miles and Directions

0.0 START from Bridge of the Gods Toll Booth Park in Cascade Locks.

0.2 Junction with Gorge Trail 400, turn left (east).

2.0 Junction with jeep road at bridge over Dry Creek, turn right (south).

2.2 Dry Creek Falls, turn around.

4.4 Return to Bridge of the Gods.

29 Pacific Crest Trail to Wahtum Lake

A difficult overnight route with loop options back onto the Herman Creek Trail.

Start: Herman Creek Horse Camp.
Distance: 14.2 miles point to point.
Approximate hiking time: Overnight.
Difficulty: Difficult.
Traffic: Moderate.
Trail type: Well maintained.
Best season: June through October.
Total climbing: 6,500 feet.
Other trail users: Horses.
Canine compatibility: Dogs are allowed on leashes only.

Nearest town: Cascade Locks.
Fees and permits: A Northwest Forest Pass is required.
Maps: Carson and Wahtum Lake USGS, Bonneville Dam Green Trails, and Maptech Oregon: Carson.
Trail contacts: Mount Hood National Forest, 16400 Champion Way, Sandy, OR 97055; (503) 668-1700; www.fs.fed.us/r6/mthood.

Finding the trailhead: You have two possible routes to the start of this trail. You could start at the Bridge of the Gods, but it's much better to drop a car off at Wahtum Lake and have your shuttle friends drive you back to either Bridge of the Gods or Herman Creek Horse Camp.

The best way is to take Interstate 84 east from Portland to the weigh station exit, just after exit 44, Cascade Locks. Drive through the weigh station area and turn right onto Herman Creek Road. Follow the road for 2 miles to the well-marked Herman Creek Horse Camp. This is the work station for trail maintenance in the Columbia Gorge. If you miss the weigh station, take exit 47, Herman Creek Road, then turn right, heading west, for 0.5 mile to the Herman Creek Recreation Site on the south side of the road. Drive up toward the campground, bearing right at the junction with the campground road. The trailhead is at the far end of the loop next to PACIFIC CREST TRAIL 2000 and HERMAN CREEK TRAIL 406 signs. Bathrooms are available at the trailhead, along with ample parking.

Walking this route point to point requires leaving a vehicle at Wahtum Lake, or having someone pick you up there. To get to Wahtum Lake, drive east to exit 62, Hood River, and turn right, following the signs to the city center on Oak. At the 13th Street stoplight, turn right, heading south. Follow the main route. Stay left on Tucker Road, following the signs to Dee after bending left and right. At Dee, turn right onto Lost Lake Road, cross the railroad tracks, and stay left at the fork. Follow the well-marked, paved Forest Road 1310 for 10 miles to the Wahtum Lake Trailhead, which is on the right.

The Hike

The Pacific Crest Trail 2000 (PCT 2000) is probably not the most popular trail in the gorge, but it runs a close third behind Multnomah Falls and Eagle Creek. This particular section of the PCT 2000 is strenuous and dry, especially the climb from Herman Creek up to the Benson Plateau. There isn't much water along the way, except for Teakettle Spring and the slightly out-of-the-way Ruckel Creek, until

Mount Hood from Chinidere Mountain.

Wahtum Lake. The trail up and the trail along the plateau offer several views of the broken-topped forest of Herman Creek and majestic Tomlike Mountain Ridge.

From the trailhead, the trail drops slightly before one switchback and the first junction, which is unmarked. The trail on the right descends to the work center; the left-hand trail continues to climb south up gradual switchbacks. The trail passes underneath power lines and crosses a jeep road as it climbs.

At 0.6 mile is the junction with Herman Bridge Trail 406E. Stay right for the main trail; left is Herman Creek Trail 406. This section technically is a shortcut to the PCT rather than starting at the Cascade Locks Trailhead. The trail drops, crossing a bridge over Herman Creek, and then climbs through maple and fir forest to a talus slope at the junction with the PCT.

After 1.9 miles, turn left, heading southwest on the PCT, and gently traverse the slope toward the Herman Creek Valley before starting the steep climb up the ridge. The next 4.5 miles of climbing gains 2,940 feet, but it's nothing compared to the Starvation Ridge Trail. Still, it's more than most of the population is fit for. Bring water: It's 3.5 miles from the junction to Teakettle Spring. Before you reach this

Pacific Crest Trail to Wahtum Lake

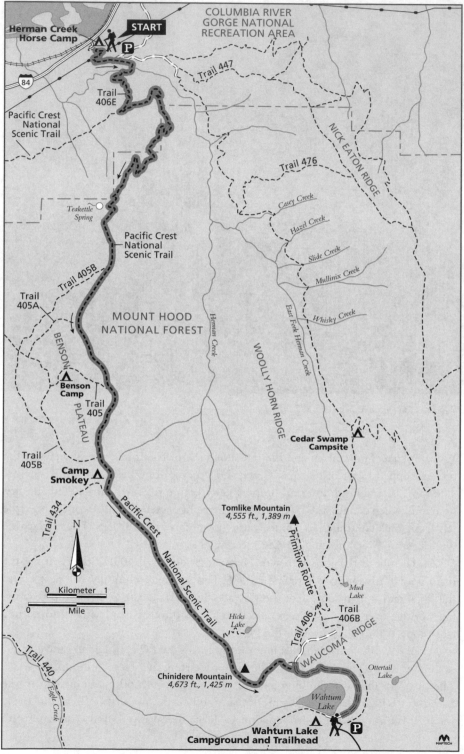

Herman Creek Horse Camp

START

Trail 447

COLUMBIA RIVER
GORGE NATIONAL
RECREATION AREA

84

Trail 406E

Pacific Crest
National
Scenic Trail

Trail 476

NICK EATON RIDGE

Casey Creek

Hazel Creek

Teakettle Spring

Pacific Crest
National
Scenic Trail

Slide Creek

Mullinix Creek

Trail 405B

Trail 405A

BENSON

MOUNT HOOD
NATIONAL FOREST

Herman Creek

Whisky Creek

East Fork Herman Creek

WOOLLY HORN RIDGE

Benson Camp

Trail 405

PLATEAU

Trail 405B

Cedar Swamp Campsite

Camp Smokey

Trail 434

N

Tomlike Mountain
4,555 ft., 1,389 m

Primitive Route

Pacific Crest

0   Kilometer   1

0   Mile   1

National Scenic Trail

Hicks Lake

Trail 406

Trail 406B

Mud Lake

WAUCOMA RIDGE

Trail 440

Eagle Creek

Chinidere Mountain
4,673 ft., 1,425 m

Ottertail Lake

Wahtum Lake

**Wahtum Lake
Campground and Trailhead**

P

MAPTECH

spring, there are several small, flat lookouts that could possibly harbor a tent, if you're willing to walk at least 0.5 mile to the spring for water.

At 5.4 miles is Teakettle Spring. It had clear water when I visited in late September, but you can expect a little mud-lined pool about 3 feet in diameter when you arrive. You probably won't care, because thirst and iodine do mix.

After Teakettle Spring, Trail 2000 continues to climb up to the plateau into a forest of mountain hemlock. Soon after the trail levels out, at 6.4 miles, is the junction with Benson Way Trail 405B.

If you wish to camp soon and don't have much water, I recommend taking a right for Ruckel Creek. Ruckel Creek has several good campsites and water almost year-round, but don't count on it late in the season, and if you push on to Camp Smokey you're unlikely to find water. One site is right at the junction with Ruckel Creek Trail 405; it's called Hunters Camp on the gorge map. It has room for three or four tents and a fire ring. You can return to the PCT by continuing south on Trail 405B or C.

▶ You can continue on the PCT to Mount Hood. See *Hiking Oregon's Mount Hood and Badger Creek Wildernesses* (Falcon 1998) by Fred Barstad.

Next on Trail 2000, past the Benson Way junction, is the junction with Benson–Ruckel Trail 405A at 7.1 miles. This trail is faint and little used, probably because most travelers decide to go to Ruckel Creek earlier on and don't rejoin the PCT until the other end of Benson Plateau.

The junction with Ruckel Creek Trail 405, at 7.8 miles, is another opportunity to turn right for a camp spot. The Benson Camp is the last campsite near water before Wahtum Lake.

At 8.7 miles, after a brief view to the east, the last Benson Plateau trail, 405B, joins the PCT. Trail 405B is a fairly well-used path, and many of the hikers who camp at Ruckel Creek use it to return to the PCT.

At 9.1 miles is Camp Smokey and the junction with Eagle–Benson Trail 434, which receives relatively light use by hikers descending to Eagle Creek. Still, it's not too hard to follow. There is room for two to three tents and an established fire ring. Camp Smokey is rumored to have a spring, but I didn't find any water there when I arrived. I recommend camping on the Benson Plateau or at least getting your water there.

Stay left after Camp Smokey and follow the trail as it breaks out of the trees around an old burned ridgetop. One of the benefits of the burn is the excellent views of Tomlike Mountain to the east and Tanner Butte to the west.

As the trail reenters the dense forest, it starts to climb steadily. There isn't much of a view until just before the spur trail to Chinidere Mountain. You can see up the open slope of the mountain, but don't try to scramble up—there's a well-maintained trail just a few hundred yards farther.

At mile 12.2 is the marked junction with the trail to the top of Chinidere Mountain. Turn left for the climb or skip it and continue straight to Wahtum Lake.

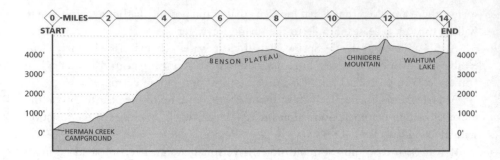

It's about 0.5 mile to the top of Chinidere Mountain on steep switchbacks. The top is composed of loose rock, and several wind shelters built by previous visitors are obvious. The view from Chinidere Mountain of Mount Hood is one of the best in the scenic area, but that's not all that you can see: Mount Defiance and the Washington Cascades are also visible.

Once you're back down on the main trail, 0.2 mile later comes the junction with Herman Creek Trail 406. Stay right for Wahtum Lake unless you plan to complete a loop back to Herman Creek.

Miles and Directions

0.0 **START** from Herman Creek Horse Camp.

0.1 Junction with trail to work center, stay left (south).

0.6 Junction with Herman Bridge Trail 406E to PCT 2000, stay right.

1.9 Junction with PCT 2000, turn left (southwest).

5.4 Teakettle Spring.

6.4 Junction with Benson Way Trail 405B, stay left (south). Turn right (west) for campsites on Ruckel Creek.

7.1 Junction with Benson–Ruckel Trail 405A, stay left (south).

7.8 Junction with Ruckel Creek Trail 405, stay left (south). Turn right for campsites at Benson Camp.

8.7 Junction with Benson Plateau Trail 405B, stay left (south).

9.1 Camp Smokey and Eagle-Benson Trail 434, stay left (south).

12.2 Junction with Chinidere Mountain Trail, continue straight (east). **Option:** Climb Chinidere Mountain for views of Mount Hood, Mount Defiance, and the Washington Cascades.

12.4 Junction with Herman Creek Trail 406, stay right (southeast).

13.9 Wahtum Lake.

14.2 Wahtum Lake Trailhead.

Herman Creek Area

Herman Creek is a good area to hike in because the old-growth forest and the many trails help keep hiker density down, even when the trailhead parking lot is full. Several loop options exist here; two of the best are the Indian Point Loop from the Gorton Creek Trail, and the Casey Creek Loop. The best extended trip is up to the Benson Plateau and back on the Pacific Crest Trail. For a simple overnight, also consider a trip to Cedar Swamp.

The Herman Creek Work Center is a home away from home for scenic area trail crews, however please give the crews some space. There is no trail access from the work center. All the hikes in the area start at the west end of the Herman Creek Horse Camp. This campground has seven sites, available on a first-come, first-served basis; no reservations accepted. The fee is $10 per night.

30 Herman Creek Trail to Wahtum Lake

A good overnight route with loop options back on the Benson Plateau.

Start: Herman Creek Horse Camp.
Distance: 12.1 miles point to point.
Approximate hiking time: Overnight.
Difficulty: Intermediate.
Traffic: Moderate to heavy.
Trail type: Maintained.
Best season: Late May through October.
Total climbing: 3,800 feet.
Other trail users: Horses.
Canine compatibility: Dogs are allowed on leashes only.

Nearest town: Cascade Locks.
Fees and permits: A Northwest Forest Pass is required.
Maps: Carson and Wahtum Lake USGS, Bonneville Dam Green Trails, and Maptech Oregon: Carson.
Trail contacts: Mount Hood National Forest, 16400 Champion Way, Sandy, OR 97055; (503) 668-1700; www.fs.fed.us/r6/mthood.

Finding the trailhead: From Portland, take Interstate 84 east to the weigh station exit just after exit 44, Cascade Locks. Drive through the weigh station area and turn right onto Herman Creek Road. Follow the road for 2 miles to the well-marked Herman Creek Recreation Site. If you miss the weigh station exit or are coming from Hood River, take exit 47, Herman Creek Road, then turn right, heading west for 0.5 mile to the Herman Creek Recreation Site on the south side of the road. Drive up toward the campground, keeping right at the junction with the campground road. The trailhead is at the far end of the loop, next to a PACIFIC CREST TRAIL 2000 sign. Bathrooms are available at the trailhead, along with ample parking.

To make the trip one-way, you must leave a vehicle at Wahtum Lake or arrange to be picked up there. Drive east to exit 62, Hood River, and turn right. Follow the signs toward the city center on Oak. At the 13th Street stoplight, turn right, heading south on the main route. Stay left on Tucker Road and follow the signs to Dee. At Dee, turn right onto Lost Lake Road, cross some railroad tracks, and stay left at the fork. Follow the well-marked, paved route for 10 miles to the Wahtum Lake Trailhead, which is on the right.

The Hike

Herman Creek is known for its old-growth fir and cedar forest. The best trees are past the Casey Creek junction. For an overnight stay among the cedars, hike to Cedar Swamp and spend a night, or continue on to Mud Lake for a second night. You can either end your hike at Wahtum Lake or loop back on the Benson Plateau via Pacific Crest Trail 2000 (PCT). Several easy climbs along the way include Chinidere and Tomlike Mountains.

From the trailhead, the trail descends slightly before you reach a switchback and the first junction, unmarked. Stay left as the trail continues to climb on switchbacks. After you pass underneath some power lines, you'll cross a jeep road, keeping straight south.

The route up Tomlike Mountain from Herman Creek Trail

At 0.6 mile is the next junction with Herman Bridge Trail 406E to Pacific Crest Trail 2000. Stay left, heading east. Trail 406 becomes more roadlike as you proceed. There are no real views of Herman Creek until the Casey Creek Trail junction, where a spur trail leads to a lookout above the creek.

Next, pass an unmarked junction where several old roads meet. Keep heading due east, bearing straight and to the right. At 1.4 miles is the clearing junction with Gorge Trail 400, Gorton Creek Trail 408, and Herman Creek Trail 406. Stay right, heading south on the main Herman Creek Trail 406. The trail is broad and level.

Just 0.1 mile farther is a junction with Nick Eaton Ridge Trail 447. Stay right. Continuing on the Herman Creek Trail, the grade is gentle, almost flat. The sound of Herman Creek muffles any residual noise from the interstate. After passing some Oregon oak, the trail climbs more steadily to a cascading falls about 60 feet high. Crossing the stream below the falls isn't hard, but another stream 0.5 mile farther along the trail is likely to get your feet wet. At 1.5 miles from the junction, another cascade crosses the trail, but this is an easy ford.

The Casey Creek Trail 467 junction is on your left after 4 miles, just before a campsite on the right. There isn't much of a view. A water source is farther along on Herman Creek Trail 406. To get a look at Herman Creek, you have to hike down a spur trail. Find this to the right as you push west through the campsite area for 0.3 mile to a lookout. The whitewater is still 50 feet below.

Past the Casey Creek junction, the trail climbs gradually uphill through increasingly dense old-growth forest. At 7.3 miles is the Cedar Swamp Camp, where, unsurprisingly, there are quite a few large cedars. Several tent sites make enough room for multiple camping parties. There are signs of heavy use and several fire rings. A water source runs conveniently through the camp. If Cedar Swamp doesn't suit you, there are a couple of smaller sites about 0.5 mile farther.

Past Cedar Swamp, the trail fords Herman Creek and begins to climb through even more overgrown forest. A couple of open spots provide views of the forested slopes of the Herman Creek Valley.

At 9.2 miles is a marked junction; turn left, heading east, onto a spur trail if you want to visit Mud Lake. The 0.3-mile trail down to the lake is less maintained than Trail 406, but not too hard to follow. There are few tent sites, however; it would be difficult to get more than two tents on flat ground here. The campsite is back out of sight of the lake. Mud Lake is boggy, but offers a nice view of the talus slopes to the east, where the vine maple is awfully pretty in its fall colors.

Past the Mud Lake junction, the trail continues to climb more steeply on switchbacks. At the crest of the climb, just before the junction with Anthill Trail 406B, an unmarked path on the right leads off to the north. This is the beginning of an off-trail route to the top of Tomlike Mountain. If you want to make the ascent, hug the east edge of the ridge, staying on top until you get a view of the mountain. Then follow the ridge line over boulders, subalpine fir, and open meadows to the top. Give yourself about two hours to make the side trip.

Fifty feet beyond the Tomlike Mountain Trail (10.1 miles on the main trail) is the junction with Anthill Trail 406B to the Wahtum Lake Trailhead. If you left a vehicle there or plan to camp, hang a left. Wahtum Lake has brook trout and several good campsites, but gets heavy use from the Eagle Creek Trail and the PCT.

Herman Creek Trail 406 continues to the right for Chinidere Mountain and Pacific Crest Trail 2000. About 0.2 mile later is an unmarked trail on your left; stay right. As another, well-maintained trail comes in from the left, continue to keep right, heading west. At 11.1 miles, the Herman Creek Trail ends at the junction with the Pacific Crest Trail. Stay right for the PCT and Chinidere Mountain; left takes you to Wahtum Lake.

Benson Plateau Loop Option

To make this an extended trip of longer than one or two nights, follow a loop route from Herman Creek Trail 406 to Pacific Crest Trail 2000 and back to the work center via Benson Plateau. If you don't have any water, you'd better go down to Wahtum Lake and fill up, because there is no water on the PCT until the upper reaches of Ruckel Creek at Benson Camp. Don't count on water at Camp Smokey. At 0.2 mile past the trail to Wahtum Lake lies a marked junction with the trail to the top of Chinidere Mountain. It's about 0.5 mile to the top of Chinidere Mountain on

Herman Creek Trail to Wahtum Lake

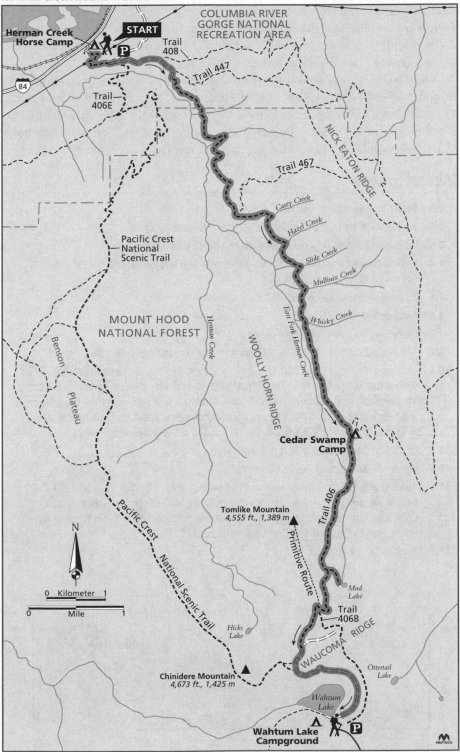

START

Herman Creek
Horse Camp

COLUMBIA RIVER
GORGE NATIONAL
RECREATION AREA

Trail
408

Trail 447

84

Trail
406E

NICK EATON RIDGE

Trail 467

Casey Creek

Hazel Creek

Pacific Crest
National
Scenic Trail

Slide Creek

Mullinix Creek

Whisky Creek

MOUNT HOOD
NATIONAL FOREST

Herman Creek

WOOLLY HORN RIDGE

East Fork Herman Creek

Benson

Plateau

Cedar Swamp
Camp

Pacific Crest

Trail 406

National Scenic Trail

Tomlike Mountain
4,555 ft., 1,389 m

N

Primitive Route

Mud
Lake

Trail
406B

0   Kilometer   1

0   Mile   1

Hicks
Lake

WAUCOMA RIDGE

Ottertail
Lake

Chinidere Mountain
4,673 ft., 1,425 m

Wahtum
Lake

Wahtum Lake
Campground

P

MAPTECH

steep switchbacks. The top is loose rock, and several wind shelters built by previous visitors are obvious. The view of Mount Hood from Chinidere Mountain is one of the best in the scenic area, but that's not all that you can see: Mount Defiance and the Washington Cascades are also visible.

Once you're back down on the main trail, to complete the loop continue right on the PCT toward the Benson Plateau. Follow Pacific Crest Trail 2000 back to the Herman Creek Horse Camp at Benson Camp or Ruckel Creek, depending upon whether there is still water at Benson Camp late in the season. Ruckel Creek holds water year-round. See Hike 29 for the Pacific Crest Trail.

Miles and Directions

0.0 **START** from Herman Creek Horse Camp.

0.6 Junction with Herman Bridge Trail 406E, stay left (east).

0.8 Unmarked junction with old logging roads, continue straight (east).

1.4 Marked clearing junction with Gorton Creek Trail 408 and Gorge Trail 400, stay right (south) on Herman Creek Trail 406.

1.5 Junction with Nick Eaton Trail 447, stay right (south).

4.0 Junction with Casey Creek Trail 476, stay right (east).

7.3 Cedar Swamp Camp, stay right (south).

9.2 Junction with trail to Mud Lake. Turn left and go 0.3 mile to visit the lake.

10.1 Junction with Anthill Trail 406B, stay right (southwest) to stay on Herman Creek Trail 406. **Option:** Turn left (south) onto Anthill Trail 406B for a shorter route to Whatum Lake campsites and trailhead. **Option:** To climb Tomlike Mountain turn right (north) at the junction just before Anthill Trail 406B and stay on the east side of the ridge until you see the mountain, then follow the ridge to the top. The trip will take about two hours.

10.3 Unmarked trail junction, stay right (southwest).

10.7 Unmarked trail junction, stay right (west).

11.1 Junction with PCT 2000, stay left (south). **Option:** For an extended trip follow PCT 2000 through Benson Plateau back to the Herman Creek Work Center. You can also climb Chinidere Mountain by going right at the next trail junction. Get water at Whatum Lake; it will be hard to find until you reach the trailhead.

12.1 Wahtum Lake Trailhead.

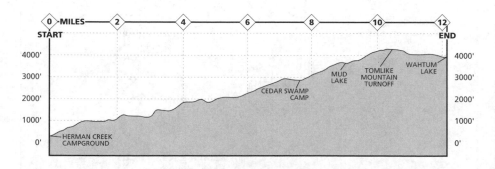

31 Casey Creek Loop

A healthy day hike with a good climb up Nick Eaton Ridge from the Herman Creek Trail.

Start: Herman Creek Horse Camp.
Distance: 11.2-mile loop.
Approximate hiking time: 6 to 8 hours.
Difficulty: Difficult.
Traffic: Moderate to light.
Trail type: Maintained.
Best season: June through October.
Total climbing: 3,840 feet.
Other trail users: Horses.

Canine compatibility: Dogs are allowed on leashes only.
Nearest town: Cascade Locks.
Fees and permits: A Northwest Forest Pass is required.
Maps: Carson USGS, Bonneville Dam Green Trails, and Maptech Oregon: Carson.
Trail contacts: Mount Hood National Forest, 16400 Champion Way, Sandy, OR 97055; (503) 668-1700; www.fs.fed.us/r6/mthood.

Finding the trailhead: From Portland, take Interstate 84 east to the weigh station exit just after exit 44, Cascade Locks. Drive through the weigh station area and turn right, heading east, onto Herman Creek Road. Follow the road for 2 miles to the well-marked Herman Creek Recreation Site. This is the work station for much of the trail maintenance in the Columbia Gorge. If you miss the weigh station exit or are coming from Hood River, take exit 47, Herman Creek Road, then turn right, heading west, for 0.5 mile to the Herman Creek Recreation Site, on the south side of the road. Drive up toward the campground, keeping right at the junction with the campground road. The trailhead is at the far end of the loop next to a PACIFIC CREST TRAIL 2000 sign. Bathrooms are available at the trailhead, along with ample parking.

The Hike

The Casey Creek Loop is an 11.2-mile day hike with an overnight option at the Casey Creek Trail junction. The climb up to Nick Eaton Ridge isn't easy, but you're rewarded with great views across the valley to the Benson Plateau.

From the trailhead, Trail 406 drops slightly before reaching one switchback and the first junction, unmarked. Stay left; the trail continues south, climbing gradually on switchbacks. Then pass underneath some power lines and cross a jeep road, keeping straight.

At 0.6 mile, you'll reach the next junction with Herman Bridge Trail 406E to Pacific Crest Trail 2000. Stay left, and watch for wild strawberries on the uphill side of the trail. Trail 406 becomes more roadlike as you progress. You can hear Herman Creek burbling off to your right, but there won't be much of a view of the creek until you reach the Casey Creek Trail 467 junction.

Next, pass an unmarked junction where several old roads meet. Keep heading straight and to the right. At 1.4 miles is the large clearing junction, where Gorge

Casey Creek Loop

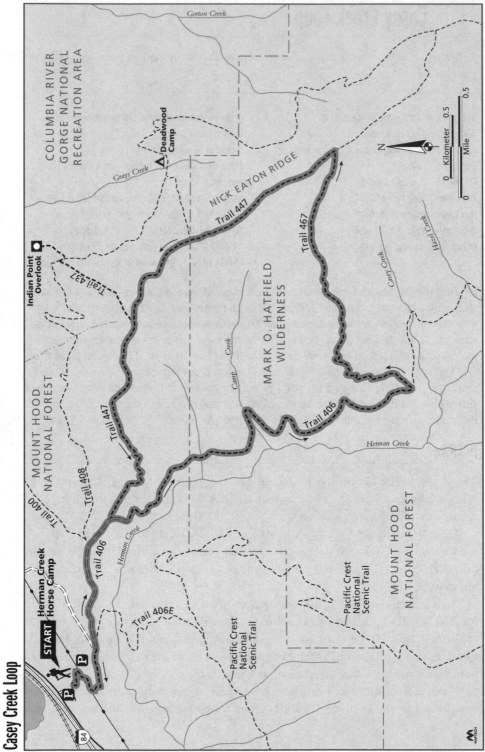

Trail 400 (on the left), Gorton Creek Trail 408 (on the left and straight, to the southeast), and Herman Creek Trail 406 (to the right, following the main road) all meet. Take Herman Creek Trail 406 heading south, which continues to the right on a wide trail. At 0.1 mile past the junction is another junction, this time with Nick Eaton Ridge Trail 447. You can do the loop either way. If you're eager to climb, turn left. If you want to climb later, stay right. Farther on Herman Creek Trail 406, the grade is gentle, almost level. The sound of Herman Creek muffles any residual sound from the interstate. After passing some Oregon oak and blooming lupine, the trail climbs more steadily to a cascading falls about 60 feet high. Crossing the stream below the falls isn't hard, but another stream 0.5 mile farther down the trail is likely to get your feet wet. Around 1.5 miles from the last two junctions, another cascade crosses the trail; this is easily forded.

▶ **Always filter or carry plenty of water prior to a lengthy climb.**

At 4.0 miles, you'll reach a junction with Casey Creek Trail 467 on the left, just before a campsite appears on the right, a bit farther along Herman Creek Trail 406. To get a look at Herman Creek, you have to hike down a spur trail through the campsite area for 0.3 mile to a lookout 50 feet above the whitewater of the creek. The camp has a few cedars, but large Douglas fir and dense, younger western hemlock predominate. Turn left up the Casey Creek Trail. (Water is seasonally available 0.1 mile past the junction on Trail 406.)

The Casey Creek Trail is very steep and dry; no water is available, despite its namesake. Several spots offer views of Tomlike Mountain and the Benson Plateau. The last stretch to the top is almost completely vertical. Once you get to the top, you might want to hang a right for a 0.1-mile walk to a craggy open space, where you can get a good view of Mount Adams. Then retrace your steps to take the left trail onto Nick Eaton Ridge Trail 447. The trail follows the ridge down with several fine viewpoints. Leave the Columbia Wilderness at Deadwood Junction.

It's 0.5 mile on Deadwood Trail down to Gorton Creek Trail 408; you can turn here for more miles, but I would stay straight on Nick Eaton Ridge Trail 447. After a nice view of Mount Hood, you'll reach the junction with Ridge Cutoff Trail 437. It's 0.8 mile farther to use Gorton Creek Trail 408 and Indian Point. If you want to extend the trip a little, make the side trip to Indian Point. Otherwise keep left on Nick Eaton Ridge Trail 447 to rejoin Herman Creek Trail 406, which leads back to the trailhead.

Miles and Directions

0.0 **START** from Herman Creek Horse Camp.

0.6 Junction with Herman Bridge Trail 406E to Pacific Crest National Scenic Trail 2000, stay left (east).

0.8 Unmarked junction with old logging roads, continue straight (east).

1.4 Marked clearing junction with Gorton Creek Trail 408 and Gorge Trail 400, stay right (south) to stay on Herman Creek Trail 406.

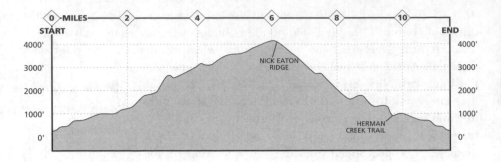

1.5 Junction with Nick Eaton Ridge Trail 447, stay right (south). **Option:** This is the beginning of the loop, and you can do the loop in either direction. Turn left to begin climbing.

4.0 Junction with Casey Creek Trail 467, turn left (northeast). **Option:** Continue on Herman Creek Trail for a campsite and a spur trail to a view of Herman Creek.

6.1 Junction with Nick Eaton Ridge Trail 447, turn left (northwest).

7.3 Junction with Deadwood Trail, stay left (northwest).

7.8 Junction with Ridge Cutoff Trail 437 to Indian Point, stay left (west). **Option:** Turn right to go to Indian Point. This can be an out-and-back trip or you can turn left (west) on Gorton Creek Trail to return to Herman Creek Horse Camp.

9.7 Junction with Herman Creek Trail 406, turn right (northwest). This is the end of the loop.

11.2 Return to Herman Creek Horse Camp.

32 Indian Point Loop

A good day-hike loop up around Nick Eaton Ridge, with spectacular views of the gorge.

Start: Herman Creek Horse Camp.
Distance: 8.4-mile loop.
Approximate hiking time: 4 to 6 hours.
Difficulty: Difficult.
Traffic: Heavy.
Trail type: Maintained.
Best season: Late May through October.
Total climbing: 2,720 feet.
Other trail users: Horses.

Canine compatibility: Dogs are allowed on leashes only.
Nearest town: Cascade Locks.
Fees and permits: A Northwest Forest Pass is required.
Maps: Carson USGS, Bonneville Dam Green Trails, and Maptech Oregon: Carson.
Trail contacts: Mount Hood National Forest, 16400 Champion Way, Sandy, OR 97055; (503) 668-1700; www.fs.fed.us/r6/mthood.

Finding the trailhead: From Portland, take Interstate 84 east to the weigh station exit, just after exit 44, Cascade Locks. Drive through the weigh station area and turn right, heading east, onto Herman Creek Road. Follow the road for 2 miles to the sign for the Herman Creek Recreation Site. If you miss the weigh station exit or are coming from Hood River, take exit 47, Herman Creek Road. Then turn right, heading west, for 0.5 mile to reach the Herman Creek Recreation Site on the south side of the road. Drive toward the campground, keeping right at the junction with the campground road. The trailhead is at the far end of the loop, next to a PACIFIC CREST TRAIL 2000 sign. Bathrooms are available at the trailhead, along with ample parking.

Special considerations: Actual Indian Point proves to be a very scary place for those sensitive to drop-offs and heights, but spectacular nevertheless.

The Hike

The Gorton Creek Trail passes through old-growth Douglas fir trees, offering multiple views of the gorge and the Cascades to the north. For day hiking, the best route is a hike to Indian Point. Take the Ridge Cutoff Trail and return on Nick Eaton Ridge Trail 447.

From the trailhead, Trail 406 dips slightly, then climbs on switchbacks. Stay left at the first, unmarked junction, heading south as the trail continues to climb gradually on switchbacks. After passing underneath some power lines, cross a jeep road and continue straight, due south. The disturbed area under the power lines offers ideal germination sites for invasive species such as Himalayan blackberry and Scotch broom. Past the power lines, the vegetation tends toward snowberry and thimbleberry, both native species.

Indian Point Loop

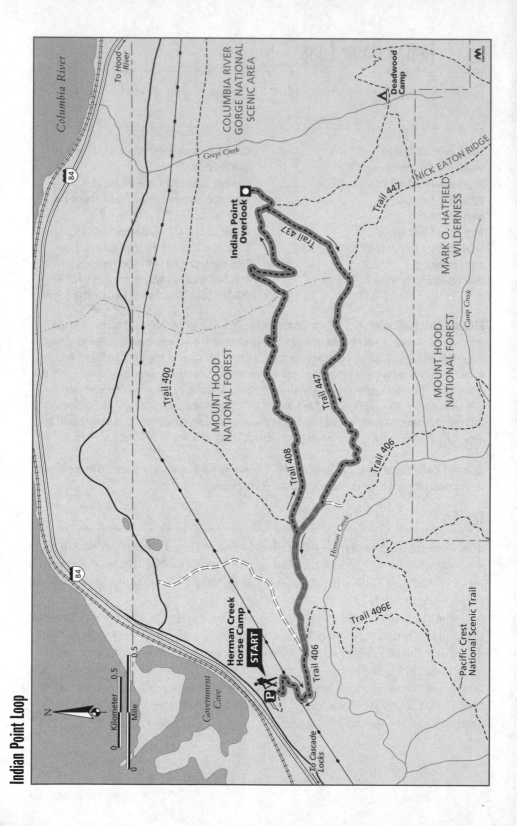

At 0.6 mile, you'll reach a junction with Herman Bridge Trail 406E to the Pacific Crest Trail 2000. Keep left, continuing east, as the trail becomes more roadlike.

Next is an unmarked junction with several old roads; continue straight and to the right. The forest here is in early succession, densely packed with young trees. There is little vegetation on the excessively shaded forest floor. This area offers a nice contrast to the old-growth forest farther up the trail, where the vegetation is lush and the density of trees low.

At 1.4 miles is the clearing junction, where Gorge Trail 400 (on the left), Gorton Creek Trail 408 (on the left and straight, to the southeast), and Herman Creek Trail 406 (to the right, following the main road) all meet. Take Gorton Creek Trail 408. After you leave the junction, the trees will be older than those you've seen previously; they are fewer in number but much larger. The forest floor teems with common bushy plants like young vine maple. The trail is cool and shady as it climbs gradually through this old-growth forest on a series of switchbacks.

At about 2.9 miles, the trail crosses a seasonal creek; you might be able to filter water here, but don't count on it, especially late in the season. At 4.0 miles from the trailhead is the junction with Ridge Cutoff Trail 437 from the Nick Eaton Ridge Trail. Before you take it, go 40 feet past the junction of the Gorton Creek Trail to the spur trail to Indian Point. It's a short, steep descent to the top of a prominent rock structure for excellent views.

Go back to Ridge Cutoff Trail 437 and turn southwest. After a short, gradual climb to Nick Eaton Ridge Trail 447, turn right, heading west, on this well-maintained trail, which descends steeply on switchbacks to Herman Creek Trail 406. Turn right again, continuing northwest, to the trailhead.

Miles and Directions

0.0 **START** from Herman Creek Horse Camp.

0.6 Junction with Herman Bridge Trail 406E to PCT 2000, stay left (east).

0.8 Unmarked junction with old logging roads, continue straight (east).

1.4 Marked clearing junction with Gorton Creek Trail 408 and Gorge Trail 400, turn left (east) onto Gorton Creek Trail 408. This is the beginning of the loop.

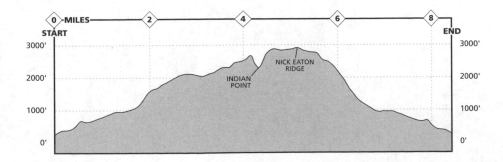

4.0 Junction with Ridge Cutoff Trail 437 and the spur trail to Indian Point. Continue past the junction then turn left (north) onto the spur trail to Indian Point. After returning to Gorton Creek Trail, turn left (southwest) onto Ridge Cutoff Trail 437.

5.0 Junction with Nick Eaton Ridge Trail 447, turn right (west).

6.9 Return to Herman Creek Trail 406, turn right (northwest).

7.0 Junction with Gorton Creek Trail 408 and Gorge Trail 400, stay left (west) on Herman Creek Trail 406. This is the end of the loop.

8.4 Return to Herman Creek Horse Camp.

33 Gorton Creek Trail to Rainy Lake

A one- or two-day backpack climb up around Nick Eaton Ridge, with great views, dark forest corridors, and a clear, freshwater wilderness destination.

Start: Herman Creek Horse Camp.
Distance: 10.8 miles point to point.
Approximate hiking time: All day or overnight.
Difficulty: Difficult.
Traffic: Moderate.
Trail type: Maintained.
Best season: Late May through October.
Total climbing: 4,576 feet.
Other trail users: Horses.

Canine compatibility: Dogs are allowed on leashes only.
Nearest town: Cascade Locks.
Fees and permits: A Northwest Forest Pass is required.
Maps: Carson USGS, Bonneville Dam Green Trails, and Maptech Oregon: Carson.
Trail contacts: Mount Hood National Forest, 16400 Champion Way, Sandy, OR 97055; (503) 668-1700; www.fs.fed.us/r6/mthood.

Finding the trailhead: From Portland, take Interstate 84 east to the weigh station exit just after exit 44, Cascade Locks. Drive through the weigh station area and turn right onto Herman Creek Road. Follow the road for 2 miles to a sign for the Herman Creek Recreation Site. If you miss the weigh station exit or are coming from Hood River, take exit 47, Herman Creek Road. Then turn right, heading west, for 0.5 mile to the Herman Creek Recreation Site on the south side of the road. Drive up toward the campground, keeping right at the junction with the campground road. The trailhead is at the far end of the loop, next to signs for the Pacific Crest Trail (PCT) and the Herman Creek Trail.

To leave a car at the Rainy Lake Trailhead, drive east to exit 62, Hood River, then turn right and follow the signs toward the city center on Oak. At the 13th Street stoplight, turn right, heading south, and follow the main route. Stay left on Tucker Road, following the signs to Dee. At Dee, turn right onto Lost Lake Road, cross some railroad tracks, and turn right onto Punch Bowl Road. Green Road veers to the left 0.2 mile later, but keep right, heading north. After 1 mile, turn left onto Dead Point Road, heading west up Dead Point Creek on Forest Road 2820. At 7.5 miles is a junction with Forest Road 620; stay left on FR 2820. At 9.4 miles is another junction, this time with Forest Road 2821, but stay left, heading west on Forest Road 2820. At 12.6 miles from Dee is an unmarked junction with a less well-maintained road on your right. Take this right fork on the north side of the road, and 0.2 mile later you'll reach the Rainy Lake Picnic Area and Trailhead. If you continue on FR 2820, it dead-ends next to Black Lake; if you reach the lake, you've gone too far.

The Hike

Gorton Creek Trail passes through a forest of old-growth Douglas fir trees and offers multiple views of the gorge and the Cascades to the north. For day hiking, the best route is the hike to Indian Point. Take the Ridge Cutoff Trail and return on Nick Eaton Ridge Trail 447.

From the trailhead, Trail 406 dips slightly, then climbs on switchbacks. Stay left at the first, unmarked junction, heading south as the trail continues to climb gradually on switchbacks. After passing underneath power lines, cross a jeep road and continue straight, due south. The disturbed area under the power lines offers ideal germination sites for invasive species such as Himalayan blackberry and Scotch broom. Past the power lines, the vegetation tends toward snowberry and thimbleberry, both native species.

At 0.6 mile, you'll reach a junction with Herman Bridge Trail 406E to the PCT. Keep left, continuing east, as Trail 406 becomes more roadlike.

Next is an unmarked junction with several old roads; continue straight and to the right. The forest here is in early succession, densely packed with young trees. There is little vegetation on the excessively shaded forest floor. This area offers a nice contrast to the old-growth forest farther up the trail, where the vegetation is lush and the density of trees low.

At 1.4 miles is the clearing junction, where Gorge Trail 400 (on the left), Gorton Creek Trail 408 (on the left and straight, to the southeast), and Herman Creek Trail 406 (to the right, following the main road) all meet. Take Gorton Creek Trail 408. After you leave the junction, the trees will be older than those you've seen previously; they are fewer in number but much larger. The forest floor teems with common bushy plants like young vine maple. The trail is cool and shady as it climbs gradually through this old-growth forest on a series of switchbacks.

▶ To reduce camping impact, it's better to use an already heavily impacted area than to trample the plants in an unused spot.

At about 2.9 miles, Trail 408 crosses a seasonal creek; you might be able to filter water here, but don't count on it, especially late in the season. At 4.0 miles from the trailhead is the junction with Ridge Cutoff Trail 437 from Nick Eaton Ridge Trail 447. Go 40 feet past the junction of the Gorton Creek Trail to the spur trail to Indian Point. It's a short, steep descent to the top of a prominent rock structure for excellent views.

Return to Gorton Creek Trail 408 and continue southeast to the junction with the Deadwood Trail, which climbs steeply to Nick Eaton Ridge. Stay left at the Deadwood junction and hop across a small stream. To the left is the first decent campsite.

Deadwood Camp gets heavy use and may already be occupied. It has a fire ring and cut logs to sit on beneath large firs, which offer cool shade. The next possible campsite is about 1.5 miles farther, but is much less desirable and might not have water.

The trail past Deadwood climbs around the ridge, then traverses across open talus slopes with good views of the gorge. At the second or third opening, you can hear rushing water underneath the rocks, and an opening allows limited access to the source. Farther into the trees, the ground is just flat enough for a couple of tents, and

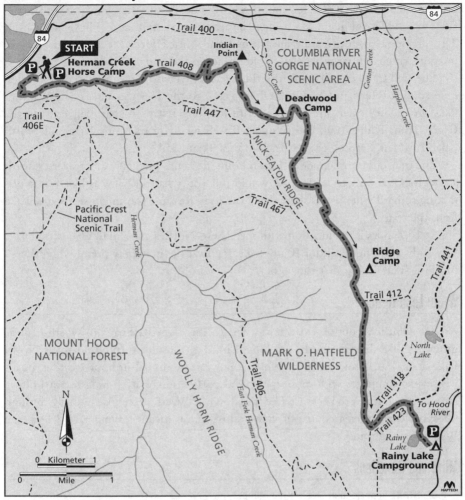

with this water source provides a possible campsite. The next campsite is past the junction with Nick Eaton Ridge Trail 447 and also has limited access to water.

The trail climbs steeply on switchbacks for another 1.1 miles to the junction with Nick Eaton Ridge Trail 447. When you reach this point, you have done most, but not all, of your climbing. Stay left, continuing south; just after this junction, the trail levels out. A plateau-like area to the right offers good tent sites for several parties at least. Getting water requires a trek down to Gorton Creek to the left, but this is manageable. The lodgepole pine covering doesn't offer much protection from the rain, but does break much of the wind's force. Through the trees to your left you can see the Gorton Creek Valley and a little of the gorge beyond.

After this flat stretch, Trail 408 switchbacks up again to a signed junction. Green Point Ridge Cutoff Trail 412 is faintly visible to your left, but stay right and south on Gorton Creek Trail 408. It winds upward gradually and then levels off into a corridor of middle-age hemlocks. Often the trail is as straight as any hospital hallway. This corridor effect gives the area a medieval, "black forest" feeling, and you can imagine knights in tarnished armor riding down the trail.

The trail travels south across the ridge to the Green Point junction at 9.5 miles. Due south is Herman Creek Cutoff Trail 410 to the Herman Creek and Wahtum Lake areas. They offer other loop options for longer trips. A sharp left leads to the Green Point Ridge Trail. The second left will take you to Rainy Lake and North Lake. Turn left, heading east on Trail 423 for Rainy Lake.

The trail, cut into the side of Green Point, descends gradually as it traverses north across rocky and forested slopes. I would tell you what the view is like, but it was raining so hard when I was there that I can't say for sure. You might see Rainy Lake from the trail.

At 10.1 miles is the junction with the trail to North Lake and to Wyeth Trail 411. Stay right, heading south for Rainy Lake. Rainy Lake is awfully pretty when there's sunshine. The fishing isn't bad, either.

Wyeth Loop Option

An excellent loop option exists for a two- to three-day backpack to Wyeth Campground. For a shorter shuttle and longer hiking, consider turning north to North Lake at the 10.1-mile junction. North Lake can be dismal in poor weather, but it has several campsites with room for several parties. There are fishing opportunities, but not much room to backcast. The trail down to Wyeth descends gradually through trees, but does offer a couple of views. This option means leaving a vehicle at the Wyeth Campground.

Miles and Directions

0.0   **START** from Herman Creek Horse Camp.

0.6   Junction with Herman Bridge Trail 406E to PCT 2000, stay left (east).

0.8   Unmarked junction with old logging roads, continue straight (east).

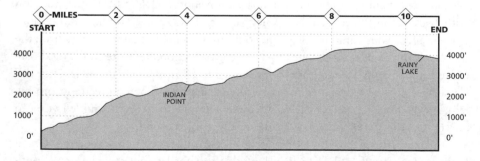

1.4 Marked clearing junction with Gorton Creek Trail 408 and Gorge Trail 400, turn left (east) onto Gorton Creek Trail 408.

4.0 Junction with Ridge Cutoff Trail 437 and spur trail to Indian Point. Stay left at the junction with Ridge Cutoff Trail 437 then turn right at the spur trail to Indian Point. **Option:** You can also go out to Indian Point by descending the steep spur trail.

4.8 Junction with Deadwood Trail, stay left (east).

7.4 Junction with Nick Eaton Ridge Trail 447, stay left (south).

8.0 Junction with Green Point Ridge Cutoff Trail 412, stay right (south).

9.5 Green Point junction, with Trail 423 to Rainy Lake, Herman Creek Cutoff Trail 410, and Green Point Ridge Trail 418, turn left (east).

10.1 Junction with trail to North Lake, stay right (south). **Option:** Turn left onto Wyeth Trail 411 for an extended backpack to North Lake and Wyeth Campground.

10.8 Rainy Lake Campground.

34 Wyeth Trail to North Lake

A good day hike or overnight backpack trip to a less visited mountain lake.

Start: Wyeth Campground.
Distance: 6.2 miles point to point.
Approximate hiking time: 6 to 8 hours or overnight.
Difficulty: Moderate.
Traffic: Moderate.
Trail type: Maintained.
Best season: April through October.
Total climbing: 3,940 feet.
Other trail users: Horses.

Canine compatibility: Dogs are allowed on leashes only.
Nearest town: Hood River.
Fees and permits: A Northwest Forest Pass is required.
Maps: Mount Defiance and Carson USGS, and Bonneville Dam and Hood River Green Trails.
Trail contacts: Mount Hood National Forest, 16400 Champion Way, Sandy, OR 97055; (503) 668-1700; www.fs.fed.us/r6/mthood.

Finding the trailhead: From Portland, take Interstate 84 east to exit 51, Wyeth. Follow the off-ramp, turn right, then right again, heading west on Herman Creek Road for 0.2 mile. Wyeth Campground is on the left, to the south. If the gate is locked, park near the entrance without blocking the gate. Either hike or drive through the campground. Stay right past the first two loops to the Gorton Creek Trailhead. There is ample parking, and public restrooms are located after the first loop in the campground.

To leave a car at Bear Lake Trailhead, drive east to exit 62, Hood River, then turn right and follow the signs toward city center on Oak. At the 13th Street stoplight, turn right, heading south on the main route. Stay left on Tucker Road, following the signs to Dee. At Dee, turn right onto Lost Lake Road, cross some railroad tracks, and turn right onto Punch Bowl Road. Green Road veers off to the left 0.2 mile later, but stay right, heading north. After 1 mile, turn left onto Dead Point Road, heading west up Dead Point Creek on Forest Road 2820. At 7.5 miles is Forest Road 620; stay left on FR 2820. At 9.4 miles, pass the junction with Forest Road 2821, keeping left (west) on FR 2820. At 11.7 miles, where there is an unmarked bend in the road to the left, a trailhead will be on the right, to the north, back from the road in the trees. Parking is available on the south side of the road. If you continue on FR 2820, it dead-ends next to Black Lake, so if you've reached the lake, you've gone too far.

The Hike

Wyeth Trail 411 offers fishing, good views, old trees, and a solid workout. It can be either an out-and-back hike from Wyeth or a point-to-point trek. From the trailhead, the trail runs on a level grade for several hundred yards and soon reaches a junction with Gorge Trail 400. Stay left, heading east, for Wyeth Trail 411. Straight ahead is an old road; a bridge to the right crosses Gorton Creek. The trail winds

Ancient Douglas firs highlight the Wyeth Trail. ▶

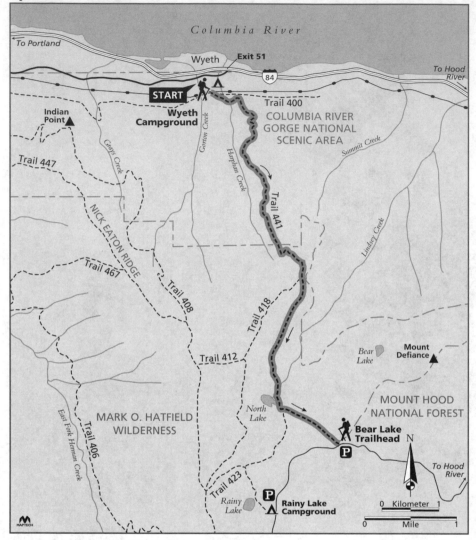

around the hillside above the campground and then passes under power lines before reaching Harphan Creek. Ford the creek and continue straight. The trail climbs gradually but steadily on long switchbacks. There isn't much of a view at this point.

After about 2.0 miles, cross a small stream to get your first good look at the elevation you've climbed. Then continue to another lookout at the edge of Gorton Creek Valley, where you can see Carson across the gorge and, some days, Mount St. Helens.

There are several moss-covered openings with glacier lily and silky phacelia. At the Mark O. Hatfield Wilderness boundary is a register. Filling out your permit is

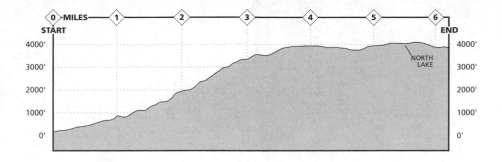

not required, but does provide the USDA Forest Service with information on hiker use.

As you crest the big climb, you'll see a lot of light through the trees on the left. You have almost made it to Green Point Ridge Trail 418.

At the junction with Trail 418, stay left, heading south, on the Wyeth Trail to North Lake. The trail proceeds gently, with a climb just before the lake. Cross Lindsey Creek before the junction with Wyeth Trail 411 to the Bear Lake Trailhead. Turn right for North Lake. This lake offers views of forested Green Point, and there are several good campsites on it. It's not that far from the Rainy Lake Campground and receives relatively heavy use. North Lake also contains fish.

▶ **North Lake is close enough to Rainy Lake to warrant bringing some extra garbage bags to keep stuff dry.**

From the junction with the North Lake spur, after spending the night, turn left, heading east, to the Bear Lake Trailhead. The trail is mostly level, with a few slight ups and downs through middle-age hemlock forest, for the 0.7 mile to the Bear Lake Trailhead.

This trailhead is kind of peculiar. It's easy to see the road from the trail, but hard to see the trail from the road. I sat and watched several confused hiking parties drive by it several times before I waved to them. If you didn't leave a shuttle, follow the main trail back to the trailhead. Or consider a loop option with the Gorton Creek Trail, Mount Defiance Trail, or Herman Creek Trail.

Miles and Directions

0.0 **START** from Wyeth Campground and the trailhead for Wyeth Trail 411.

0.1 Junction with Trail 400, stay left (east).

3.8 Junction with Green Point Ridge Trail 418, stay left (south).

5.5 Junction with spur trail to North Lake, turn right. Turn left (east) on the Wyeth Trail to continue to Bear Lake Trailhead.

6.2 Bear Lake Trailhead.

Starvation Falls, Viento State Park, and Mitchell Point Area

This section of the gorge is bypassed by most visitors except those in the know. It offers some healthy climbs up the side of Mount Defiance, waterfalls, little-visited creeks, and escape from the crowds. Most of the bordering land was donated to the state of Oregon, and current public holdings include a series of state parks: Starvation Creek State Park, Viento State Park, Wygant State Natural Area, Vinzenz Lauzmann Memorial State Natural Area, and Seneca Fouts Natural Area.

Starvation Creek State Park took its name from the stranded train passengers who spent three weeks here in 1884. Starvation Falls, visible from the interstate, is easily the most spectacular waterfall east of Elowah Falls in the gorge. You can also access the Starvation Falls area via a short connecting trail from Viento State Park.

Viento is the Spanish word for wind, but supposedly the state park received its name from the combination of the first letters of three railroad men, Villard, Endicott, and Tollman. We are, however, starting to get close to Hood River—sailboarding capital of the world.

The remaining parks provide public land holding around Mitchell Point. Interestingly, the Mitchell Point tunnels were destroyed with the building of Interstate 84, but they were some of the most adventuresome features of the Historic Columbia River Highway when it ran through this section. You can still walk a little of them when you camp at Viento State Park and talk a stroll to Starvation Falls.

Viento State Park Campground

The campground is open March through November, with a $3.00 daily use fee. Campsites are first come, first served; with fifty-seven electrical and eighteen tent sites, there are bound to be a few spaces available even in the busy season.

35 Lancaster Falls

A short hike to one of the gorge's least-visited waterfalls, starting from spectacular Starvation Falls.

Start: Starvation Falls Rest Area, exit 54.
Distance: 2.2 miles out and back.
Approximate hiking time: 1 hour.
Difficulty: Difficult.
Traffic: Moderate.
Trail type: Maintained.
Best season: Year-round.
Total climbing: 280 feet.
Other trail users: None.

Canine compatibility: Dogs are allowed on leashes only.
Nearest town: Hood River.
Fees and permits: None.
Maps: Mount Defiance USGS, Maptech Oregon: Mount Defiance, and Hood River Green Trails.
Trail contacts: Mount Hood National Forest, 16400 Champion Way, Sandy, OR 97055; (503) 668-1700; www.fs.fed.us/r6/mthood.

Finding the trailhead: From Portland, take Interstate 84 east to exit 54, Starvation Creek Rest Area, just after the Wyeth exit heading east. If you get to Viento State Park, you've gone too far. The rest area is accessible only from the eastbound side. Mount Defiance Trail 413 starts on the right, just to the west, before the parking lot. Bathrooms are no longer available at the trailhead.

The Hike

The Mount Defiance Trail is known mostly for tough climbing, but the first section offers several waterfalls and requires little effort. On this short trip you can pass Starvation Falls at the trailhead, Cabin Falls (out of sight), Hole-in-the-Wall Falls back from the trail, and Lancaster Falls on top of the trail.

The Starvation Creek Rest Area receives heavy use. It offers a short nature path to the bottom of Starvation Falls, which is worth a look. Starvation Creek got its name from the stranded train passengers who spent three weeks here in 1884. The falls crash down from a height of more than 180 feet.

Start hiking on Mount Defiance Trail 413, which is found at the west end of the rest area. The path runs parallel to Interstate 84 for 0.3 mile to the junction where Starvation Ridge Cutoff Trail 414A forks to the left. Go straight, continuing west, on the Mount Defiance Trail.

After entering the trees, the trail passes near Cabin Falls, which is not easily seen from the trail. Continue straight on the Mount Defiance Trail and cross a small footbridge below Hole-in-the-Wall Falls.

At about 1.0 mile, after you cross Warren Creek, you'll reach the junction with the Starvation Ridge Trail to Warren Lake. Stay right, heading west, on Trail 413. The trail traverses the slope for another 0.1 mile before crossing underneath Lancaster

Lancaster Falls

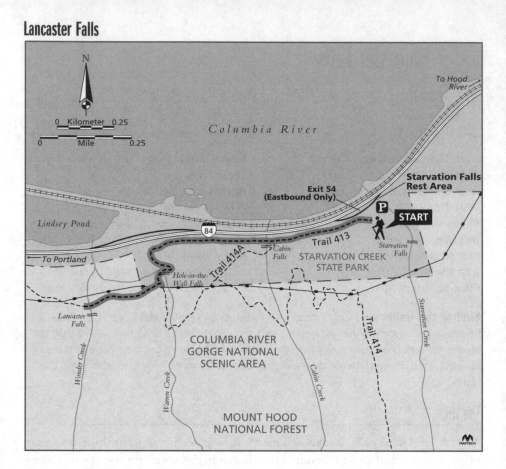

Falls—a series of cascades that rush over broken basalt, spreading across the trail and offering a welcome shower.

Return to the trailhead via the same route.

Miles and Directions

0.0 **START** from Starvation Falls Rest Area, exit 54.

0.3 Junction with Starvation Ridge Cutoff Trail 414A, continue straight (west).

1.0 Junction with Warren Creek Trail to Starvation Ridge Trail 414, stay right (west).

1.1 Lancaster Falls, turn around.

2.2 Return to Starvation Falls Rest Area.

36 Mount Defiance Trail

A steep hike to Mount Defiance, with access to Bear Lake and North Lake loop options.

Start: Starvation Falls Rest Area, exit 54.
Distance: 7.1 miles point to point.
Approximate hiking time: 5 to 6 hours one-way, all day up and back.
Difficulty: Strenuous.
Traffic: Moderate to light.
Trail type: Maintained.
Best season: Late May through October.
Total climbing: 4,840 feet.
Other trail users: None.

Canine compatibility: Dogs are allowed on leashes only.
Nearest town: Hood River.
Fees and permits: None.
Maps: Mount Defiance USGS, Maptech Oregon: Mount Defiance, and Hood River Green Trails.
Trail contacts: Mount Hood National Forest, 16400 Champion Way, Sandy, OR 97055; (503) 668-1700; www.fs.fed.us/r6/mthood.

Finding the trailhead: From Portland, take Interstate 84 east to exit 54, Starvation Creek Rest Area, just after the Wyeth exit heading east. If you get to Viento State Park, you've gone too far. The rest area is accessible only from the eastbound side. Mount Defiance Trail 413 starts on the right, just to the west, before the parking lot. Bathrooms are no longer available at the trailhead.

To leave a car at the Bear Lake Trailhead, drive east to exit 62, Hood River, turn right, and follow the signs toward city center on Oak. At the 13th Street stoplight, turn right, heading south on the main route. Stay left on Tucker Road, following the signs to Dee. At Dee, turn right onto Lost Lake Road, cross some railroad tracks, and turn right onto Punch Bowl Road. Green Road veers off to the left 0.2 mile later, but stay right, heading north. After 1 mile, turn left onto Dead Point Road, heading west up Dead Point Creek on Forest Road 2820. At 7.5 miles is Forest Road 620; stay left on FR 2820. At 9.4 miles, pass the junction with Forest Road 2821, keeping left (west) on FR 2820. At 11.7 miles, where there is an unmarked bend in the road to the left, a trailhead will be on the right, to the north, back from the road in the trees. Parking is available on the south side of the road. If you continue on FR 2820, it dead-ends next to Black Lake, so if you've reached the lake, you've gone too far.

The Hike

Rumor has it that Mount Defiance is one of the toughest trails in Oregon, if not the toughest. After climbing it, a friend of mine was asked where he went. When he responded, his inquisitor asked if he had done it for training, because it's an even tougher hike than climbing Mount Hood from Timberline Lodge. Why else would you do it? We did it for fun. Judge for yourself how tough this trail is; I say it isn't as hard as Starvation Ridge Trail 414.

The top of Mount Defiance offers some of the best views of the Oregon and Washington Cascades and the Hood River Valley. It's 5.6 miles and 4,840 feet of

Mount Defiance as viewed from Dog Mountain

elevation gain to the top. The trail switchbacks most of the way. At several points the grade levels out a bit, but generally the trail climbs straight up the ridge.

The Starvation Creek Rest Area receives heavy use. It has a short nature path to the bottom of Starvation Falls, which is worth a look. A water fountain along the way is a good place to fill water bottles.

Start hiking on Mount Defiance Trail 413, the beginning of which is at the west end of the rest area. The path runs parallel to Interstate 84 for 0.3 mile to a junction where Starvation Ridge Cutoff Trail 414A forks off to the left. Go straight, continuing west, on the Mount Defiance Trail.

After entering the trees, the trail passes near Cabin Falls, which is not easily seen from the trail. Continue straight on Mount Defiance Trail 413. The path crosses a small footbridge across Warren Creek, below Hole-in-the-Wall Falls.

At about 1.0 mile, after crossing Warren Creek, you'll reach the junction with the Starvation Ridge Trail to Warren Lake. Stay right on Trail 413. The trail traverses the slope for 0.1 mile before crossing underneath Lancaster Falls—a series of cascades that rush over broken basalt, spreading across the trail and offering a welcome shower. This is the last place to filter water for the steep climb ahead.

The trail advances around the ridge before starting upward on steep switchbacks. The cover is mostly bigleaf maple and Douglas fir. After a hefty bit of climbing and another mile of trail, a small spur trail forks right to a viewpoint of the gorge and opposing mountains. This is a good place for a break and some water.

Next, the trail flattens out slightly through more firs and some western red cedars. You will notice many downed trees. Some are still lying across the trail, waiting for the saw, while others decompose into the soil nearby. Wind, wet soil around the roots, heavy snow on branches, and disease all contribute to fallen wood. This natural thinning of the forest reduces fire danger and facilitates the survival of the largest and strongest trees.

Soon the trail starts climbing again, becoming steeper and steeper as it passes through smaller and smaller trees. At almost 4.0 miles up, the trail enters the Columbia Wilderness; the border is marked only by a permit box. Fill out your free permit and keep climbing.

Because of the elevation, the forest now consists mostly of lodgepole and whitebark pines and subalpine firs. Then the trail breaks out onto a massive talus slope, from which you will catch your first view of the microwave tower on top of Mount Defiance. Seeing the summit will give you a second wind. Continue along the open slope, bearing left, to the junction with Mitchell Point Trail 417 to Warren Lake. Stay right for Mount Defiance.

About 0.2 mile farther, you'll reach an unmarked junction. Either trail can take you to the top, but the left trail goes straight up whereas the right trail runs gently around the mountain to the other side for a short backtrack to the top. If you are returning via the same trail, straight is quickest. If you are continuing on to the Bear Lake or North Lake area, stay right.

The trail passes through the talus slope, seen from below, and curves into dense subalpine forest. Then the trail winds upward toward the west, onto another talus slope, before leaving the Columbia Wilderness. Below and to the west, Bear Lake is visible, surrounded by forested slopes in an old glacial cirque. The same glaciers also sculpted the volcanic rock of Mount Defiance into a steep point. After leaving the wilderness, cross another talus slope to a junction. Turn left for the summit, right for North Lake. The 0.2 mile to the summit passes through subalpine fir trees stunted by wind and cold. The summit offers incredible views in all directions.

The radio facility at the top, and the roads nearby, make this achievement not as unique as you might like it after the challenging climb from the gorge, but it is spectacular and not everybody can say they climbed Mount Defiance the "real" way.

Upon your triumphant climb of Mount Defiance, continue past the junction with Bear Lake. The trail levels out before a cut area through the trees, to the left signals the wilderness boundary and the intersection with FR 2820, Wyeth Trail 411, and Bear Lake Trailhead.

You also have several other options for getting back to civilization from the top of Mount Defiance. The simplest of these is to hike back down to your vehicle the way you came. Another route is to return via the Starvation Ridge Trail. Both of these options are hard on the knees. It may be more enjoyable to continue to a vehicle at

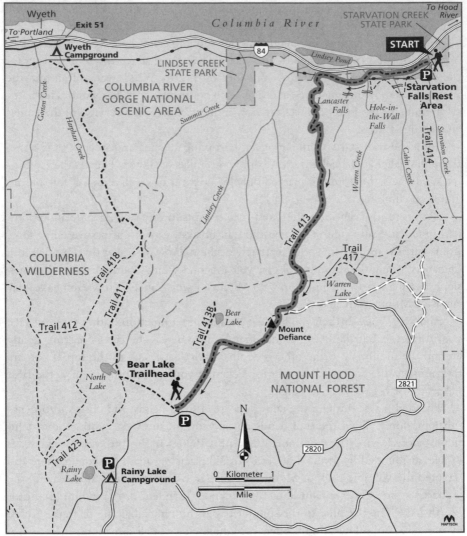

the Bear Lake Trailhead. For an easier but longer trip, you may want to consider an extended trip to North Lake and the Wyeth Trailhead. The descent down the Wyeth Trail is much less severe than either the Starvation or the Mount Defiance Trails.

Bear Lake Option

From the junction with Mount Defiance Trail 413 and the trail running around Mount Defiance, the path descends steadily for 0.9 mile to the junction with Bear Lake Trail 413B. The junction is marked by a large pile of rocks, somewhat like a cairn, but not obvious. Turn right, heading north for Bear Lake, and gently descend through lodgepole pines to the lake. It's surrounded by trees, but offers good views of the mountain above. There are at least two sites and room for multiple tents, plus a fire pit and fishing opportunities.

North Lake Option

To make an even larger loop, you can leave a car at the Wyeth Trailhead. Continue past the junction with Bear Lake. The trail levels out before a cut area through the trees, to the left, signals the wilderness boundary and the intersection with FR 2820 and Wyeth Trail 411. Turn right onto Wyeth Trail 411 for North Lake. The trail is mostly level, with slight ups and downs through middle-age hemlock forest for 0.7 mile to the junction with the Rainy/North Lake Trail and Wyeth Trail 411. Turn left, and 100 yards later turn right for North Lake.

North Lake offers views of Green Point and good campsites on both ends of the lake. It's not that far from the Rainy Lake Campground and receives relatively heavy use. North Lake is rumored to have fish, but it was raining so hard when I got there that I didn't feel much like fishing.

From North Lake, follow Wyeth Trail 411 6.2 miles to Wyeth Trailhead.

Miles and Directions

0.0 **START** from Starvation Falls Rest Area, exit 54.

0.3 Junction with Starvation Ridge Cutoff Trail 414A, continue straight (west).

1.0 Junction with Warren Creek Trail to Starvation Ridge Trail 414, stay right (west).

1.1 Lancaster Falls.

5.1 Junction with Mitchell Point Trail 417 to Warren Lake, stay right (south).

5.3 Junction with steeper route to top. **Option:** Continue straight if you plan to return to Starvation Falls Rest Area. If you plan continue to North Lake stay right.

5.6 Mount Defiance, and junction with more gradual route. **Option:** Turn around and return to Starvation Falls Rest Area using the same route you came up.

6.5 Junction with Trail 413B to Bear Lake, continue straight (south). **Option:** Turn right (north) to descend to Bear Lake.

7.1 Bear Lake Trailhead and FR 2820. **Option:** Turn right onto Wyeth Trail 411 to make a long loop past North Lake to Wyeth Campground.

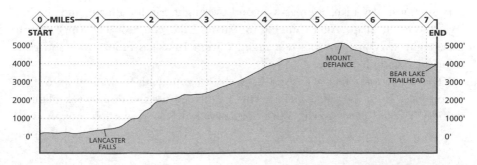

37 Starvation Ridge Trail

A very strenuous hike to Warren Lake and Mount Defiance, with some loop options.

Start: Starvation Falls Rest Area, exit 54.
Distance: 5.6 miles point to point.
Approximate hiking time: 5 hours one-way; all day up and back.
Difficulty: Strenuous.
Traffic: Light.
Trail type: Maintained.
Best season: April through October.
Total climbing: 3,640 feet.
Other trail users: None.

Canine compatibility: Dogs are allowed on leashes only.
Nearest town: Hood River.
Fees and permits: None.
Maps: Mount Defiance USGS, Maptech Oregon: Mount Defiance, and Hood River Green Trails.
Trail contacts: Mount Hood National Forest, 16400 Champion Way, Sandy, OR 97055; (503) 668–1700; www.fs.fed.us/r6/mthood.

Finding the trailhead: From Portland, take Interstate 84 east to exit 54, Starvation Creek Rest Area, just after the Wyeth exit heading east. If you get to Viento State Park, you've gone too far. The rest area is accessible only from the eastbound side. Mount Defiance Trail 413 starts on the right, just to the west, before the parking lot. Bathrooms are no longer available at the trailhead.

A point-to-point hike necessitates a shuttle from the Warren Lake Trailhead. Drive east to exit 62, Hood River, and turn right, following the signs to the city center on Oak. At the 13th Street stoplight, turn right, heading south along the main route. Stay left on Tucker Road, following the signs to Dee. At Dee, turn right onto Lost Lake Road, cross some railroad tracks, and turn right onto Punch Bowl Road. Green Road veers left 0.2 mile later, but stay right, heading north. After 1 mile, turn left onto Dead Point Road, heading west up Dead Point Creek on Forest Road 2820. At 7.5 miles is Forest Road 620; stay left on FR 2820. At 9.4 miles is the junction with Forest Road 2821; stay right, heading east. At 9.8 miles, the road is blocked by a gate. Another road to the right is blocked by a dirt pile.

The Hike

The Starvation Ridge Trail is not easy. It climbs more than 3,000 feet in less than 4 miles. The trail doesn't switchback much, climbing straight up the ridge. The Starvation Ridge Trail isn't as well known as the Mount Defiance Trail but is in my opinion the toughest hike in the Columbia Gorge, especially with a pack. This is a very strenuous day hike, but makes a good overnight trip for athletes and climbers trying to get in shape. After climbing to Warren Lake, you probably won't want to leave right away anyway, so stay a night. Warren Lake has brook trout and good camping, despite heavy use.

The Starvation Creek Rest Area has a short nature path to the bottom of Starvation Falls. Both the ridge and the falls are named for the three-week plight of stranded railroad passengers in 1884–85. Starvation Falls is worth a look. A water

Looking west from Starvation Ridge Trail.

fountain nearby is a good place to fill water bottles. The climb up Starvation Ridge requires a lot of sweat and does not provide water after Cabin Creek.

Start on Mount Defiance Trail 413, which begins at the west end of the rest area. The path runs parallel to Interstate 84 for 0.3 mile to the junction with Starvation Ridge Cutoff Trail 414A. The fork left is the most direct route to the Starvation Ridge Trail. It immediately switchbacks up for 0.5 mile before rejoining the main Starvation Ridge Trail. You will get plenty of steep climbing, so it might be a good idea to follow Defiance Trail 413 and take the more gradual scenic route up Starvation Ridge Trail 414 just after the Warren Creek crossing. This allows for a short warm-up.

Stay right, heading west on Mount Defiance Trail 413, which passes Cabin Falls; the falls isn't easily seen from the trail. Continue straight on the Mount Defiance Trail to a footbridge just below Hole-in-the-Wall Falls. These falls are human-made, created after the construction of the original Columbia Gorge Highway.

A short mile beyond Warren Creek, you'll reach the junction with the Starvation Ridge Trail to Warren Lake. Turn left and climb gradually around the ridge to

Starvation Ridge Trail

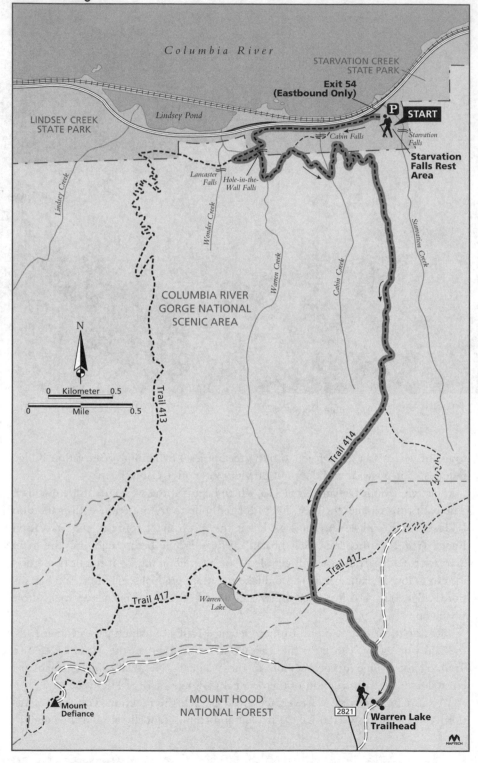

Warren Creek, which you must ford. The trail switchbacks up onto a steep grassy meadow, rich in wildflowers and skirted by Oregon oak. The power lines above distract slightly from the view, but the familiar profiles of Dog and Wind Mountains are easily seen across the gorge.

After leaving the meadow behind, round the second ridge and cross Cabin Creek in the trees. This is your last chance for water until Warren Lake, which is 4.0 miles farther uphill. At 2.0 miles, Starvation Ridge Cutoff Trail 414A rejoins the main trail. Once you hit this junction, I hope you're warmed up, because it's all uphill from here. This trail deserves respect, and if you don't respect it now, you will in a couple of miles.

From the junction, the trail climbs steeply on switchbacks until cresting the ridge for more views west, down the gorge. After the trail crests the ridge, the nice switchbacks end and the ridgetop crawl begins. There is only about one place along the way to get a view. Try to focus on the increasing sense of peace as you get higher and higher, away from the highway, the smell of pine, the vision of an alpine lake, and the healthy heart.

After 2.3 miles of straight-up climbing from the Starvation Ridge Cutoff junction, the trail veers to the right as an old trail to Viento Ridge veers left. At this point, most of the steep climbing is done; the remaining trail to Warren Lake follows a gentle uphill grade. The view in this area is subject to human intervention and an abundance of tree harvesting. After turning right, continue to keep right as an old road forks left, and enjoy another viewpoint before passing through another logged area by the junction with Mitchell Point Trail 417. Stay right and fill out your wilderness permit at the end of the logged area. You are now entering the Columbia Wilderness.

Warren Lake is 0.3 mile farther and has several good campsites with well-used fire rings. Above Warren Lake are several talus slopes, which give the lake an alpine feel and a beautiful panoramic setting, especially if you wade out to catch a fish.

After climbing this trail, you may need someone to pick you up, take you home, and put you to bed. I can't guarantee that Mom will meet you at FR 2821, but you might want to make vehicle arrangements anyway. From the junction with Mitchell Point Trail to Warren Lake, head southeast on Trail 417A for the 0.25 mile to the car.

Otherwise, return to the trailhead via the same route.

Mount Defiance Trail Loop Option

After resting a night at Warren Lake, climb west on the Mitchell Point Trail to the Mount Defiance Trail. Go left and south the rest of the way up the mountain; right takes you back to the Starvation Creek Rest Area on a grade similar to the one you climbed up.

Miles and Directions

0.0 **START** from Starvation Falls Rest Area, exit 54.

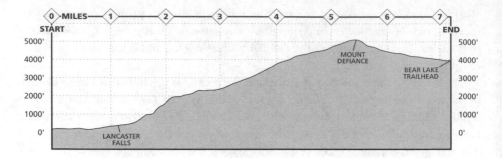

0.3 Junction with Starvation Ridge Cutoff Trail 414A, continue straight (west). **Option:** Turn left for the steepest and most direct route to Trail 414.

1.0 Junction with Starvation Ridge Trail 414, turn left (east).

2.0 Junction with rejoining Starvation Ridge Cutoff Trail 414A, stay right (east).

4.3 Junction with Viento Ridge Spur Trail 417, turn right (southwest).

5.3 Junction with Mitchell Point Trail 417 to Warren Lake, turn right (west) to go to Warren Lake. **Option:** To climb Mount Defiance from Warren Lake, continue on Trail 417 and turn left onto Mount Defiance Trail 413 to the top. A loop to Starvation Falls Rest Area can be made by turning around at the top of the mountain and following Trail 413 back to rest area.

5.6 Warren Lake.

5.9 Junction with Trail 414 and Trail 417A. Turn right (south) to Warren Lake Trailhead.

6.1 Warren Lake Trailhead.

38 Wygant Trail and Perham Creek Loop

A steep day hike up Wygant Point, with shorter scenic options along Perham Creek.

Start: Wygant Trailhead off exit 58, Mitchell Point (eastbound only).
Distance: 8.0 miles out and back.
Approximate hiking time: 4 to 6 hours.
Difficulty: Difficult to top of mountain; moderate for loop.
Traffic: Light.
Trail type: Maintained.
Best season: Year-round, depending upon frost line.
Total climbing: 2,050 feet.

Other trail users: None.
Canine compatibility: Dogs allowed on leashes only.
Nearest town: Hood River.
Fees and permits: None.
Maps: Hood River and Mount Defiance USGS, Maptech Oregon: Hood River, and Hood River Green Trails.
Trail contacts: Mount Hood National Forest, 16400 Champion Way, Sandy, OR 97055; (503) 668-1700; www.fs.fed.us/r6/mthood.

Finding the trailhead: From Portland, take Interstate 84 east to Mitchell Point, about 3 miles before the first Hood River exit. Follow the off-ramp up to the Mitchell Point parking lot. The Wygant Trail starts at a gated jeep trail on the right, to the west, just before the parking lot. Bathrooms are available at the trailhead. (Note that the trailhead is only accessible from eastbound Interstate 84.)

The Hike

One of the lesser-known gorge trails, the Wygant Trail has some spectacular views. Wygant Point is quiet and pristine, but getting to it isn't easy. A hike to the top is 8.0 miles, round trip. The Perham Creek Loop option (5.0 miles round trip) offers an easier hike, with rushing streams and cool cedar trees.

The trail begins at the gate at Mitchell Point, along an abandoned stretch of the old gorge highway, which parallels the interstate for 0.25 mile. Then, after a small clearing, a jeep trail curves uphill to the left while the Wygant Trail forks right. Next, the trail crosses seasonally wet Mitchell Creek. A nice new footbridge makes the crossing easier. Soon after crossing Mitchell Creek, the trail rejoins the overgrown highway.

At 0.7 mile the trail forks left, leaving the old highway, which disappears in the direction of Interstate 84. Remnants of a small landslide caused by flooding in 1996 are visible above the junction. The faint trail follows the scoured creekbed. In several places the trail is washed out, and scrambling up to the next switchback is necessary. The trail climbs steeply out of the gully, and two short switchbacks later levels out. It passes several old Douglas fir trees and younger, moss-covered Oregon oaks.

At 1.0 mile, the Perham Loop Trail joins the Wygant Trail from the south (left). This trail up to the Perham Creek Loop climbs steadily, until dropping down to cross Perham Creek. It rejoins the Wygant Trail in another 1.5 miles. It's better for the return trip, so stay right, continuing west.

This trail proceeds 50 feet to a T junction. The right fork, to the north, is a spur trail to a viewpoint. Stay left, continuing west, as the Wygant Trail descends into the Perham Creek Valley. The floods of 1996 destroyed the old log footbridge that used to cross this creek. You can follow the remaining pieces of the old bridge part of the way across, but at some point it will be necessary to get your feet wet. Be careful: It is difficult to negotiate the fallen debris. The trail isn't immediately apparent on the other side, but look upstream, to the south. About 100 yards upstream from the old bridge, you'll see the trail next to a large fir.

After Perham Creek, the trail climbs up onto a shelf. It levels out for the 1.7 miles to the Columbia River lookout. This offers prime views of Cook Hill directly across the river and Dog Mountain just to the west. This is a good spot to spy on the anglers below. In spring look for early blue violets on this grassy point. After the lookout, the trail passes underneath some power lines and begins to switchback upward.

At 2.5 miles, the Chetwoot Trail forks left for the continuation of the Perham Loop, heading east. Take the right fork, which leads directly to Wygant Point. The switchbacks continue. At the west elbow of several of the switchbacks, spur trails climb out onto steep clifftop views. These views can distract you from the burning muscles of rapid climbing. You may find that this hill suffers from a little bit of the never-ending-switchback disease. Just when you think, this is the last switchback . . . there's another one. Try to focus on the temperate forest that surrounds you. Along the way many of the trees are very old, and the trail is quiet and shady. The forest floor is home to common sword ferns and Cascade Oregon grape.

The upper reaches of this trail offer even greater isolation. Just before the crest, Wygant State Park comes to an end and the Mount Hood National Forest begins. At the marked boundary, the Perham Creek drainage is visible below to the south. The summit is a modest pile of rocks, surrounded by a stand of young firs. It's quiet enough to scare up a grouse or two.

Return the way you came.

Chetwoot Trail Option

On the way back, you might prefer to take the right fork at 5.5 miles, heading east, on the Chetwoot Trail that connects with the Perham Loop. This trail descends and traverses the contours of Wygant Ridge into a cooler, wetter environment of western red cedar. This crossing of Perham Creek is also bridgeless. Getting your feet wet might be better than slipping on exposed rocks in an attempt to hop across.

On the opposite side, the trail climbs for a short while, then descends gradually, crossing underneath the power lines again to a jeep trail. Follow the jeep trail right for 50 feet before turning north and down on the Perham Loop. Soon after, the trail rejoins the main Wygant Trail for the last mile back to the trailhead.

Wygant Trail and Perham Creek Loop

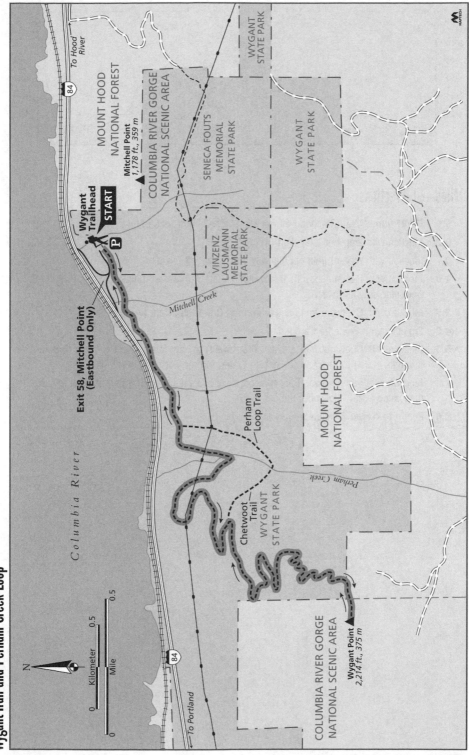

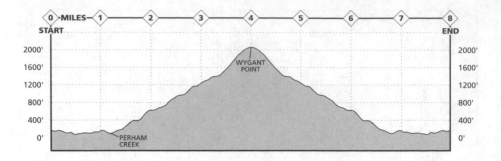

Miles and Directions

0.0 **START** from Wygant Trailhead off exit 58, Mitchell Point (eastbound only).

0.2 Junction with jeep trail, stay right (west).

0.7 Junction with Wygant Trail; old highway ends, turn left (west).

1.0 Junction with Perham Loop Trail, stay right (west). At the next junction to a spur trail to a viewpoint, stay left (west).

2.5 Junction with Chetwoot Trail back to Perham Creek, stay right (west).

4.0 Top of Wygant Point, turn around.

5.5 Junction with Chetwoot Trail, stay left (northwest) to continue to the trailhead. **Option:** Turn right (east) to descend to Perham Creek and the Perham Loop Trail.

7.0 Junction with Perham Loop Trail, stay left (east). This is the end of the optional loop from the junction with Chetwood Trail.

8.0 Return to Wygant Trailhead.

Historic Columbia River Highway State Trail

E ver since the original construction of the Historic Columbia River Highway through the Columbia River Gorge, completed in 1922, tourists and visitors have enjoyed the whitewashed fences, scenic bypasses, and well-placed tunnels along the route. Much of this aesthetic quality of the route eroded with the much more utilitarian construction of Interstate 84 and a major railroad. In fact, to make way for I–84 several crucial sections of the existing highway had to be destroyed, including the Mitchell Point Tunnels, the Toothrock section, and many others. In a move to restore some of these scenic opportunities and to provide a noninterstate east–west route through the gorge for hikers and cyclists, the Oregon Department of Transportation and the Columbia River Gorge National Scenic Area acquired funding to rebuild sections of the former highway for pedestrians and cyclists only. Two sections are now complete: the following section from Hood River to Mosier, as well as the Toothrock section between Tanner Creek and Cascade Locks.

39 Highway State Trail–Hood River to Mosier

A 4.5-mile rolling paved trail along a restored portion of the Historic Columbia River Highway.

Start: Mark O. Hatfield East Trailhead.
Distance: 9.0 miles out and back; 4.5 miles point to point.
Approximate hiking time: 1 to 4 hours.
Difficulty: Easy.
Traffic: Moderate.
Trail type: Paved, with a firm surface.
Best season: Year-round. The trail should be clear and dry all year.
Total climbing: 1,360 feet.
Other trail users: Mostly used by cyclists from Hood River; no horses.

Canine compatibility: Dogs are allowed on leashes only.
Nearest town: The trail basically connects Mosier to Hood River for nonmotorists.
Fees and permits: $3.00 day-use fee; yearly passes are available at the west-end visitor center.
Maps: Maptech Oregon: White Salmon.
Trail contacts: Oregon State Parks, 725 Summer Street NE, Suite C, Salem, OR 97301; (503) 986-0707; www.prd.state.or.us.

Finding the trailhead: Take exit 69 in Mosier, head south toward Mosier for about 0.25 mile, then turn left, heading north and circling back under the way you came in before climbing up Rock Creek Road. The Mark O. Hatfield East Trailhead is on the left just past the actual start of the Highway State Trail. This is a fully developed trailhead with all the amenities and its own pay station to collect your money.

The 4.5 miles of trail really isn't long enough to warrant a shuttle—I suggest an out-and-back hike—but you might like to start or end from the west end. Take exit 64 in Hood River, head north on the main route, Oregon Highway 35, then turn left (east) at the first stoplight. The road winds up the hill to the Mark O. Hatfield West Trailhead, which includes a visitor center and all the amenities. In case you hadn't already figured it out, Mark O. Hatfield was the longtime senior U.S. senator from Oregon who got a lot of federal funding for his home state—hence the move to plaster his name on trails and wildernesses in the Columbia River Gorge.

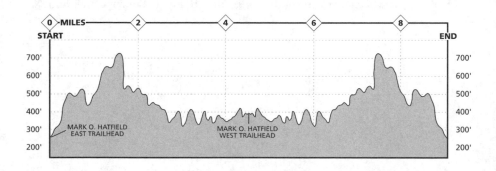

The Highway State Trail between Hood River and Mosier

Special considerations: You might consider biking this route instead. It made me wish I had brought my road bike along to Hood River.

The Hike

From the trailhead, walk down the hill 200 yards and cross Rock Creek Road, passing through the gate onto the wide-paved Highway State Trail, heading west. The first section climbs gradually through ponderosa forest. If the path weren't so wide, I might advise you to be careful for poison oak—this is certainly the right climate for it. After a short climb, the path drops into what is billed as the Twin Tunnels. The amount of cement and number of metal bars will surprise you and makes you feel glad to be protected from yourself and the rocks above.

After the tunnels, the path climbs and rolls a bit through a transition zone. The ecosystem is actually quite fascinating. You might notice it most as you move east through the gorge, the climate gets increasingly arid. This is evidenced here by the trees changing from Douglas fir to a mostly ponderosa pine forest. Farther east when you visit the Deschutes River, there won't be many trees at all, just sagebrush covered hillsides.

Highway State Trail–Hood River to Mosier

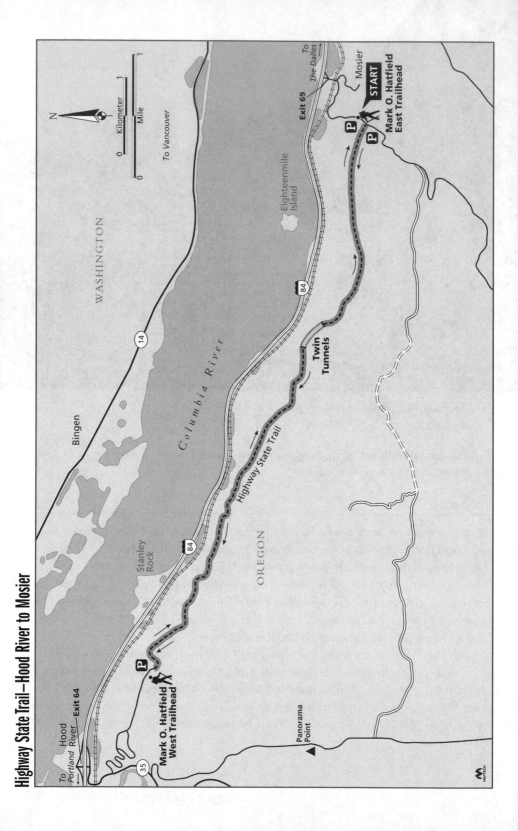

Twin Tunnels

Miles and Directions

0.0 **START** from Mark O. Hatfield East Trailhead.

4.5 Mark O. Hatfield West Trailhead, turn around.

9.0 Return to the Mark O. Hatfield East Trailhead.

Mayer State Park and Tom McCall Preserve

N amed for a former Oregon governor, the Tom McCall Preserve is a combi-nation of state land in Mayer State Park, national forest, and private land owned by The Nature Conservancy (TNC), a nonprofit organization that manages the area without state funding and offers periodic wildflower walks and conservation opportunities. Because thousands of people visit each year, TNC asks that you follow several use guidelines designed to preserve the natural heritage of the area. A "stay-on-the-trail" ethic on the part of visitors keeps the landscape pristine despite heavy visitation.

The preserve is famous for its wildflowers, especially the radiant purple Colum-bia desert parsley. It's also a great place for bird-watching. There is no drinking water or restrooms on the preserve.

For volunteer habitat restoration opportunities, contact:

The Nature Conservancy of Oregon
821 SE Fourteenth Avenue
Portland, OR 97214
(503) 230–1221

Tom McCall Preserve Regulations

- No dogs, horses, or bicycles.
- Adhere to a zero impact ethic.
- Groups of ten or more must have prior permission to visit the preserve.
- Leave the area cleaner than you found it and report any management problems to The Nature Conservancy.

40 Rowena Plateau

A gentle nature walk on Mayer State Park, USDA Forest Service, and Nature Conservancy land famous for wildflowers.

Start: Rowena Crest Viewpoint on the Historic Columbia River Highway.
Distance: 2.4 miles out and back.
Approximate hiking time: 1 to 2 hours with wildflower stops.
Difficulty: Easy.
Traffic: Heavy.
Trail type: Maintained.
Best season: March through June for wildflowers.
Total climbing: 230 feet.
Other trail users: None.
Canine compatibility: No pets are allowed on the preserve.
Nearest town: Mosier.

Fees and permits: A donation is requested; groups of ten or more must contact The Nature Conservancy to arrange for a staff member or volunteer to accompany the group.
Maps: Lyle USGS, and Maptech Oregon: Lyle.
Trail contacts: The Nature Conservancy of Oregon, 821 SE Fourteenth Avenue, Portland, OR 97214; (503) 230-1221.
Mount Hood National Forest, 16400 Champion Way, Sandy, OR 97055; (503) 668-1700; www.fs.fed.us/r6/mthood.
Oregon State Parks, 725 Summer Street NE, Suite C, Salem, OR 97301; (503) 986-0707; www.prd.state.or.us.

Finding the trailhead: From Portland, take Interstate 84 east to exit 69 at Mosier. Turn right (east) onto the Historic Columbia River Highway and drive 6.5 miles. The trailhead is on the left, opposite the loop road to Rowena Crest Viewpoint.

The Hike

At 2.4 miles, the hike out onto the Rowena Plateau isn't much of a workout; it's perhaps better suited for those in a nature-loving mood. Rowena Plateau offers a diverse group of wildflowers, from balsamroot and Columbia desert parsley to monkey flowers, buttercups, and broad-leafed lupine.

At the trailhead, there is a sign-in board that helps The Nature Conservancy monitor the number of people who visit the preserve. Please sign in and look over the information provided about the preserve by TNC. The interpretive display provides a preview of the flora and fauna commonly seen at Tom McCall.

From the trailhead, the grade is level to slightly downhill, following a singletrack people path. Soon the trail curves right, toward the gorge, and then left through an old stone fence from the days when this plateau was grazed. The plateau has cliffs on all sides except this entrance, and only a small fence was needed to contain cattle. The aftermath of this, however, is that there isn't as much balsamroot on this plateau, because cows like the big, soft leaves. The area hasn't been grazed recently,

Rowena Plateau

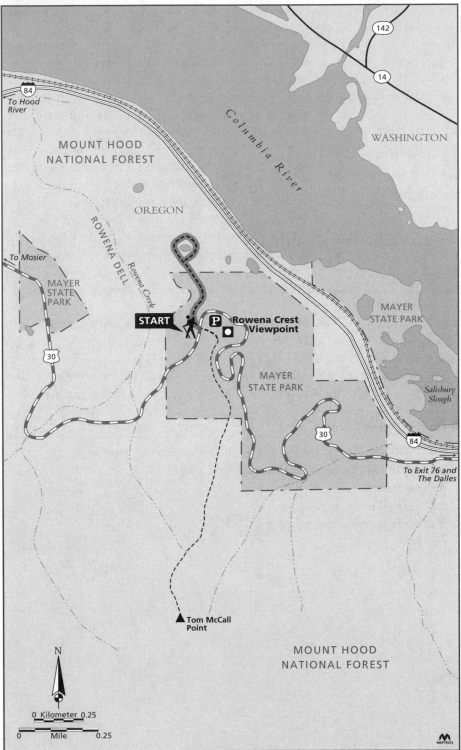

but balsamroot is still sparse past the stone fence. TNC is working to restore some of the native plant populations on several portions of the plateau.

At 0.3 mile is the junction with the top loop around one of two vernal ponds. Going right at the unmarked junction takes you around the pond for a view of Lyle and the Klickitat Valley beyond. Left continues down the plateau.

Heading west, there is a side trail down to the pond for a bird-watching stop. Shortly after the loop trail rejoins the main trail, continue left farther out onto Rowena Plateau. The scenery is much the same, with fields of flowers and grasses and Oregon oak in the surrounding ponds. This can be dull if you don't like the little things, or it can be exhilarating to look for the smallest flower and listen for the slightest variation in the songs of the birds.

▶ It's a good idea to carry your favorite flower or bird book on this walk. You are guaranteed plenty of chances to use it.

At the second vernal pond, there is another side trail down to the edge, but this one is skirted by poison oak. The understory, aside from poison oak, is composed primarily of snowberry and serviceberry. You can also tell that this preserve is drier than many of the places west in the gorge, because of the absence of moss on the oak trees.

Continue on down the plateau through the open mound-and-swale topography to a lookout. A spur trail forks right, on top of the basalt cliffs of the gorge. You might feel some of the updrafts from below that could lift your wings, if you had any.

Continuing down the trail offers much of the same, with more areas for plant exploration and identification. The return trip is slightly uphill along the same trail.

Miles and Directions

0.0　**START** from Rowena Crest Viewpoint on Historic Columbia River Highway.

0.3　Junction with top loop around vernal pond.

0.8　Second vernal pond.

1.2　Spur trail to lookout over gorge.

2.4　Return to Rowena Crest Viewpoint.

41 McCall Point

A gentle ascent of McCall Point.

Start: Rowena Crest Viewpoint on the Historic Columbia River Highway.
Distance: 3.0 miles out and back.
Approximate hiking time: 1 to 2 hours.
Difficulty: Moderate.
Traffic: Moderate to heavy.
Trail type: Well maintained.
Best season: May through October; closed to public access during winter.
Total climbing: 1,100 feet.
Other trail users: None.
Canine compatibility: No pets are allowed on the preserve.

Nearest town: Mosier.
Fees and permits: A donation to The Nature Conservancy is appreciated.
Maps: Lyle USGS, and Maptech Oregon.
Trail contacts: The Nature Conservancy of Oregon, 821 SE Fourteenth Avenue, Portland, OR 97214; (503) 230-1221.
Mount Hood National Forest, 16400 Champion Way, Sandy, OR 97055; (503) 668-1700; www.fs.fed.us/r6/mthood.
Oregon State Parks, 725 Summer Street NE, Suite C, Salem, OR 97301; (503) 986-0707; www.prd.state.or.us.

Finding the trailhead: From Hood River, take Interstate 84 east to exit 69 at Mosier. Turn right (east) onto the Historic Columbia River Highway. Drive 6.5 miles and turn right onto a loop road to Rowena Crest. The trailhead is just to the right of the paved turnaround; this is the best place to park.

The Hike

The trail to the top of McCall Point isn't strenuous, but neither is it easy. The trail offers many views due to only a sparse covering of Oregon oaks and ponderosa pines. From the top, on a clear day, the view of Mount Hood is spectacular. The area receives heavy, but surprisingly polite foot traffic. Off-trail habitat is preserved remarkably well and offers places for many species of birds, flowers, and other wildlife. One of these species is the rattlesnake: beautiful but dangerous.

The trail starts along the grassy scab land left by the ancient Missoula floods, following a level old road that winds toward the forested hillside above. Several large ponderosa pines sculpted by the wind offer resting spots for the common birds of the area. Kestrels and red-tailed hawks are commonly seen on the preserve. As the trail enters the more forested area, watch out for poison oak along the side of the old road. This

▶ Caution: Typical trail dangers occur on the preserve, including cliffs, rattlesnakes, ticks, and poison oak. In rattlesnake country it's best to stay on the trail. Rattlesnakes generally avoid areas of heavy human traffic, and are most common on the rocky slopes away from the trail.

Lyle from McCall Point Trail.

is also a good place to see Columbia desert parsley with its bright purple flowers and pillowy green leaves. The trail rounds the edge of the hillside and traverses along the east slope until reaching a marked junction. This is the where the main trail forks right off the old road. The old road keeps heading straight for a while.

The trail continues to climb through moss-covered oaks and snowberry plants. In spring you can sometimes catch a glacier lily in bloom along the way. Next, switchbacks follow the ridge up, with views of the gorge below and to the east.

There's about 0.5 mile of switchbacks to reach the summit. From the top, on a clear day, you can get a good view of Mount Hood and Mount Adams. A faint trail continues farther, but is on private land; please respect this boundary. The summit of McCall Point is a great place to have lunch and enjoy the surrounding vista before returning via the same trail. Please choose your lunch spot to minimize impact on the vegetation.

McCall Point

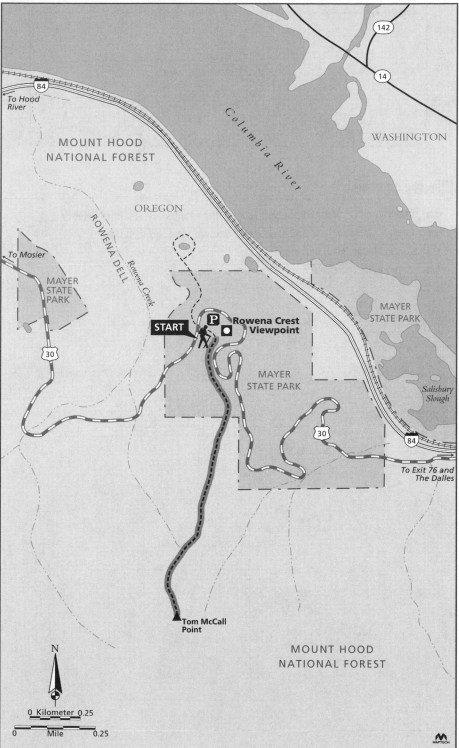

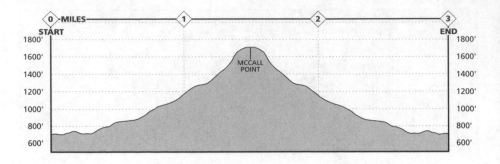

Miles and Directions

0.0   **START** from Tom McCall Preserve Trailhead on Historic Columbia River Highway.

0.7   Junction with dead-end trail at NATURE CONSERVANCY sign, stay right (south).

1.5   Top of McCall Point, turn around.

3.0   Return to Tom McCall Preserve Trailhead.

Deschutes River Recreation Area

When you have an arid plain and a lush river runs through it, all life seems to gravitate to the river, and such is the case with the Deschutes River in north-central Oregon. From the signs at the boat launch and campground, you should get a pretty good idea that almost every outdoorsperson and her dog has visited or continues to visit the Deschutes River, either to raft, fish, hike, mountain bike, ride a horse, or just plain sit in a lawn chair and drink a beer. It's easy to see why; the Deschutes is world renowned for whitewater and fly fishing. The campground is pleasant with lots of shade and space. It really seems to exude a calm in the mist of immense demand for recreation. The mountain bike route goes up the river for 17 miles. Horses can travel on it only in spring.

Deschutes River Campground

This extensive campground includes thirty-three electrical sites, twenty-five primitive sites, and four group sites. One extra vehicle is allowed per site. For reservations, call (800) 452–5687; for more information, call (541) 739–2322 or (800) 551–6949. Fees range from $5.00 for a primitive site up to $60.00 for a group site, with most sites going for between $8.00 and $12.00 during peak season.

42 Deschutes River Trail

A gorgeous dry-land sagebrush stroll along and above the famous Deschutes River.

Start: Deschutes River State Park, at the southernmost paved parking lot.
Distance: 5.3 mile loop.
Approximate hiking time: 3 to 4 hours.
Difficulty: Moderate.
Traffic: Heavy to light.
Trail type: Maintained.
Best season: Year-round.
Total climbing: 700 feet.
Other trail users: There are separate horse and mountain bike trails. The Middle and River Trails are for hikers only.

Canine compatibility: Dogs are allowed on leashes only.
Nearest town: Biggs.
Fees and permits: None for day use; floating, camping, or fishing requires a permit.
Maps: Maptech Oregon: Emerson.
Trail contacts: Bureau of Land Management Prineville District Office, 3050 NE Third Street, Prineville, Oregon 97754; (541) 416-6700; www.or.blm.gov/prineville.

Finding the trailhead: From the west, take Interstate 84 to exit 104, Biggs, heading immediately south on U.S. Highway 97; turn right at the first intersection, heading west for Deschutes River State Park. Head west on the frontage road for 4.4 miles and turn south on the east side of the Deschutes River bridge.

From the west, driving from The Dalles, take east exit 97. Turn east onto the frontage road; continue for 2.5 miles, passing Heritage Landing (a massive river access site onto the west side of the Deschutes River bridge); and cross the bridge to Deschutes River State Park.

The mountain bike access is immediately on the left at the junction, but stay right, driving through the campground to the farthest paved parking area. Keep going—it's a narrow paved path all the way to the southernmost part of the campground. The trail starts at the far end of the grassy field to the south.

Special considerations: Watch for the rare rattlesnake and some poison oak along the river.

The Hike

After parking your car, walk across a nice green picnic area lawn to the TRAILHEAD sign. Begin hiking on the Atiyeh Deschutes River Trail or Lower Trail. It starts in the shade with nice views of a major side channel of the river. Stay right past a junction with the middle and equestrian trails.

A well-maintained and well-beaten dusty path along the river closely follows the banks of the Deschutes past a USGS gauging station and several knarled bunches of Himalayan blackberry, sagebrush, and bunchgrass. After about 2.0 miles, the trail tops a nice basalt cliff, perfect for a snack break above the river to watch the geese below. Geese visit the wheat fields above the canyon to feed and return to the river bottom for its cool waters.

Natural Arch along the Deschutes River Trail

About 2.2 miles in, the trail crosses the doubletrack mountain bike route. Just below the intersection is a small natural basalt arch, with social trails continuing along the river. The maintained route crosses the doubletrack and climbs gradually up and around to Ferry Springs. A curious river rat may want to continue upstream on the doubletrack and watch some weekend boaters float through Rattlesnake Rapids, which definitely look like they'd require some snaking to navigate.

Climbing to Ferry Springs, pass through some old-growth sagebrush and patches of blooming lupine in spring. After the climb to Ferry Springs, it's a quick descent back to the doubletrack and down to the trailhead.

Miles and Directions

0.0 **START** from far end of picnic area at Deschutes Campground.

0.1 Junction with the Middle and Equestrian Trails, stay right (south).

2.0 Junction with Middle Trail, stay right (south).

2.2 Junction with mountain bike/horse doubletrack, cross the doubletrack and turn left (east).

3.2 Ferry Springs.

Deschutes River Trail

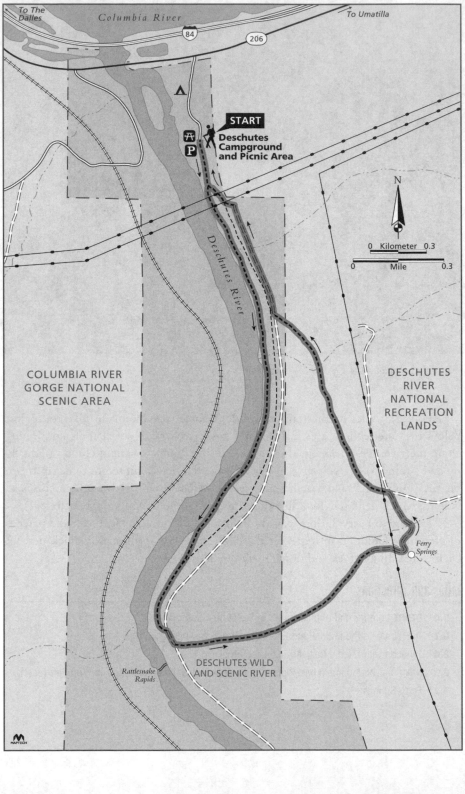

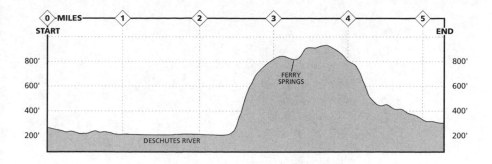

4.2 Junction with mountain bike/horse doubletrack, turn right (north).

5.0 Leave road.

5.3 Return to Deschutes Campground.

Beacon Rock State Park

Beacon Rock marks the place where Lewis and Clark first noticed the rise and fall of the tides. They then knew they were finally on the last leg of their journey to the Pacific. The area is now one of the premier hiking spots on the Washington side of the gorge, and has a well-maintained trail to the top of Beacon Rock. In addition, the Hamilton Mountain Trail offers both easy and difficult day hiking. It's an easy 1.4-mile hike to Rodney and Hardy Falls, and a 4.0-mile trek to the summit of Hamilton Mountain—almost all uphill past the falls.

Beacon Rock State Park was established in 1935, encompasses 4,500 acres, and is open year-round. It also offers a great picnic area, with two kitchen shelters and fifty-three unsheltered picnic tables. For group reservations, call (888) 226–7688. At the campground, sites are available on a first-come, first-served basis from May 15 through September. Certain areas of Beacon Rock State Park are periodically closed to rock climbers; call (509) 427–8265 for more information.

43 Beacon Rock

A short, steep day hike to the top of Beacon Rock.

Start: Beacon Rock Trailhead off WA 14.
Distance: 2.2 miles out and back.
Approximate hiking time: 2 hours.
Difficulty: Moderate.
Traffic: Heavy.
Trail type: Guardrail-protected path.
Best season: Year-round, depending upon frost line.
Total climbing: 600 feet.
Other trail users: None.

Canine compatibility: No pets are allowed.
Nearest town: Cascade Locks.
Fees and permits: None.
Maps: Bridal Veil USGS, Geo-Graphics Trails of the Columbia Gorge, and Maptech Washington: Bridal Veil.
Trail contacts: Washington State Parks and Recreation Commission, 7150 Cleanwater Lane, P.O. Box 42650, Olympia, WA 98504; (360) 902–8844; www.parks.wa.gov.

Finding the trailhead: From Portland, take Interstate 84 east to exit 44, Cascade Locks. Cross the Columbia River on the Bridge of the Gods for a toll of 75 cents. Turn left, heading west, on Washington Highway 14 for 7 miles to milepost 35. Two parking lots for Beacon Rock State Park are available on the left, south side. The trailhead is at the west end of the first parking lot; public restrooms are at the east end. From Vancouver, you can also drive 35 miles east on WA 14 to the trailhead.

Special considerations: More an amusement attraction than a hike, but spectacular nonetheless.

The Hike

Originally purchased and constructed by Henry J. Biddle in 1935, the Beacon Rock Trail winds its way around the basalt core of an ancient volcano.

The heavily traveled trail to the top of Beacon Rock is paved in some places, boardwalked in others, and surrounded by a safety guardrail most of the way up. It's less a wilderness experience than an urban park. The view is spectacular, and the location deeply historical.

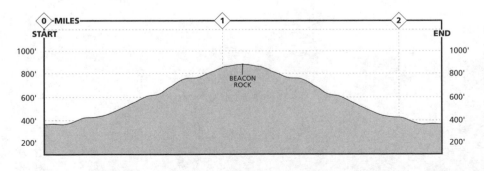

Beacon Rock

You will probably see many kids and families; however, I don't recommend this trail for children because it hikes up a cliff and the guardrail is a single pipe, offering insufficient protection. I recommend Rodney and Hardy Falls instead.

The trail climbs around the west side of Beacon Rock to a steel-gated enclosure on the cliff. The enclosure consists of a large metal plate with a door cut into it, and it's surrounded by razor wire. To get around this obstacle when the trail is closed would be practically impossible.

Past the metal gate, the trail climbs switchbacks upward. Wooden planks hold you up as you proceed along the cliff, with views of the gorge and Munra Point across the river. Upriver there is a good view of the Bonneville Dam and Cascade Locks. This trail proves that engineers can build a trail anywhere they want to.

Farther up, the trail enters a fir stand atop the rock and climbs to the final lookout. From this vantage point there are good views of Hamilton Mountain and Table Mountain to the northeast.

Beacon Rock

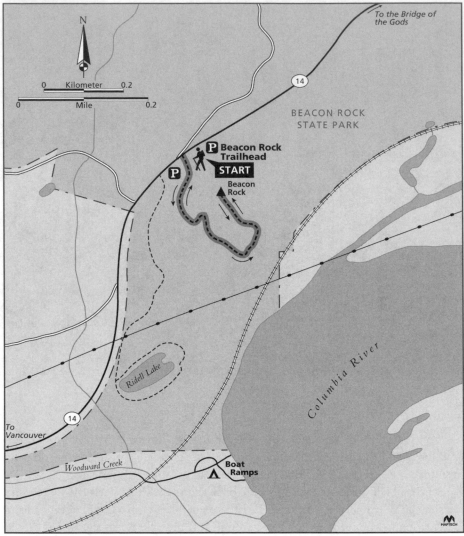

Miles and Directions

0.0 **START** from Beacon Rock Trailhead off WA 14.

1.1 Top of Beacon Rock, turn around.

2.2 Return to Beacon Rock Trailhead.

44 Rodney and Hardy Falls

A gentle day hike to Hardy and Rodney Falls.

Start: Beacon Rock Picnic Area.
Distance: 2.8 miles out and back.
Approximate hiking time: 2 to 3 hours.
Difficulty: Easy.
Traffic: Moderate to heavy.
Trail type: Well maintained.
Best season: Year-round, depending upon frost line.
Total climbing: 600 feet.
Other trail users: None.

Canine compatibility: Pets are allowed on leashes only.
Nearest town: Cascade Locks.
Fees and permits: None.
Maps: Beacon Rock USGS, Bridal Veil Green Trails, Geo-Graphics Trails of the Columbia Gorge, and Maptech Washington: Beacon Rock.
Trail contacts: Washington State Parks and Recreation Commission, 7150 Cleanwater Lane, P.O. Box 42650, Olympia, WA 98504; (360) 902-8844; www.parks.wa.gov.

Finding the trailhead: From Portland, take Interstate 84 east to exit 44, Cascade Locks. Cross the Columbia River on the Bridge of the Gods for a toll of 75 cents. Turn left and head west on Washington Highway 14 for 7 miles. Turn right at Beacon Rock State Park, just opposite Beacon Rock. Follow the park road for 0.25 mile to the first picnic area on the right. The trailhead is at the east end of the parking lot, behind the public restrooms.

The Hike

Instead of climbing Hamilton Mountain, you can opt for the less strenuous hike to Rodney and Hardy Falls. The trail is graded gently uphill and is a better choice for children than Beacon Rock (Hike 43). There aren't very many waterfalls on the Washington side of the Columbia River Gorge, but these are two of the gems.

From the picnic area, the trail climbs gradually through large Douglas firs and a mix of smaller deciduous trees. At 0.5 mile, the trail intersects with the campground trail, just underneath the power lines. One disadvantage of the Washington side of the gorge is that almost all the hiking trails must pass beneath these lines, whereas many of the Multnomah Falls area hikes on the Oregon side do not. Stay right, continuing north, for the falls.

At 1.3 miles is a spur trail to the Hardy Falls overlook. The right, unmarked fork, on the south side of the trail, descends downhill for 200 yards to a circular set of benches above Hardy Creek. Hardy Falls is just barely visible from this overlook.

At 1.4 miles, another spur trail forks left, on the northeast side of the trail, to the Pool of the Winds and Rodney Falls. Pool of the Winds is a deep bowl carved out of the rock by Rodney Falls, which has just a small vertical slit in the rock for an outlet. The short spur trail climbs up to the area just outside the pool. A guardrail prevents hikers from falling on the slick rock, and a log bench offers the weary a

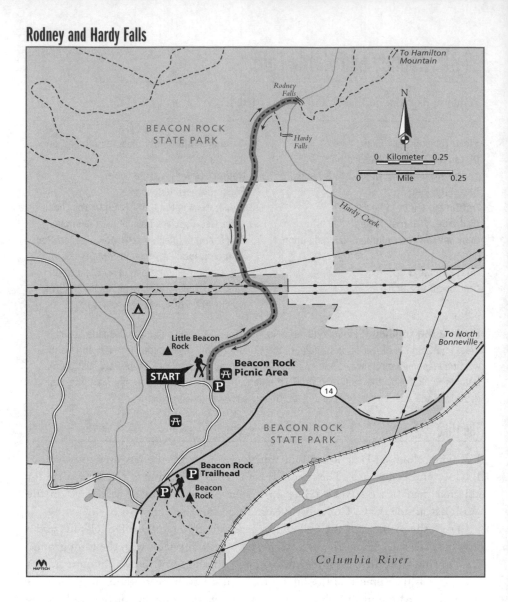

cool resting spot. It is necessary to follow the guardrail all the way to the end in order to see inside the bowl. Don't be surprised if you get a cool blast of mist on your face. The mist is responsible for the slick rock, and despite the guardrail caution is warranted.

Return to the trailhead via the same route, or continue on to Hamilton Mountain.

Miles and Directions

0.0 **START** from Beacon Rock Picnic Area.

0.5 Junction with campground trail, stay right (north).

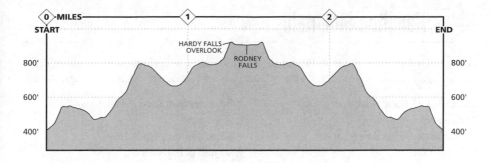

1.3 Junction with spur trail to Hardy Falls overlook, stay left (north).

1.4 Junction with Pool of the Winds spur trail to Rodney Falls, turn around.

2.8 Return to Beacon Rock Picnic Area.

45 Hamilton Mountain

A steep day hike to the top of Hamilton Mountain, passing Hardy and Rodney Falls.

Start: Beacon Rock Picnic Area.
Distance: 9.0-mile loop.
Approximate hiking time: 6 hours.
Difficulty: Difficult.
Traffic: Moderate to heavy.
Trail type: Well maintained.
Best season: Year-round, depending upon frost line.
Total climbing: 3,230 feet.
Other trail users: None.

Canine compatibility: Pets are allowed on leashes only.
Nearest town: Cascade Locks.
Fees and permits: None.
Maps: Beacon Rock USGS, Bridal Veil Green Trails, Geo-Graphics Trails of the Columbia Gorge, and Maptech Washington: Beacon Rock.
Trail contacts: Washington State Parks and Recreation Commission, 7150 Cleanwater Lane, P.O. Box 42650, Olympia, WA 98504; (360) 902–8844; www.parks.wa.gov.

Finding the trailhead: From Portland, take Interstate 84 east to exit 44, Cascade Locks. Cross the Columbia River on the Bridge of the Gods for a toll of 75 cents. Turn left, heading west, on Washington Highway 14 for 7 miles. Turn right at Beacon Rock State Park, just opposite Beacon Rock. Follow the park road for 0.25 mile to the first picnic area on the right. The trailhead is at the far end of the parking lot, behind the public restrooms.

The Hike

The Hamilton Mountain Trail climbs 4 miles to the top of Hamilton Mountain, and past the Rodney Falls it's almost all uphill. This portion of Beacon Rock State Park offers spectacular views, but some sections of the trail are very steep; think carefully before taking the southern route to the top. There is a less treacherous route, described as the return route for this hike, that runs to the north after Rodney Falls.

From the picnic area, the trail climbs gradually until it intersects the campground trail at 0.5 mile. Stay right, heading north and east for Hamilton Mountain. At 1.3 miles is a spur trail to the Hardy Falls overlook, from which the falls are just barely visible. After visiting the falls, continue northeast, bearing left, on the main trail.

At 1.4 miles, another spur trail forks left, northeast, to the Pool of the Winds and Rodney Falls. Pool of the Winds is a deep bowl carved out of the rock by Rodney Falls. You can follow a guardrailed path all the way to the end of the spur trail for a look into the Pool of the Winds. The rocks are slick, so be careful.

Next, continue on the Hamilton Mountain Trail. The trail descends on weathered switchbacks and crosses Hardy Creek on a footbridge. Then you begin climbing steep switchbacks.

At 1.8 miles is an unmarked fork. The left trail, to the north, goes up the Hardy Creek drainage. This is a longer, more gradual route to the top. The right trail, to the

Hamilton Mountain

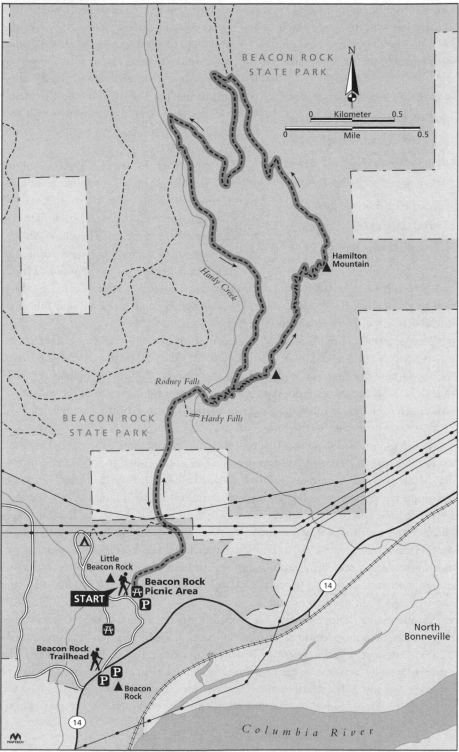

east, is a continuation of the Hamilton Mountain Trail that climbs steeply, often close to the edge, with the gorge visible below. If you don't like being on the edge, take the left fork. The right trail is better for people impatient to get to the top, who don't mind steep switchbacks. The left trail is for people who like to take a somewhat longer but less crowded route. The elevation gain is the same for both routes, but the left route up the Hardy Creek drainage is a mile longer to the top. If you take the left fork, follow the description of the upper loop in reverse.

▶ Below Hamilton Mountain moves are under way to develop a trail to Aldrich Butte and a new trailhead along Hamilton Creek or in the Greenleaf Slough area by North Bonneville. Check the Columbia River Gorge National Scenic Area's Web site at www.fs.fed.us/r6/columbia for updates on the planning process.

The right fork, to the east, keeps climbing after the junction. After about a mile of switchbacks, the trail levels off a bit. It follows the ridge before reverting to switchbacks for the final ascent. The summit of Hamilton Mountain is covered by brush, so the views along the way are better. Table Mountain, Mount Hood, and Nesmith Point are all visible on a clear day. Take a rest while deciding which way to go down. I recommend the ridge trail that continues left beyond the summit. Better views await you down the ridge.

The loop trail continues along the ridge, dropping down several switchbacks, and opens up into a lava field. This is great place to spend a few contemplative moments; the views here are superior to those from the summit. Mount St. Helens is sometimes visible in the distance, adding to the gorge panorama. At the other end of the lava clearing, there are three trail/logging roads to choose from. Take the left one, heading west, to complete the loop.

This logging road descends 1.0 mile into the Hardy Creek drainage. There are some huge stumps here and there among the trees of a young deciduous and fir forest. Most of these stumps have burn marks, and the unattached snag is usually decomposing somewhere nearby. These clues indicate a burn rather than a harvest.

Just before you reach a clearing, a logging road forks right up the drainage. Stay left, heading south and west, on the loop. At the clearing, the logging road crosses over Hardy Creek, to the west. The loop trail forks left, continuing south, before crossing the creek on a small catwalk. Just remember to keep left. The loop trail continues another 1.2 miles to rejoin the Hamilton Mountain Trail. Turn right for the last 1.8 miles back to the trailhead.

Consider the campground trail for variety on the return route. It follows the power lines, then drops through "Hadley's Grove," marked by a petrified stump dedicated to the first superintendent of Beacon Rock State Park, Clyde B. Hadley. His grove is actually a young stand of fir, much smaller than the ancient trees in the campground just a little farther on. The trail terminates at the upper end of the campground loop. From the campground, it's a short walk down the paved road to the picnic area.

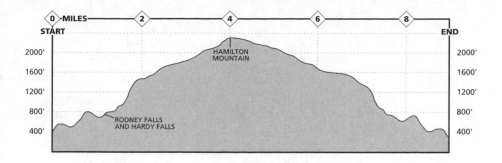

Miles and Directions

0.0 **START** from Beacon Rock Picnic Area.

0.5 Junction with campground trail, stay right (north).

1.3 Junction with spur trail to Hardy Falls overlook, stay left (north).

1.4 Junction with Pool of the Winds spur trail to Rodney Falls, stay right (east).

1.8 Junction with loop trail from Hamilton Ridge, stay right (east). This is the end of the loop. **Option:** For a more gradual ascent of Hamilton Mountain, turn left and follow the loop in reverse. The summit is a mile farther this way.

4.0 Top of Hamilton Mountain.

5.0 Junction with logging road on loop, turn left (west).

6.0 Junction with loop trail, turn left (south) and leave old logging road.

7.2 Junction with Hamilton Mountain Trail, turn right (west).

9.0 Return to Beacon Rock Picnic Area.

Pacific Crest Trail, Washington

Pacific Crest Trail National Scenic Trail 2000 (PCT) extends from Mexico to Canada and encompasses miles of trail. The PCT was designated a national scenic trail by Congress in 1968. The section through the Columbia River Gorge offers at least four good hiking options—more if you like. On the Washington side the best way to break the trail up is to make a short day hike to Gillette Lake or a long day to Table Mountain and beyond.

For more information:

Pacific Crest Trail Association
5325 Elkhorn Boulevard, PMB 256
Sacramento, CA 95842-2526
(888) 728–7245
www.pcta.org

The Westway Trail to the top of Table Mountain off the Pacific Crest Trail was built and maintained by the Mazama Trail Club and is not officially designated USDA Forest Service route. For information on volunteer opportunities with the Mazamas, contact:

Mazamas
909 NW Nineteenth Ave
Portland, OR 97209
(503) 227–2345
www.mazamas.org

46 Gillette Lake

A 5-mile round-trip day hike to Gillette Lake on the famous Pacific Crest Trail.

Start: Tamanous Trailhead off WA 14.
Distance: 5.0 miles out and back.
Approximate hiking time: 3 to 4 hours.
Difficulty: Easy.
Traffic: Moderate.
Trail type: Well maintained.
Best season: Year-round.
Total climbing: 1,200 feet.
Other trail users: None.
Canine compatibility: Pets are allowed on leashes only.

Nearest town: Cascade Locks.
Fees and permits: A Northwest Forest Pass is required.
Maps: Bonneville Dam USGS, Bonneville Dam Green Trails, and Pacific Crest National Scenic Trail Washington Southern Section USFS.
Trail contacts: Gifford Pinchot National Forest, 10600 NE 51st Circle, Vancouver, WA 98682; (360) 891-5000; www.fs.fed.us/gpnf.

Finding the trailhead: From Portland, take Interstate 84 east to exit 44, Cascade Locks and cross the Columbia River on the Bridge of the Gods, paying a toll of 75 cents. Turn left, heading west on Washington Highway 14, for 1.5 miles. The trailhead is on the right, to the north, opposite the Bonneville Visitor Center turnoff.

The Hike

This trail offers easy day hiking. The terrain is dominated by second-growth Douglas fir trees averaging sixty to eighty years or younger. Most of the hiking is through the trees, but several points offer unique views of the Columbia River Gorge and Table Mountain.

The first 0.5 mile follows a singletrack path that crosses several jeep trails and offers views of the Columbia River. The strong current is visible here in the rippling and churning of the river. The trail actually runs on top of a train tunnel, and the passing of a freight train might startle you. This section that connects with the Pacific Crest Trail 2000 from the Bridge of the Gods is the Tamanous Trail, named for a Native American vision quest.

At 0.5 mile, the Tamanous Trail intersects the PCT 2000. Turn left, heading north, to head for Gillette Lake. Several ponds to the west give the forest a smooth green tint. The trail winds around for 0.5 mile or so until it reaches a Washington State Department of Natural Resources sign promoting sustainable yield and multiple-use timber harvest in the forest. The sign is an interesting cultural exhibit, considering how dissenters have altered the message with graffiti. After another 0.5 mile, the trail passes through a clear-cut from 1991 that was replanted a year later. The end of the clear-cut affords a western view of the gorge and Beacon Rock.

Gillette Lake

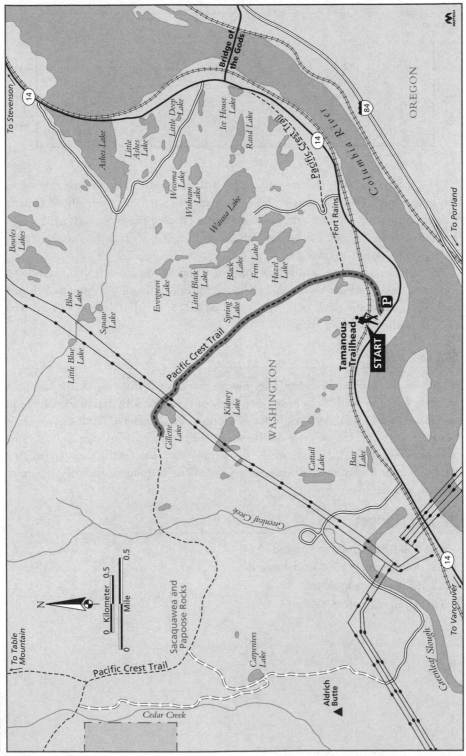

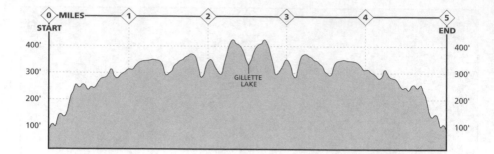

Just before reaching Gillette Lake, cross a forest road and continue underneath the power lines. The trail drops a little, traverses the northeast slope above Gillette Lake, and then descends to the lake's elevation. Despite the proximity of the road and power lines, Gillette Lake is very quaint and natural. It's common to see waterfowl swimming in the calm water.

At an old tractor tire, a path forks off to the left, heading south, and leads down to a well-used campsite by the shore. The right fork, heading northwest, continues the PCT. Follow the same trail back to the trailhead, and don't forget to turn west back onto the Tamanous Trail.

Bass Lake Side Trip

Before or after a trip to Gillette Lake, you might consider stopping at the Bass Lake Wildlife Area in North Bonneville. Just south of the Tamanous Trailhead, turn right under the underpass and stay right for 0.5 mile to the Bass Lake Wildlife Area Trailhead on the right. If you drive all the way around Greenleaf Slough, you've gone too far. After a short 0.3- to 0.5-mile stroll down the path to the east, you reach a duck blind for bird-watching and good views of lots of resident waterfowl, herons, ospreys, and the like.

Miles and Directions

- **0.0** **START** from Tamanous Trailhead off WA 14.
- **0.5** Junction with PCT 2000, turn left (north).
- **2.5** Gillette Lake, turn around.
- **5.0** Return to Tamanous Trailhead.

47 Table Mountain

A tough, 15-mile round-trip climb to the top of Table Mountain on the Pacific Crest Trail.

Start: Tamanous Trailhead off WA 14.
Distance: 15.5 miles out and back.
Approximate hiking time: All day.
Difficulty: Strenuous.
Traffic: Moderate to light.
Trail type: Well maintained to the Eastway junction; primitive to the summit.
Best season: Year-round.
Total climbing: 6,000 feet.
Other trail users: Horses.
Canine compatibility: Dogs are allowed on leashes only.

Nearest town: Cascade Locks.
Fees and permits: A Northwest Forest Pass is required.
Maps: Bonneville Dam USGS, Bonneville Dam Green Trails, Pacific Crest National Scenic Trail Washington Southern Section USFS, and Maptech Washington: Bonneville Dam.
Trail contacts: Gifford Pinchot National Forest, 10600 NE 51st Circle, Vancouver, WA 98682; (360) 891-5000; www.fs.fed.us/gpnf.

Finding the trailhead: From Portland, take Interstate 84 east to exit 44, Cascade Locks and cross the Columbia River on the Bridge of the Gods, paying a toll of 75 cents. Turn left and head west on Washington Highway 14 for 1.5 miles. The trailhead is on the right, opposite the Bonneville Visitor Center turnoff.

Special considerations: To protect fragile resouces the Eastway/Heartbreak Ridge route is not recommended.

The Hike

This trail is one of the better gorge power climbs. The terrain is dominated by second-growth Douglas fir trees. Most of the hiking is through the trees, but the summit of Table Mountain is one of the more satisfying and spectacular destinations in the gorge.

The first 0.5 mile follows a singletrack path that crosses several jeep trails and offers some views of the Columbia River. The trail is actually right on top of a train tunnel, and the passing of a freight train might startle you. The section that connects with the Pacific Crest Trail 2000 from the Bridge of the Gods is called the Tamanous Trail.

At 0.5 mile, the Tamanous Trail intersects the PCT 2000. Turn left, heading north, to head for Gillette Lake. Several ponds to the west give a smooth green tint to the forest. After another 0.5 mile, the trail passes through a clear-cut from 1991. The end of the clear-cut affords a western view of the gorge and Beacon Rock.

Just before reaching Gillette Lake, the trail crosses a forest road and continues underneath the power lines. The trail drops down to traverse the northeast slope above Gillette Lake, then drops farther to the lake's elevation. Despite the proximity of the road and power lines, Gillette Lake is very quaint and natural looking. It's common to see waterfowl swimming in the calm water.

At an old tractor tire, a spur trail forks off to the left, heading south. It leads down to a well-used campsite by the shore. Camping is allowed, but expect to see a few day hikers.

The main trail to the right, heading northwest, continues the PCT. Soon after leaving the lake, the trail crosses Gillette Creek on a log bridge. No fording is necessary.

The trail climbs gradually until it crosses a jeep road; follow the singletrack trail with PCT 2000 markers west. Then pass a small pond to the south, just before Greenleaf Creek. A well-maintained footbridge across the creek affords views of Table Mountain. This is also a good place to filter some water.

After Greenleaf Creek, the trail proceeds up steeper switchbacks for 0.25 mile to a break in the trees. This overlook offers views of Kidney Lake and across the gorge to Wauna Point.

After the lookout is another unmarked junction; continue straight to a four-way junction and keep going straight. As Cedar Creek comes into view on the left and Papoose Rock becomes visible through the trees on the right, the trail crosses another jeep road. Stay straight again, heading north. Just 0.3 mile later, recross the jeep road and head up and right to the north. The left trail leads to a campsite where water is available.

Soon after, the trail reaches the Eastway Trail/Heartbreak Trail. The Mazamas, the Washington Department of Natural Resources, and the Forest Service strongly encourage hikers to stay off the Eastway Trail due to resource concerns. For a slightly less steep—but still far from easy trail—continue northwest to the Westway Trail.

The top of Table Mountain is just as spectacular as it looks from the interstate, and you can see a hell of a lot more . . . if it isn't foggy.

When you reach the summit, the trail forks to the right and heads east to a nice clifftop lunch spot. The trail to the left, heading west, leads to shelter in the trees and the Westway Trail. You can follow the trail along the cliffs or through the trees. If you go through the trees, then head right (north) as the trail forks, to follow the ridge to the PCT. The left trail, to the south, heads down on the Westway Trail. It's steep, but a little easier on your knees than the Eastway. When you reach the bottom, turn left on the PCT and head for home.

If you have enough overnight gear or really need a workout, it's another 4.9 miles to the junction with the 0.75-mile trail up Three Corner Rock, giving you well over a 20-mile day.

Table Mountain

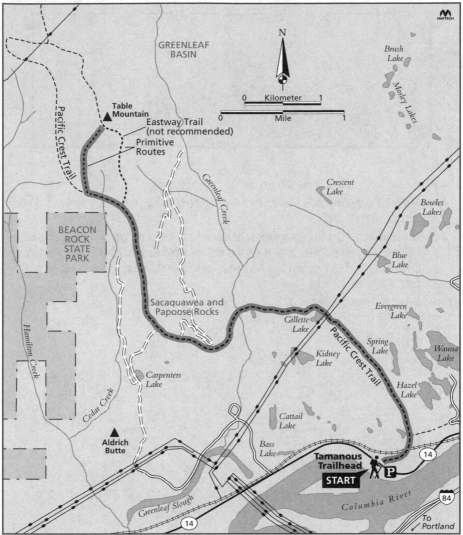

Miles and Directions

- **0.0**   **START** from Tamanous Trailhead off WA 14.
- **0.5**   Junction with PCT 2000, turn left (north).
- **2.5**   Gillette Lake.
- **4.0**   Overlook.
- **4.1**   Unmarked trail junction, continue straight.
- **4.4**   Four-way trail junction, continue straight (northwest).

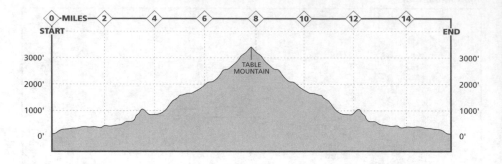

4.7   Second junction with unmarked jeep trail, turn right (north)

6.7   Stay left (northwest) on PCT 2000, then turn right (north) on the Westway Trail and follow it to the summit.

7.7   Table Mountain, turn around. **Option 1:** Turn around to follow the Westway Trail back the PCT, then turn left (southeast) to reach the trailhead. **Option 2:** Turn right (north) to follow the ridge to the PCT and then turn left (west) for a longer loop back to the junction with the Eastway Trail.

15.5   Return to Tamanous Trailhead.

Dog Mountain
Trail System

D og Mountain is best known for sunny skies and blooming balsamroot, but the area also offers good healthy climbing and access to a public hiking area rare in this part of the gorge. Private land dominates most of the Washington side of the gorge east of the Bridge of the Gods, but Dog Mountain is a wonderful exception. A growing addition to the system has been the Augspurger Mountain Trail, which will hopefully provide access to Grassy Knoll and points north.

48 Dog Mountain Loop

A steep day hike up Dog Mountain.

Start: Dog Mountain Trailhead off WA 14
Distance: 6.8-mile loop.
Approximate hiking time: 3 to 6 hours.
Difficulty: Difficult.
Traffic: Heavy, but the trail can absorb a lot of use without feeling crowded.
Trail type: Well maintained.
Best season: Year-round, or March through December, depending upon frost line.
Total climbing: 2,828 feet.
Other trail users: Not suitable for mountain bikes.

Canine compatibility: Dogs are permitted on leashes only.
Nearest town: Stevenson.
Fees and permits: A Northwest Forest Pass is required.
Maps: Mount Defiance USGS and Hood River Green Trails.
Trail contacts: Gifford Pinchot National Forest, 10600 NE 51st Circle, Vancouver, WA 98682; (360) 891-5000; www.fs.fed.us/gpnf.

Finding the trailhead: From Portland, take Interstate 84 east to exit 44, Cascade Locks. Cross the Bridge of the Gods after paying a toll of 75 cents. Turn right, heading east on Washington Highway 14 for 12.5 miles to the well-marked Dog Mountain Trailhead on the left at milepost 53. Bathrooms are available 100 yards up from the old Dog Mountain Trailhead at the east end of the parking lot. The newer Augspurger Mountain Trailhead is just 50 feet west.

Special considerations: Increasingly poison oak has become a problem along many parts of the Dog Mountain trail system, so beware or wear long pants.

The Hike

The Dog Mountain trail system is heavily used by hikers, and the summit is often crowded on weekends; still, the mountain provides a peaceful and scenic hike. On a clear day, Mount Hood, Mount St. Helens, and Mount Adams are all visible from the top. Dog Mountain is also well known for wildflowers, especially during spring and early summer.

There are several different routes up the peak. The most scenic starts at the old trailhead at the east end of the parking lot. Take the "scenic" option on the first loop and return either the same way or via the more gradual route down the back side—this description follows the latter route. You could reverse this by taking Augspurger Trail 4407 up, which takes 3.7 miles to get to the top and is not as steep. I believe it makes a better route down, because a steep climb followed by a more gradual descent is easier on the knees.

From the east end of the parking lot, Dog Mountain Trail 147 climbs less than 0.1 mile to the public restrooms. Because of the trail's heavy use, it's better to use these now than to have to go along the trail somewhere. The trail continues to climb

Hikers on Dog Mountain Trail.

steeply up dry, partially exposed switchbacks through fir and oak trees. The trail reaches the first junction at 0.5 mile. The right trail, to the east, is the more gradual and scenic option. The left trail, to the north, is the oldest route up Dog Mountain and has no views, lots of shade, and steep grades.

After taking the right trail, climb past a couple of good viewpoints of the Columbia River and across to Mount Defiance. At 2.0 miles, the scenic and old trails rejoin. (A shorter option is to turn back at this point, descending on the opposite loop trail.) The main trail climbs in the shade for another 0.5 mile until it opens up to the Flowering Inferno. You might suppose this is a misprint or a bad pun on the "Towering Inferno," but that's what the junction sign says. As the trail opens up into a meadow, the blooms of paintbrush and balsamroot are spectacular. Even before these more noticeable flowers bloom, goldstars and buttercups add a yellow tint to the fresh green grass.

At 2.5 miles is a junction with a loop. This viewpoint junction is actually Puppy Dog Mountain, just a little bit smaller than the real thing. It used to be the site of a fire lookout, but this lookout—in use off and on since 1920—was dismantled in 1967. It is easy to see why from the view. The left route, to the northwest, is more scenic, especially if the balsamroot is in full bloom. It stays in the open, allowing a full view of the flowers, river, and the mountains beyond. The right trail to the east is a slightly longer option with fewer views.

After turning left, traverse the west face of Dog Mountain to the intersection with the summit trail. Continuing straight north is the Augspurger Trail; turning right, a little to the east, takes you to the top and the loop trail to the "Puppy Dog" junction. Turn right to reach the top. Just before the summit, the trail keeps going straight and passes a short spur trail on the left, to the north, through some low brush. This path is necessary to actually reach the highest point, but the view is better just below. The meadow below is a comfortable lunch and water spot.

▶ On steep climbs, drinking lots of water helps prevent the ill effects of dehydration and exhaustion. These are two major contributors to hypothermia, on warm and cool days alike.

From inside the grove of trees at the summit, you can see Mount Adams (and, through the branches, Mount St. Helens) to the north. Mount Hood and Mount Defiance are easily seen to the south across the river.

To return to the trailhead, there are three options: the way you came; the return trail to Puppy Dog junction; and the gentle, longer route back down the Augspurger Trail. For the last option, turn right down the 0.1-mile trail to the junction with the Augspurger Connector Trail. Turn right again, heading northwest, for the additional 3.7 miles back to the trailhead. The Augspurger Trail along the west face of Dog Mountain descends gradually, entering the trees after 0.5 mile. At 0.9 mile from the top, it intersects with Augspurger Trail 4407.

Augspurger Trail 4407 continues north for 4.0 miles to the top of Augspurger Mountain. This side route offers occasional views through temperate forest. The Forest Service hopes to connect this ridge route with the Grassy Knoll Lookout Trail and access to the Pacific Crest Trail at Big Huckleberry Mountain. Turn left, heading south on Augspurger Trail 4407 for the trailhead, just 2.8 miles farther. The trail

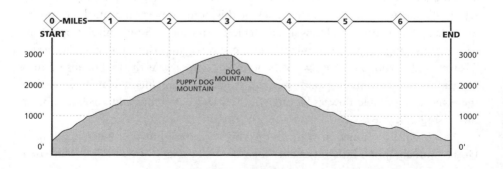

Dog Mountain Loop

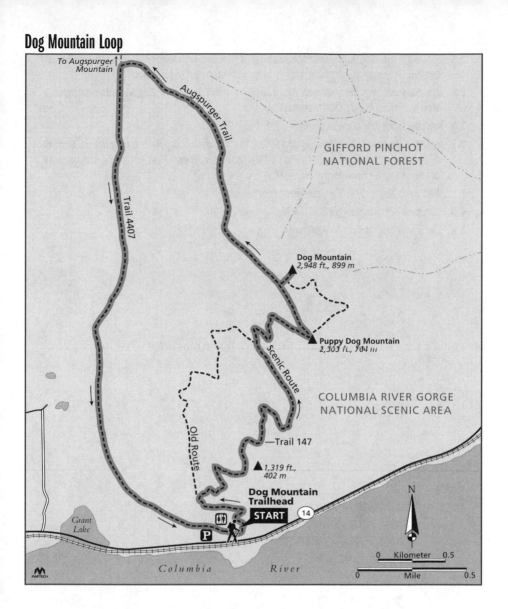

descends gradually along the side of Dog Mountain back toward the gorge, down a couple of switchbacks and some dry, exposed scree slopes. Watch for poison oak.

Miles and Directions

0.0 **START** from Dog Mountain Trailhead off WA 14.

0.1 Public restrooms.

0.5 Junction with scenic and old routes, turn right (east).

2.0 Junction with return of scenic and old routes, stay right (north). **Option:** For a short hike, turn around and follow the old route back to the trailhead.

2.5 Flowering Inferno, Puppy Dog Mountain, and junction with loop trail, turn left (northwest). **Option:** Stay right (east) for a slightly longer climb to Dog Mountain.

2.8 Junction with summit trail, turn right (east) to reach the top of Dog Mountain and the loop trail from Puppy Dog Mountain.

3.0 Junction with the Augspurger Trail.

3.1 Summit. **Option 1:** Turn around and follow the same route back to the trailhead. **Option 2:** Follow the loop trail back to Puppy Dog Mountain, then follow either the scenic route or the old route back to the trailhead.

3.2 Return to Augspurger Trail, turn right (northwest).

4.0 Junction with Augspurger Trail 4407, turn left (south).

6.8 Return to Dog Mountain Trailhead.

The Dalles Area

f you live in Portland or Vancouver, The Dalles is sunshine heaven and, although there are not as many mountains to climb or waterfalls to visit, there is a lot of history and geology. The Dalles has been a center of trade for natives and settlers. The center of the area today is the massive The Dalles Dam with its fish ladders, generators, and locks. While in The Dalles, any visitor to the gorge should do two things: walk along Horsethief Butte and visit the Columbia Gorge Discovery Center and Wasco County Historical Museum, just west of the city of The Dalles. This granddaddy of a modern museum and interpretive paradise is worth the price of admission.

Columbia Gorge Discovery Center
5000 Discovery Drive
The Dalles, OR 97058
(541) 296–8600
www.gorgediscovery.org

Special Regulations for the Catherine Creek Area

- No fires.
- No motorized vehicles.
- All other modes of travel are legal.

49 Catherine Creek Natural Arch

A short day hike to a natural basalt arch.

Start: Catherine Creek Trailhead off Old Highway 8, just east of Lyle.
Distance: 1.4 miles out and back.
Approximate hiking time: 1 to 2 hours.
Difficulty: Easy.
Traffic: Moderate.
Trail type: Jeep trail.
Best season: Year-round.
Total climbing: 700 feet.
Other trail users: Horses, mountain bikes.

Canine compatibility: Dogs are allowed on leashes only.
Nearest town: Lyle.
Fees and permits: None.
Maps: Lyle Wash USGS, and Maptech Washington: Lyle.
Trail contacts: Gifford Pinchot National Forest, 10600 NE 51st Circle, Vancouver, WA 98682; (360) 891-5000; www.fs.fed.us/gpnf.

Finding the trailhead: From Portland, take Interstate 84 east to Hood River. Take the Hood River exit, cross the 75-cent toll bridge, and turn right, heading east, on Washington Highway 14 for 6 miles. Then turn left, heading north, on Old Highway 14 for 1.5 miles. A Forest Service gate is on the left before the washed-out bridge over Catherine Creek.

The Hike

There is a controversy in this area over what types of use are permitted. Motorized vehicles aren't currently allowed, but the Forest Service is studying the issue. If there is a trailhead questionnaire, filling it out and relaying that you used this area for hiking might help determine future management.

At the trailhead, there are two jeep roads; take the one on your right, heading northeast, dropping into the Catherine Creek gulch. Catherine Creek will most likely not have much water, if any, but it does have plenty of poison oak.

At 0.3 mile, stay right, heading northeast, at the fork. The road soon passes an old corral to the west. Look up to the east, on the right, to see the natural arch. If the old ranch and this view of the arch are enough entertainment, return via the same route. If you'd like a better view from atop the arch, continue up the jeep road to the north. The forest consists of Oregon oak, ponderosa pine, and some poison oak.

After a climb, the road divides again; stay right, heading east. Just a little farther, under the power lines, is a faint path veering right, to the south. A cross-country route leads across the brown grass atop the basalt to a lookout above the arch.

Looking up valley above Catherine Creek Natural Arch ▶

Catherine Creek Natural Arch

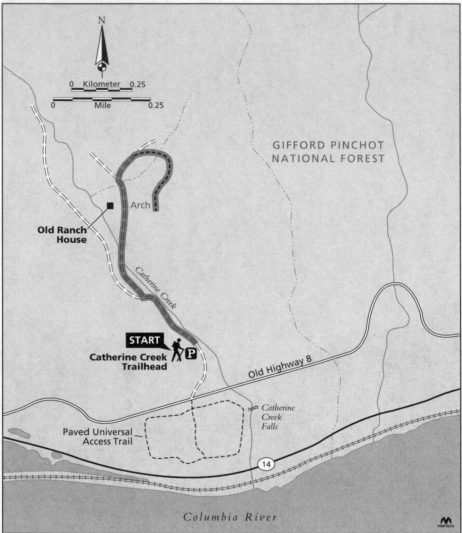

The view of the arch is a bit eerie, as a narrow slit allows light to slip between the arch and the side of the gulch. You might be tempted to scramble down underneath the arch to the gulch, but this route involves some tricky talus-slope sliding on large, loose pieces of basalt—a very coarse surface against your skin if you fall. It's better to return via the original route.

Miles and Directions

0.0   START from Catherine Creek Trailhead off Old Highway 14.

0.3   Jeep road forks, stay right (northeast).

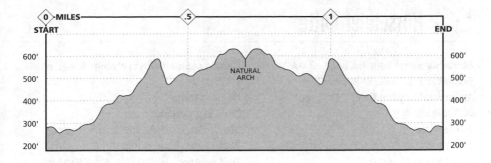

0.4 Jeep road forks, stay right (east).

0.7 Natural arch overlook, turn around.

1.4 Return to Catherine Creek Trailhead.

50 Horsethief Butte

Start: Horsethief Butte Trailhead off WA 14.
Distance: 2.0 miles out and back.
Approximate hiking time: 1 to 2 hours.
Difficulty: Easy.
Traffic: Heavy.
Trail type: Maintained with primitive routes.
Best season: Year-round.
Total climbing: 140 feet.
Other trail users: Rock climbers.

Canine compatibility: Pets are allowed on leashes only.
Nearest town: The Dalles.
Fees and permits: None.
Maps: Stacker Butte USGS, and Maptech Washington: Stacker Butte.
Trail contacts: Washington State Parks and Recreation Commission, 7150 Cleanwater Lane, P.O. Box 42650, Olympia, WA 98504; (360) 902-8844; www.parks.wa.gov.

Finding the trailhead: Eastbound from The Dalles, take exit 87, Celilo Park, off Interstate 84 and cross the Columbia River on U.S. Highway 197 below the Dalles Dam. Turn right, heading east on Washington Highway 14. Drive east for 2.8 miles, or just 1.2 miles past the Horsethief Lake State Park turnoff. You'll find limited parking and primitive trailhead facilities. You may have to park on the opposite side of WA 14; use caution crossing this heavily-traveled road.

Special considerations: The petroglyphs at Horsethief Lake State Park have been closed to public access due to vandalism. To prevent similar access restriction on Horsethief Butte, please respect artifacts and antiquities.

The Hike

Horsethief Butte is a large outcropping of basalt on the dry hills above the Dalles Dam area. It rises right in your face from the start of the trailhead and is a popular place for history buffs and rock climbers alike. There are social trails all over the butte, but a somewhat major trail circles its southwestern flank, with a spur trail climbing up into the craggy knolls in the middle. Lots of signs warn visitors not to

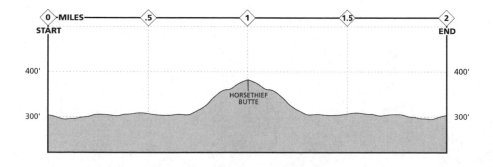

Horsethief Butte

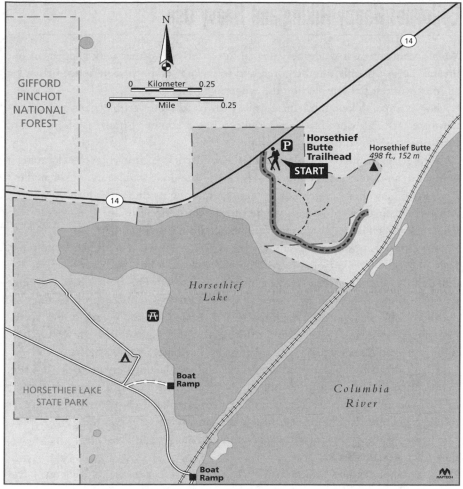

deface the Native drawings on some of the more hidden rock faces. Similar damage has caused the more well-known cliff-drawings at Horsethief Lake State Park to be restricted to ranger-escorted hikes only.

Miles and Directions

- **0.0**   **START** from primitive Horsethief Butte Trailhead on WA 14.
- **1.0**   End of trail on far side of butte, turn around.
- **2.0**   Return to Horsethief Butte Trailhead.

Epilogue: Happy Hiking and Heavy Use

We all want our own wilderness area all to ourselves, but that only happens in our dreams. Lots of people use the gorge, and to make everyone's experience better, we all must work at politely sharing the wilderness.

For example, hikers must share trails with backcountry equestrians and mountain bikers. Both groups have every right to be on approved trails, so please do not turn an encounter into a confrontation.

Another example of politely sharing the wilderness is choosing your campsite. If you get to a popular lake late in the day and all the good campsites are taken, don't crowd in on another camper. This is most aggravating, as these sites rightfully go on a first-come, first-served basis. If you're late, it's your responsibility to move on or to take a less desirable site at a respectful distance from other campers.

Also, special considerations are warranted for very popular trails like Multnomah Falls and Eagle Creek. Going to Multnomah Falls on a busy summer weekend is a different experience for the veteran hiker. It's crowded. The trail is paved. Orange fences section off rehabilitation areas. Signs at every switchback promise fines for cutting. People in high heels with radios and dressed for a city park tromp up the path. Increasingly, areas like Multnomah Falls that receive extremely heavy use have to be managed like city parks, and other areas may have a similar future.

I have hiked up to the falls many times and would not hesitate to do it again. People have told me that other hikers are necessarily a negative when choosing a hike. Yet people will always keep coming to Multnomah Falls. More diverse groups of hikers get a firsthand look at nature here than anywhere else in the gorge. Everyone has the right to care for the preservation of Multnomah Falls. The more wilderness advocates, the better.

Even so, places like Multnomah Falls require extra patience and energy. I recommend these guidelines for happy hiking with heavy use:

- A simple, friendly howdy or hello is worth a thousand nods or shrugs.
- Yield generously to other hikers, especially tiny ones.
- Don't bring noisemakers.
- Avoid excessive public displays of affection.
- Support the volunteers and public workers who have the difficult job of managing our treasures.

Appendix: Checklists

Table 1: Day-Hiking Checklist

For day hiking wear baggy shorts, trail-running shoes or boots, synthetic socks, a T-shirt, and your favorite hiking hat. You can go as light as just an extra shell, water, snacks, and survival kit, but it helps to carry other comfort and safety items. You might also wish to carry binoculars, a camera, film, and fishing gear.

Individual Items	Weight (oz.)
1-liter water bottle (full of water)	36
Day pack	48
Extra clothing: rain pants, rain jacket, wool gloves, stocking cap, wool or synthetic sweater (may vary with climate)	86
Survival kit	20.5
Map (a copy for each person)	3.5
Money, credit card, driver's license	2
Sunglasses (in breakproof case)	3
Weight of individual items	199 oz.

Group Items (for three hikers)	Weight (oz.)
Water filter (carry backup iodine, too)	19
Plastic trowel, toilet paper	10
Bug repellent in sealed plastic bag	2
Keys (attached to inside of pack)	3
Snacks	20
Sunscreen	2
Headlamp (with fresh batteries)	8.5
First-aid kit (from Backpacking Essentials list)	27.3
Weight of group items	91.8 oz. (30.6 oz./person)
Weight of day-hiking items (per hiker)	229.6 oz. (14.3 lbs.)

Table 2: The Backpacking Essentials

The list below represents a basic checklist for a three-day, two-night backpack for three people. If you go by yourself, you will need to shave off a few pounds, most likely with a lighter tent and less cookware.

The checklist starts with items that all parties should carry, then adds in their percentage of the group's weight if the group items are divided equally. Food isn't listed as a group item, because each person would carry the same amount of food with or without a group. The list includes articles of clothing you wear on the first day, and hence have to carry the rest of the trip.

Individual Items	**Weight (oz.)**
1-liter water bottle (full of water)	36
Lightweight backpack (internal frame, doubles as partial emergency sleeping shell)	72
Synthetic sleeping bag (20 degree F rating, in a garbage bag and stuffed into a stuff sack)	61
Pack fly or poncho (to cover pack while hiking and while breaking camp; can also be used as a ground cloth)	12
Foam sleeping pad	9
Feminine hygiene products	10
Waterproof journal and pencil	4
Toothbrush and toothpaste	4
Food (per person—85 oz. total)	
Drink bag: 6 tea bags, 3 apple cider packets, 6 soup packets, 5 lemon-flavor packets	10
Snacks/breakfast: 6 breakfast bars, 2 cups trail mix, bag of almonds, 3 boxes raisins	36
Meal bag 1: baguette and 12 oz. sharp cheddar cheese	23
Meal bag 2: Noodles-and-sauce or rice-and-sauce dinners	12
Insulated plastic cup with lid	3
Plastic spoon and fork	1.5
Weight of individual items	539 oz. (33.7 lbs.)

Group Items	**Weight (oz.)**
Camp stove (with cigarette lighter)	24
Fuel bottle (full of gas, 32 oz.; may vary with fuel efficiency of stove)	29
Pans (2 pans, lids, handles)	21
Pepper spray (in bear country)	16
50 feet of cord	4
Tent (three-person)	91
Water filter (carry backup iodine in personal survival kit)	19
Permit (if required)	0.1
First-aid kit	
Ace bandage	2.5
Adhesive bandages (Band-Aids)	1.5
Adhesive tape (1 roll)	3
Antibiotic ointment packets (or small tube of Neosporin)	0.5
Cravat (triangular bandage)	1.8
Gauze pads (four, each 4 inches square)	1.6
Gauze rollers	2
Medications (laxative, anti-diarrhea, allergy, aspirin, ibuprofen)	2
Nonadhesive bandage (for burns)	0.5

Nylon bag	4
Rubber/vinyl gloves (2 pairs)	1.4
Safety pins	0.5
Scissors	3
Tweezers (forceps)	0.5
Wound closure strips	0.5
Moleskin or Molefoam pieces	2
Weight of group items	231.4 (77.1 oz. per person)
Weight per person	616.1 oz. (38.5 lbs.)

If you have any special conditions or allergies (such as bee stings), you should consult with your physician before taking a backpacking trip. If you are allergic to bee stings, carry an anaphylaxis emergency kit. If you are diabetic, be sure to include necessary insulin and glucose paste for emergencies. If you are traveling in snake country, be sure to carry a snakebite kit. For more information on wilderness first-aid kits, see *Wilderness First Aid* by Gilbert Preston, MD (Falcon 1997).

Table 3: Post-Trip Checklist

Once you return to the trailhead and change clothes, stop at a pizza place, and grab a cold beverage, don't forget your post-trip duties. It is in your best interest to do a little post-trip maintenance, especially if your trip has been a dirty one. Probably the most important thing you can do to preserve your gear is to make sure it is clean and dry before storing it.

- Call or notify those with whom you left your itinerary. This way they know you got back safely and won't call for a massive search. A search for someone who isn't lost is costly and embarrassing.

- For your own safety and that of other wilderness travelers, report all trail dangers to the local ranger district.

- Clean all gear and repair any items damaged during the trip, so you're ready for the next trip.

- Take your sleeping bag out of the stuff sack and put it loosely in a storage bag.

- Dry out your tent, fly, and rain gear before storing.

- Dump your garbage, but don't fill trailhead garbage cans. Drive it in. Drive it out.

- Replenish survival and first-aid items used unexpectedly, so you don't forget them on the next trip.

Columbia River Gorge National Scenic Area Contacts

Columbia River Gorge National
Scenic Area
902 Wasco Avenue, Suite 200
Hood River, OR 97031
(541) 308–1700, TTY (541) 386–8758
www.fs.fed.us/r6/columbia/forest

Skamania Lodge
1131 SW Skamania Lodge Drive
Stevenson, WA 98648
(509) 427–2528
Located off Washington Highway 14 in
Stevenson.

Multnomah Falls Lodge
Off Interstate 84 or on the Historic
Columbia River Highway (Oregon
Highway 30)
(503) 695–2376
www.multnomahfallslodge.com

Mount Hood National Forest
Forest Headquarters
16400 Champion Way
Sandy, OR 97055
(503) 668–1700
www.fs.fed.us/r6/mthood

Hood River Ranger District
6780 Highway 35 South
Mt. Hood-Parkdale, OR 97041
(541) 352–6002

Barlow Ranger District
P.O. Box 67
Dufur, OR 97021
(541) 467–2291

Gifford Pinchot National Forest
Forest Headquarters
10600 NE 51st Circle

Vancouver, WA 98682
(360) 891–5000
www.fs.fed.us/gpnf

Mount Adams Ranger District
2455 Highway 141
Trout Lake, WA 98650
(509) 395–3400

Columbia River Gorge Commission
P.O. Box 730
White Salmon, WA 98672
(509) 493–3323
www.gorgecommission.org

Chinook Trail Association
(360) 695–7149
www.chinooktrail.org

Nature of the Northwest
800 NE Oregon Street, Suite 177
Portland, OR 97232
(503) 872–2750

Oregon State Parks
(800) 551–0321

Washington State Parks
(800) 233–0321

Oregon Department of Fish and
Wildlife
(503) 872–5268

Washington Department of Fish and
Wildlife
(360) 696–6211
(541) 386–3300

Columbia River Gorge Visitors
Association
404 West Second Street
The Dalles, OR 97058

(800) 98–GORGE
www.gorge.net/crgva

Gresham Area Chamber of Commerce
150 West Powell
Gresham, OR 97030
(503) 665–1131

Bonneville Lock and Dam Visitor
Center
U.S. Army Corps of Engineers
Cascade Locks, OR 97014–0150
(541) 374–8820

Cascade Locks Marine Park
Visitor Center and Sternwheeler
P.O. Box 307
Cascade Locks, OR 97014
(541) 374–8619

Hood River County Chamber of
Commerce and Information Center
405 Portway Avenue
Hood River, OR 97031
(541) 386–2000, (800) 366–3530
www.gorge.net/hrccc

The Dalles Area Chamber of
Commerce
404 West Second Street
The Dalles, OR 97058
(541) 296–2231, (800) 255–3385

The Dalles Lock and Dam
Visitor Center and Train
U.S. Army Corps of Engineers
P.O. Box 564
The Dalles, OR 97058
(541) 296–9778

Troutdale Chamber of Commerce
P.O. Box 245
Troutdale, OR 97060
(503) 669–7473

Camas-Washougal Chamber of
Commerce
P.O. Box 915
422 NE Fourth Avenue
Camas, WA 98607
(360) 834–2472

Skamania County Chamber of
Commerce
P.O. Box 1037
167 NW 2nd
Stevenson, WA 98648
(509) 427–8911, (800) 989–9178
www.skamania.org

Mt. Adams Chamber of Commerce
P.O. Box 449
White Salmon, WA 98672
(509) 493–3630

Klickitat County Tourism Committee
131 West Court Street, MSCH-24
Goldendale, WA 98620
(509) 773–3466, (800) 785–1718
www.klickitatcounty.org

Columbia Gorge Interpretive Center
990 SW Rock Creek Drive
Stevenson, WA 98648
(509) 427–8211

Columbia Gorge Discovery Center and
Wasco County Historical Museum
P.O. Box 998
5000 Discovery Drive
The Dalles, OR 97058
(541) 296–8600
www.gorgediscovery.org

About the Author

Russ Schneider grew up hiking the wilds of
the West. He moved to Portland to attend
Reed College. While earning a degree, Russ
visited the gorge often for a taste of the
wilderness. Its accessibility from the city and
its truly wild character kept Russ hiking,
and pretty soon he had hiked every one of
the trails in this book.

As a veteran hiker, guide, and author,
Russ loves showing people the land. In
addition to *Hiking the Columbia River Gorge,*
he has authored *Fishing Glacier National
Park* and *Backpacking Tips.* He is also an active editor and contributor to many other
FalconGuides.